Get the eBook FREE!

(PDF, ePub, Kindle, and liveBook all included)

We believe that once you buy a book from us, you should be able to read it in any format we have available. To get electronic versions of this book at no additional cost to you, purchase and then register this book at the Manning website.

Go to https://www.manning.com/freebook and follow the instructions to complete your pBook registration.

That's it!
Thanks from Manning!

Publishing Python Packages

Publishing Python Packages

TEST, SHARE, AND AUTOMATE YOUR PROJECTS

DANE HILLARD

Foreword by DAVID BEAZLEY

MANNING

SHELTER ISLAND

For online information and ordering of this and other Manning books, please visit
www.manning.com. The publisher offers discounts on this book when ordered in quantity.
For more information, please contact

    Special Sales Department
    Manning Publications Co.
    20 Baldwin Road
    PO Box 761
    Shelter Island, NY 11964
    Email: orders@manning.com

Manning Publications Co.
20 Baldwin Road
PO Box 761
Shelter Island, NY 11964

Development editor:	Toni Arritola
Technical development editor:	Al Krinker
Review editor:	Aleksandar Dragosavljević
Production editor:	Andy Marinkovich
Copy editor:	Pamela Hunt
Proofreader:	Melody Dolab
Technical proofreader:	Alex Agarkov
Typesetter:	Dennis Dalinnik
Cover designer:	Marija Tudor

ISBN: 9781617299919
Printed in the United States of America

brief contents

contents

foreword

Everyone starts their Python journey in a different place. Regardless of how you start, you'll eventually start working your way upstream to experience new sights and sounds. As the river narrows and the trees thicken, you may even start to think about how to deliver a Python application to others. There you find hulls of shattered projects around the entrance to a hidden cavern at the river's headwaters. Suddenly you hear a hollow voice ask, "What's your favorite packaging tool?" right before you're flung into a chasm.

Python has something for everyone—and you'll usually find it on the Python Package Index (https://pypi.org). PyPI brings about new challenges as you start to worry about installation, dependencies, environments, and other important matters related to using your software in the real world. This is where new open source packages are created and maintained. This is the starting point for this much-needed book.

A quiet secret of most Python books is that nobody really wants to talk much about packaging (and I speak from experience). Oh, books are more than happy to talk about modules and packages in terms of software organization. A book might even provide a simple skeleton of a basic package that you can give away. However, the actual process of making a production-grade downloadable package is often "left as an exercise." As such, this book occupies a unique niche as it directly tackles this specific problem.

Even though most Python users might not be inclined to release a public package, they still often have to deliver Python code to others, and doing so can introduce considerable challenges. Much of this is a natural consequence of the complexity of the ecosystem. Python packages often involve much more than just Python. For example, they might include a mix of programming languages such as Python, C, C++, Fortran, and Rust. Packages can run in any number of operating environments such as Linux, Mac, Windows, or more recently, Web Assembly. Factor in the problem of dealing with compatibility across multiple Python versions, package dependencies, and the ever-shifting landscape of package management tools, and the problems only seem to compound.

Before writing this foreword, I had one simple question to ask—can I use the knowledge from this book to modernize some of my own projects? I've been involved with Python for over twenty-five years. Over that time, I've released and maintained several small packages. However, this has always been a part-time endeavor. Honestly, I've generally aspired to do the least amount of work possible when it comes to packaging. This means that I come here with a certain amount of skepticism, old-timer inertia, and no advice to offer with respect to packaging "best practices," because I just wouldn't know.

I'm pleased to report that I learned a lot from this book. First, it takes a wholly modern approach to the current tooling that surrounds packaging. Second, it provides a lot of background related to the problems faced by package developers before presenting practical solutions to those problems. Also, I learned several new tricks related to some of the tools I was already using (e.g., pytest, coverage, etc.). Finally, you will even find advice on creating and managing a community for your project.

All of this said, this is not necessarily an "easy" book. Even with the modern treatment, there is still no one-size-fits-all approach to packaging. You might find yourself trying different approaches and adapting the book in your own way. I think the key is to keep an open mind and to think of this book as a practical guide to what's possible. In doing so, I think you'll find it to be a useful source of inspiration.

—David Beazley (https://www.dabeaz.com), Author of *Python Distilled*

preface

I started working at ITHAKA in autumn of 2014. The team had been working tirelessly to break free of a proprietary content management system with a months-long release cycle that made it difficult to change quickly. This effort paid off handsomely, birthing a new delivery platform that could stay apace with our desired agility.

The frontend group invested in the Django web framework for new user-facing development on JSTOR (https://www.jstor.org), a choice that had a role in my coming aboard. The team also made early investment in supporting the project with installable Python packages, which proved helpful as our product offerings fragmented while retaining shared core functionality. The business domain around our content and access models was complex; these packages put useful boundaries and reusability around them. Despite taking this concept in a strong direction, we still suffered a few shortcomings.

We weren't operating a private package repository, so all our packages had to be installed from our version-control system. There was no semantic versioning, and the Git commit hashes didn't provide much insight or management of expectations around what changed between versions. We didn't maintain changelogs—commit messages were our medium of change management.

In the ensuing years, our investment in Django and Python evolved to many thousands of lines of code serving most of the traffic on JSTOR. Our packages grew in size and number, and the friction of our packaging story created cow paths. We'd pulled our packages to live alongside our application code, forsaking the ability to opt into changes for the relative ease of seeing changes reflected immediately during development. Code landed wherever was easiest.

This paradigm shifted when the core infrastructure group invested in first-class support for private packaging. Seeing this new capability and diagnosing the organizational structure we had, I sought to understand how we could leverage continuous integration and standardization to maintain our agility while improving quality and regaining the ability to opt into changes.

The apiron project (https://github.com/ithaka/apiron) was the first effort to adopt new packaging practices and went on to become ITHAKA's first actively developed open source project intended for third-party use. As the benefits of this packaging workflow became increasingly clear, we adopted the process widely. Today, ITHAKA's frontend group maintains over two dozen Python packages supporting a similar volume of applications.

ITHAKA's mission is to improve access to knowledge, and I hope this book does its part, opening your eyes in some places and enabling things you've hoped and dreamed of in others. Although practical, I also hope you'll come away with some theoretical and philosophical tools to help you and your teams become significantly more productive with automation and repeatable process. It may take a turn here or there that you disagree with, and that's lovely—it's a chance for feedback into the collective knowledge we as creators are always iterating within. I hope you enjoy and benefit and disagree and critique.

You can reach me any time with questions, success stories, and debate at pubpypack@danehillard.com.

acknowledgments

As difficult as this book was for me to get across the finish line, it would have been impossible if not for the immeasurable work done by those at the Python Software Foundation and the Python Packaging Authority. Your efforts in keeping the story for packaging in Python trending ever upward are so appreciated. Although I've collected knowledge and process here, I stand largely on the shoulders of giants.

I had the luxury of writing my first book from a high-end home furnishings store with a cozy coffee shop in the back. This book, on the other hand, was 100% home-grown—mostly across the desk from my partner, Stefanie. Thank you for your calm, your kindness, and your regular comic relief. If we can weather pandemic-induced cabin fever on top of my rampant procrastination and complaining, we'll probably take over the world together some day.

Thank you to the team at ITHAKA for your continuous enthusiasm for learning, improvement, and innovation. Your drive to do things well keeps me going.

This book almost didn't happen. Thank you to Toni Arritola, my development editor, and Mike Stephens, my acquisitions editor, for taking me in on the fly for a second endeavor. Your encouragement and feedback ensured this turned into a worthwhile pursuit.

To Al Krinker, my technical editor, I thank you for consistently asking about the motivations. This certainly improved the impact and clarity of the work.

Thank you to Marjan Bace and the rest of the team at Manning for bringing this book to life and getting it in the hands of those who need it.

To those brave souls who invested early in this book and provided feedback along the way, thank you so much. You set me on the straight and narrow and tripped over things so others won't have to.

To all the reviewers who worked on this book: Aleksei Agarkov, Cage Slagel, Clifford Thurber, Daniel Holth, David Cabrero Souto, David Cronkite, Delena Malan, Edgar Hassler, Emanuele Piccinelli, Eric Chiang, Ganesh Swaminathan, Håvard Wall, Howard Bandy, Jim Amrhein, Johnny Hopkins, Jose Apablaza, Joshua A. McAdams, Katia Patkin, Kevin Etienne, Kimberly L. Winston-Jackson, Larry Cai, Laxman Singh Tomar, Marc-Anthony Taylor, Mathijs Affourtit, Matthias Busch, Mike Baran, Miki Tebeka, Richard J. Tobias, Richard Meinsen, Robert Vanderwall, Salil Athalye, Sriram Macharla, Vasudevan Surendran, Vidhya Vinay, Vraj Mohan, and Zoheb Ainapore, your suggestions helped make this a better book.

A final thank you to anyone and everyone else who has had a positive influence—directly, intentionally, or otherwise—on this book. I cannot hope to produce an exhaustive list; names not appearing here are due expressly to the limitations of my own mind. Thank you to Ee Durbin, Dustin Ingram, Brett Cannon, Paul Ganssle, Filipe Laíns, Bernát Gábor, Łukasz Langa, Sébastien Eustace, Thomas Kluyver, Donald Stufft, Simon Willison, Will McGugan, Dawn Wages, Reuven Lerner, David Beazley, Brett Slatkin, Tzu-Ping Chung, Henry Schreiner, Pradyun Gedam, Paul Moore, Tushar Sadhwani, Sandi Metz, Jason Coombs, Jeff Triplett, Carlton Gibson, Chris Kolosiwsky, and Peter Ung.

about this book

Publishing Python Packages introduces several aspects specific to Python packaging along with several concepts applicable to almost any language that, together, can make teams and individuals more productive in software delivery. DevOps teams, product teams, and site reliability teams alike can find new practices and tools to refine their work. If you hope to automate, standardize, and orchestrate as much of the life cycle of your Python projects as possible, this could be the book for you.

Who should read this book?

Publishing Python Packages is for anyone already familiar with Python who wants to share their code—with their friends, their team, or the world. The practices contained in this book are specifically chosen to be manageable by one person but scalable to a team of almost any size. Collaboration is the key to effective software development, so these practices tend toward removing the tedium so you can focus on proper communication through code and prose.

As software continues to grow in the scientific community, packaged software is an increasingly valuable commodity. Successful open source projects have been highlighted in recent milestones as big as landing on Mars and imaging black holes. Whether you're looking to create the next big thing or simply want to make sure your lab PI can verify the code you used to generate your results, repeatable process is key.

If you haven't worked with software quality tools like unit testing and linting before, this book can help you expand on light introductions to automate the work and help you grow your quality checks into a rich automated suite. You can spend your time thinking about how to catch problems before they arise instead of putting out fires.

How this book is organized: a roadmap

Publishing Python Packages consists of 11 chapters organized in four parts. Part 1 covers the inherent value of packaging software of any kind. Part 2 takes you through building a working package with most of the bells and whistles it might need. Part 3 launches you into the automation and maintenance needs of highly collaborative projects. Part 4 shows you how to repeat this process and scale your user and contributor base.

Part 1, "Foundations," sets the stage for Python packaging and gets you in the right mindset as you start to build your own package by covering the following areas:

- Chapter 1 covers how packaging came into being and why it's still just as valuable today for sharing software. It may broaden your thinking about what counts as a package, and you'll start to see that packages target many audiences.
- Chapter 2 covers getting started with the tools from the appendices that you can use for product packaging work.
- Chapter 3 shows you the underpinnings of what it means to be a Python package, including the files and metadata involved and how they flow through the process.

Part 2, "Creating a viable package," grows your minimal Python package into something with real behavior you can expand upon after you finish the book:

- Chapter 4 shows you how to incorporate third-party dependencies, command-line interfaces, and non-Python extensions into a package.
- Chapter 5 introduces unit-testing tools for orchestrating your unit-testing activities to ensure quality in your software behavior.
- Chapter 6 builds further on quality, incorporating checks for common bugs, type safety, and consistent code formatting.

Part 3, "Going public," suggests practices you can adopt anywhere but that are especially useful for collaborating with others:

- Chapter 7 shows you the power of automation and continuous integration principles, helping you think about how you can create tight feedback loops for contributors.
- Chapter 8 covers the importance of documentation and shows how to integrate an automated documentation build system that covers both code and prose.
- Chapter 9 offers practices for keeping a Python package up to date on a regular basis with minimal effort so you can avoid accumulating technical debt.

Part 4, "The long haul," answers questions about where to go next now that you have a new skillset:

- Chapter 10 helps you turn the practices you learned in earlier chapters into a repeatable project template for use in future projects.
- Chapter 11 offers practices for building a community of users, contributors, and maintainers around your projects that thrives on the clear processes from earlier chapters.

I recommend reading *Publishing Python Packages* from cover to cover. Each new chapter builds on the last with exciting milestones along the way.

Additionally, the following appendices will help you install tooling that makes working with packaging much more enjoyable in my experience:

- Appendix A helps you install tools that make it easier to install multiple versions of Python—and other languages—and invoke the various Python interpreters and virtual environments you create in your travels.
- Appendix B helps you install project-agnostic tools that are needed for the project in the book, but which can boost your productivity on most any Python project.

About the code

This book contains many examples of source code both in numbered listings and in line with normal text. In both cases, source code is formatted in a `fixed-width font like this` to separate it from ordinary text. Sometimes code is also **`in bold`** to highlight code that has changed from previous steps in the chapter, such as when a new feature adds to an existing line of code.

In many cases, the original source code has been reformatted; we've added line breaks and reworked indentation to accommodate the available page space in the book. In rare cases, even this was not enough, and listings include line-continuation markers (➥). Additionally, comments in the source code have often been removed from the listings when the code is described in the text. Code annotations accompany many of the listings, highlighting important concepts.

You can get executable snippets of code from the liveBook (online) version of this book at https://livebook.manning.com/book/publishing-python-packages. The complete code for the examples in the book is available for download from the Manning website at www.manning.com, and from GitHub at http://mng.bz/69A5.

For each chapter, the code reflects the full state of the package as it stands at the end of the chapter. I arrived at this choice carefully—because packaging configuration requires precise syntax and values in a number of files, it can be more difficult to get right than even regular programming. To minimize your chances of frustration, I believe this is the best reference compared to organizing the code by listing.

Because packaging practices can and do change, I'll provide updated versions of this code companion over time. I'll maintain those separate from the code that accompanies this edition to minimize confusion, and I'll provide links to them from the code companion as they're available.

liveBook discussion forum

Purchase of *Publishing Python Packages* includes free access to liveBook, Manning's online reading platform. Using liveBook's exclusive discussion features, you can attach comments to the book globally or to specific sections or paragraphs. It's a snap to make notes for yourself, ask and answer technical questions, and receive help from the author and other users. To access the forum, go to https://livebook.manning.com/book/publishing-python-packages/discussion. You can also learn more about Manning's forums and the rules of conduct at https://livebook.manning.com/discussion.

Manning's commitment to our readers is to provide a venue where a meaningful dialogue between individual readers and between readers and the author can take place. It is not a commitment to any specific amount of participation on the part of the author, whose contribution to the forum remains voluntary (and unpaid). We suggest you try asking the author some challenging questions lest his interest stray! The forum and the archives of previous discussions will be accessible from the publisher's website for as long as the book is in print.

about the author

DANE HILLARD is currently a technical architect at ITHAKA, a nonprofit in higher education. His experience includes building application architecture for the JSTOR research platform supporting millions of users. His current interests lie in safety, loosely coupled systems, and formal methods.

about the cover illustration

The figure on the cover of *Publishing Python Packages* is taken from a collection by Jacques Grasset de Saint-Sauveur, published in 1797. Each illustration is finely drawn and colored by hand.

In those days, it was easy to identify where people lived and what their trade or station in life was just by their dress. Manning celebrates the inventiveness and initiative of the computer business with book covers based on the rich diversity of regional culture centuries ago, brought back to life by pictures from collections such as this one.

Part 1

Foundations

Software packaging is perhaps the most important achievement in bringing applications and behavior to the consumer market. Packages let us reuse others' work in our projects, install apps on our phones, and more. Without packaging, our decreased productivity would still have us in the dark ages of software development.

Whether you're already a maintainer of a Python package or just getting started with packaging, a solid understanding of packaging concepts will put you in the right mindset as you work through this book and other projects. This part covers what packaging is, what you'll need to get started with your own Python package, and what constitutes a minimal working package.

The what and why of Python packages

This chapter covers

- Packaging code to make it more accessible to others
- Using packages to make your own projects more manageable
- Building Python packages for different platforms

Imagine that you've written a groundbreaking piece of Python software for use in self-driving cars. Your latest work is going to change the world, and you want as many people using it as possible. You've convinced CarCorp to use your solution, and they want to retrieve the code to get started with it.

When CarCorp calls to ask how to install and use your code, you go through all the gory details of copying each file to the right directory, making some files executable so they can be run as commands, and so on. Because you wrote the software, this is all second nature to you. To your surprise, the developers on the other end of the phone are a bit lost. What happened?

You've discovered the chasm that often exists between those who create software and those who use it. These days, people are used to visiting the app store on their iPhone when they need something new. You have a bit of work to do if you want to improve the user experience of your software!

In this book, you'll learn how distributing your Python project as an installable package can make it more accessible to others. You'll also learn how to create a repeatable process for managing your projects, reducing the effort you'll spend maintaining them, so you can focus on your real aspiration: to change the world. You'll do all this by building a real project using some popular packaging tools and automating several aspects of the process. Although the Python community has developed standards for some areas of packaging, the One True Way© of doing things has not yet emerged. Nor may it ever do so!

Even if you've created or published a Python package before, you'll find something in this book for you. The suggestions and tools you'll learn in this book are time-tested approaches to some of the more loosely defined packaging practices. Python packaging has a messy history and many current alternative options, so in addition to seeing and using the tools available now, you'll also learn the methodology behind how they work to continue adapting as the landscape matures. To that end, it's important to first understand why software is packaged at all.

1.1   *What is a package, anyway?*

To save your relationship with CarCorp, you promise to come back in a few weeks with an overhauled process that will help them install your software in a snap. You know that some of your favorite Python code, like `pandas` and `requests`, are available as packages online, and you want to provide the same ease of installation to your own consumers.

Packaging is the act of archiving software along with metadata that describes those files. Developers usually create these archives, or *packages*, with the intent of sharing or publishing them.

> **IMPORTANT**   The Python ecosystem uses the word *package* for two distinct concepts. The Python Packaging Authority (PyPA) differentiates the terms in the *Python Packaging User Guide* (https://packaging.python.org) as follows:
>
> - *Import packages* organize multiple Python modules into a directory for discovery purposes (http://mng.bz/wypg).
> - *Distribution packages* archive Python projects to be published for others to install (http://mng.bz/qoNz).
>
> Import packages aren't always distributed in an archive, though distribution packages often contain one or more import packages. Distribution packages are the main subject of this book and will be disambiguated from import packages where necessary to avoid confusion.

With a probably infinite number of ways to roll software and its metadata together, how do maintainers and users of that software manage expectations and reduce manual work? That's where *package management systems* come in.

1.1.1 Standardizing packaging for automation

Package management systems, or *package managers*, standardize the archive and metadata format for software packages in a particular domain. Package managers provide tools to help consumers install dependencies at the project, programming language, framework, or operating system level. Most package managers ship with a familiar set of instructions to install, uninstall, or update packages. You may have used some of the following package managers:

- pip (https://pip.pypa.io)
- conda (https://docs.conda.io)
- Homebrew (https://brew.sh/)
- npm (https://www.npmjs.com/)
- asdf (https://asdf-vm.com/)

The early days of package management

Although developers had been packaging their code informally for some time, it wasn't until package management systems became widely available in the early 1990s that this approach took off (see Jeremy Katz, "A Brief History of Package Management," *Tidelift*, http://mng.bz/7ZG4).

The ability to declaratively define project dependencies proved a boon to developer productivity by abstracting away a major area of legwork in managing software projects.

Software repositories standardize packaging further by acting as centralized marketplaces to publish and host packages that others can install (see figure 1.1). Many programming language communities provide an official or de facto standard repository for installing packages. PyPI (https://pypi.org), RubyGems (https://rubygems.org/), and Docker Hub (https://hub.docker.com/) are a few popular software repositories.

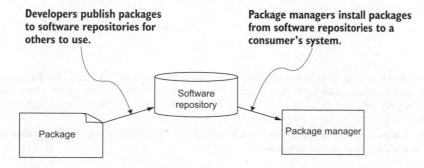

Figure 1.1 Packages, package managers, and software repositories are all critical to sharing software.

If you own a smartphone, tablet, or desktop computer and you've installed apps from an app store, that's packaging at work. Packages are software bundled together with metadata about that software, and that's precisely what an app is. Software repositories host software that people can install, and that's what an app store is.

So, packages are software and metadata rolled together in an agreed-upon format, codified in the relevant package management system. At a more granular level, packages also typically include a way to build the software on a user's system, or they may provide several prebuilt versions of the software for a variety of target systems.

1.1.2   *The contents of a distribution package*

Figure 1.2 shows some of the files you might choose to put in a distribution package. Developers often include the source code files in a package, but they can also provide compiled artifacts, test data, and whatever else a consumer or colleague might need. By distributing a package, your consumers will have a one-stop shop to grab all the pieces they need to get started with your software.

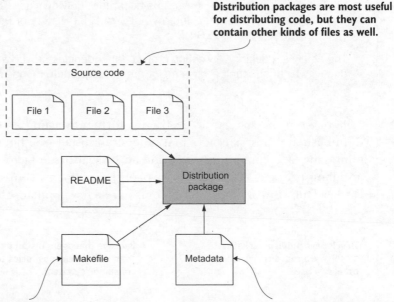

Distribution packages are most useful for distributing code, but they can contain other kinds of files as well.

You can distribute configuration and compilation code along with instructions to help the consumer build and use your software.

Metadata about the package, like the name and version, help differentiate it from other packages or other versions of the same package.

Figure 1.2   A package often includes source code, a makefile for compiling the code, metadata about the code, and instructions for the consumer.

Distributing noncode files is an important capability. Although the code is often the reason to distribute anything in the first place, many users and tools depend on the metadata about the code to differentiate it from other code. Developers usually specify the name of a software project, its creator(s), the license under which it can be reused, and so on in the metadata. Importantly, the metadata often includes the version of the archive to distinguish it from previous and future publications of the project.

> **The early days of sharing software**
>
> For more than a decade after the Unix operating system first became available, sharing software between teams and individuals remained a largely manual process. Downloading source code, compiling it, and contending with the artifacts of the compilation were all left up to the person trying to use the code. Each step in this process introduced opportunities for failure due to human error and architectural or environmental differences between systems. Tools like Make (https://www.gnu.org/software/make/) removed some of this variation from the process but stopped shy of package version, dependency, and installation management.

Now that you're familiar with what goes into a package, you'll learn how this approach to sharing software solves specific problems in practice.

1.1.3 The challenges of sharing software

Your call with CarCorp is growing tense, and you realize you forgot to have them install all your project's dependencies first. You back up a few steps and navigate them through the dependency installation. Unfortunately, you forgot to check which version you've been using for one of your major dependencies, and the latest version doesn't seem to work. You walk them through installing each previous version until you finally find one that works. Crisis narrowly averted.

As you develop increasingly complex systems, the effort to make sure you've installed the required version of each dependency correctly grows quickly. In the worst cases, you might reach a point where you need two different versions of the same dependency, and they can't coexist. This is affectionally known as "dependency hell." Detangling a project from this point can prove challenging.

Even without running into dependency hell, without a standardized approach to packaging, it can be difficult to share software in a standard way so that anyone, anywhere knows what other dependencies they need to install for your project. Software communities create conventions and standards for managing packages, codifying those practices into the package management systems you use to get your work done.

Now that you understand why packaging is good for sharing software, read on to learn about some of the advantages that packaging can provide even if you aren't always making your software publicly available.

1.2 How packaging helps you

If you're new to packaging, it may seem so far like it's mainly useful for sharing software with people across the globe. Although that's certainly a good reason to package

your code, you may also like some of the following benefits that packaging brings
when developing software:

- Stronger cohesion and encapsulation
- Clearer definition of ownership
- Looser coupling between areas of the code
- More opportunity for composition

The following sections cover these benefits in detail.

1.2.1 *Enforcing cohesion and encapsulation through packaging*

A particular area of code should generally have one job. *Cohesion* measures how duti-
fully the code sticks to that job. The more stray functionality is floating around, the
less cohesive the code is.

You've probably used functions, classes, modules, and import packages to organize
your Python code (see Dane Hillard, "The Hierarchy of Separation in Python," *Practices of the Python Pro*, Manning Publications, 2020, pp. 25–39, http://mng.bz/m2N0).
These constructs each place a kind of named boundary around areas of code that
have a particular job. When done well, naming communicates to developers what
belongs inside the boundary and, importantly, what doesn't.

Despite best efforts, names and people are rarely perfect. If you put all your Python
code in a single application, chances are some code will eventually seep into areas it
doesn't belong. Think about some of the larger projects you've developed. How many
times did you create a `utils.py` or `helpers.py` module containing a grab bag of functionality? The boundaries you create with a function or a module are readily overcome.
These "utility" areas of the code tend to attract new "utilities," with the cohesion trending down over time.

Imagine that your self-driving car system can use lidar (https://oceanservice.noaa
.gov/facts/lidar.html) as one type of input. CarCorp's vehicles don't include lidar sen-
sors. Being the diligent developer you are, you create a lidar-specific part of the code
base to separate it from other concerns. Although assessing naming and regularly
refactoring the code base can keep cohesion higher, it's also a maintenance burden.
Distribution packages increase the barrier to adding code where it may not belong in
the first place. Because updating a package necessitates going through a cycle of packaging, publishing, and installing the update, it prompts developers to think more
deeply about the changes they make. You will be less likely to add code to a package
without explicit intent that's worth the investment of the update cycle.

Creating cohesion and packaging a cohesive area of code is a gateway into *encapsulation*. Encapsulation helps you build the right expectations with your consumers
about how to interact with your code by defining whether and how the code's behavior is exposed. Think of a project you built and shared with someone to use. Now
think about how many times you changed your code, and how many times they had to
change their code in turn. How frustrating was it for them? How about for you?

Encapsulation can reduce this kind of churn by better defining the API contract that's less subject to change. Figure 1.3 shows how you might create multiple packages out of cohesive areas of code.

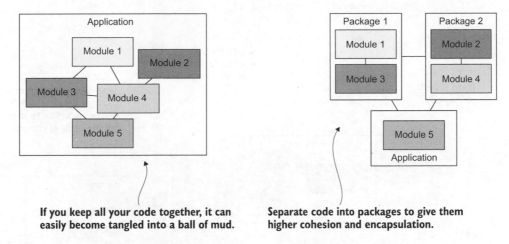

If you keep all your code together, it can easily become tangled into a ball of mud.

Separate code into packages to give them higher cohesion and encapsulation.

Figure 1.3   Packaging can reduce unexpected interdependence between areas of code by introducing stronger boundaries.

You might've felt frustration in the past when you found that a piece of code meant only for use internal to a module was being used widely throughout the code. Each time you update that "internal" code, you need to update usages elsewhere. This high-churn environment can lead to bugs when you don't propagate a change everywhere, leaving you or your team that much less productive.

Well-encapsulated, highly cohesive code will change rarely, even when used widely. This kind of code is sometimes labeled "mature." Mature code is a great candidate for distributing as a package because you won't need to republish it frequently. You can get a start in packaging by extracting some of the more mature code from your code base and then use what you know about cohesion and encapsulation to bring less mature code up to snuff.

1.2.2   *Promoting clear ownership of code*

Teams benefit from clear ownership over areas of code. Ownership often goes beyond maintaining the behavior of the code itself. Teams build automation to streamline unit testing, deployment, integration testing, performance testing, and more. That's a lot of plates to keep spinning at once. Keeping the scope of a bounded area of code small so that a team can own all these aspects will ensure the code's longevity. Packaging is one tool for managing scope.

The encapsulation you create through packaging code enables you to develop automation independent of other code. As an example, automation for a code base with little structure may require you to write conditional logic to determine which tests to run based on which files changed. Alternatively, you might run all the tests for every change, which can be slow. Creating packages that you can test and publish independently of other code will result in clearer mappings from source code to test code to publication code (see figure 1.4).

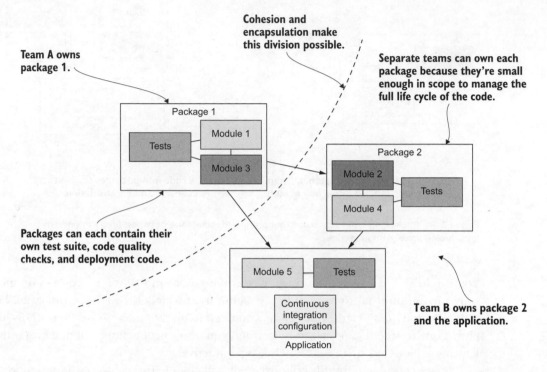

Figure 1.4   Teams can take full ownership over individual packages, defining how they want to manage the development, testing, and publishing life cycle.

A clear delineation of purpose for a package makes it likelier to have a clear delineation of ownership. If a team isn't sure what they're committing to by taking ownership of some code, they're going to be wary. Try providing a package with a clear scope, story, and operator's manual to see how the mood shifts.

1.2.3 *Decoupling implementation from usage*

You may have heard the term *loose coupling* used to describe the level of interdependence between areas of code.

> **DEFINITION**   Coupling is a measure of the interdependence between areas of code. Loosely coupled code provides multiple avenues of flexibility so you can implement and choose from a variety of execution strategies instead of being

forced down a particular path. Two pieces of code with low coupling have little or no dependence on each other, and they can be changed at different rates.

The cohesion and encapsulation practices you read about earlier in this chapter are a way to reduce the likelihood of tight coupling due to poor code organization. Highly cohesive code will have tight coupling within itself and loose coupling to anything outside its boundary. Encapsulation exposes an intentional API, limiting any coupling to that API. Your choices about packaging and encapsulation, then, help you decouple your consumers from implementation details in your code. Packaging also makes it possible to decouple consumers from implementation through versioning, namespacing, and even the programming language in which software is written.

   In a big ball of mud, you're stuck running whatever code is in each module. If you or someone on your team updates a module, all code using that module needs to accommodate the change immediately. If the update changes a call signature or a return value, it may have a wide blast radius. Packaging significantly reduces this restriction (see figure 1.5).

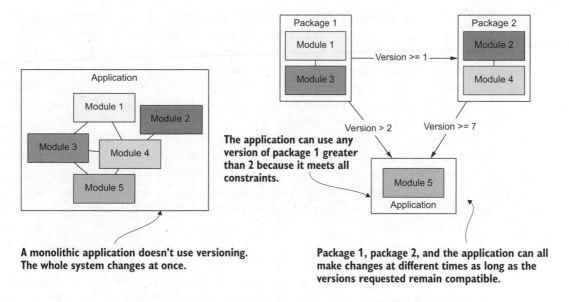

Figure 1.5   Packaging provides flexibility so two areas of code can evolve at different rates.

Imagine if each update to the `requests` package required you to react immediately by updating your own code. That would be a nightmare! Because packages version the code they contain, and because consumers can specify which version they want to install, a package can be updated many times without impacting consuming code. Developers can choose precisely when to incur the effort of updating their code to accommodate a change in a more recent version of the package.

Another point at which you can decouple code is *namespacing*. Namespaces attach values and behavior to human-readable names. When you install a package, you make it available at the namespace it specifies. As an example, the `requests` package is available in the `requests` namespace.

Different packages can have the same namespace. This means they could conflict if you install more than one of them, but it also makes something interesting possible: this flexibility in namespaces means packages can act as full alternatives to one another. If a developer creates an alternative to a popular package that's faster, safer, or more maintainable, you can install it in place of the original as long as the API is the same. As an example, the following packages all provide roughly equivalent MySQL (https://www.mysql.com) client functionality (specifically, they implement some level of compatibility with PEP 249; https://www.python.org/dev/peps/pep-0249/):

- mysqlclient (https://github.com/PyMySQL/mysqlclient)
- PyMySQL (https://github.com/PyMySQL/PyMySQL)
- mysql-python (https://github.com/arnaudsj/mysql-python)
- oursql (https://github.com/python-oursql/oursql)

Finally, Python packaging can even decouple usage in Python from the language in which a package is written! Many Python packages are written in C and even Fortran for improved performance or integration with legacy systems. Package authors can provide precompiled versions of these packages alongside versions that can be built from source by the consumer if needed. This also makes packages more portable, decoupling developers somewhat from the details of the computer or server they're using. You'll learn more about packaging build targets in chapter 3.

You might like to package some of your code to experiment with the freedom of version decoupling to see how your versioned packages evolve over time. Those that change quickly may point to low cohesion because the code has many reasons to change. On the other hand, it may indicate only that the code is still maturing. At the very least, these data points will be observable! You'll learn more about versioning in chapter 9.

1.2.4   *Filling roles by composing small packages*

The act of extracting code into multiple packages is a bit like *decomposition*. Successful decomposition requires a good handle on loose coupling. Decomposing code is an art that separates pieces of code so they can be recombined in new ways (for a wonderfully concise rundown of decomposition and coupling, see Josh Justice, "Breaking Up Is Hard to Do: How to Decompose Your Code," *Big Nerd Ranch*, http://mng.bz/5mpq).

By packaging smaller areas of your code, you'll start to identify code that accomplishes a very specific goal that can be generalized or broadened to fulfill a role. As an example, you can create one-off HTTP requests using a built-in Python utility like `urllib.request.urlopen`. Once you've done this a few times, you can see commonalities between the use cases and generalize the concept into a higher-level utility. So the `requests` package isn't built to make just one specific HTTP request; it fills a general role as an HTTP client. Some of your code may be very specific now, but as you find new areas where you need similar behavior, you may see an opportunity to identify the role it fills, generalize a bit, and create a package that can fill that role.

As you work on revamping your software for CarCorp, you remember that a major portion of the code deals with the car's navigation systems. You realize that with a bit of tweaking, the navigation code will also work for Acme Auto's vehicles. This code could fill the role of communicating with vehicle navigation systems. Because you've learned that packages can depend on other packages, and because your navigation system code is already fairly cohesive, you commit yourself to creating not one but two packages before your next CarCorp meeting.

A composition success story

You can see great examples of composition at play in packaging through Python frameworks like Django (https://www.djangoproject.com). Django is itself a package, and because it's built as a plugin-based architecture, you can extend its functionality by installing and configuring additional packages. Peruse the hundreds of packages listed on Django Packages (https://djangopackages.org) to see the kind of wide adoption the packaging approach enjoys.

Thinking about composition and decomposition highlights the fact that distribution packages can exist at any size, just as functions, classes, modules, and import packages do. Look to cohesion and decoupling as guiding lights to strike the right balance. One hundred distribution packages that each provide a single function would be a maintenance burden, and one distribution package that provides one hundred import packages would be about the same as having no package at all. If all else fails, always ask yourself, "What role do I want this code to fill?"

Now that you've learned that packaging can help you write cohesive, loosely coupled code with clear ownership that you can deliver to consumers in an accessible way, I hope you're rolling up your sleeves to dive into the details.

Summary

- Packages archive software files and metadata about the software, such as the name, creator, license, and version.
- Package managers automate installing packages and managing the interdependencies between them.
- The packaging process has a number of pitfalls that can be overcome with tools and a repeatable process.
- Software repositories host published packages for others to install.
- Packaging is a great way to separate and encapsulate code with high cohesion.

- Packaging can be used as a decoupling tool to gain flexibility in developing and maintaining code.
- Versioned packages are a great way to reduce churn across the code base for each individual update.

Preparing for package development

This chapter covers

- Managing virtual environments using venv
- Isolating project dependencies using virtual environments
- Managing virtual environment creation and activation using venv
- Listing installed dependencies using pip

At the beginning of a project, you're likely eager to get started and accomplish something tangible. This is understandable—building things and solving problems can be rewarding. But it's valuable to move slowly at first so you can move quickly later and longer as a project matures. When you're exploring a new technology or process, it can also be helpful to practice with it first so you can use it deftly. A bit of planning up front can go a long way toward your productivity and resulting morale. In this chapter, you'll use asdf and venv to create a development environment for the package you'll work on for the rest of this book.

> **IMPORTANT** Before reading on, visit appendix A to install the tools you'll need for this chapter.

2.1   *Managing Python virtual environments*

As you think more about the potential success of your CarCorp engagement, you realize that if the package you're working to publish becomes popular, people using a variety of Python versions might want to install and use it. It isn't likely that they'll always be running the latest version of Python on their production systems. It's a good practice to explicitly state the range of Python versions your package supports and test your package across all those versions. Because you're leveraging the power of asdf and python-launcher from appendix A, you've already got most of the power you need. The last step is to create a virtual environment for use in local development of your package.

When you install Python, it ships with the packages that are available in Python's *standard library*.

> **DEFINITION**   A *standard library* defines which functionality is considered the core part of a programming language. The standard library of a language is built into the language or its installation process and is available by default after installing the language's software on your system.

Python's standard library is extensive compared to some languages, but even then, it doesn't provide all the functionality you might need for your projects. Python packages, the Python Package Index (PyPI), and the pip package manager exist to share software that extends beyond, or provides alternatives to, the Python standard library.

Imagine that when you first started your project with CarCorp, you used pip to install a few packages like `requests`. You also had some other packages installed from an earlier project for Vehicle Ventures. Did you notice that all these packages ended up together in one place, regardless of the project you were using them for?

By default, pip installs packages in a location related to the Python version with which pip itself was installed, known as the *site packages* directory. That is, when you install Python 3.7 and use the copy of pip that comes with it, packages you install will be stored in Python 3.7's site packages directory. Installing all packages to this site packages directory might be manageable enough for a while, but what happens when you need different package versions for different projects? What happens if you need to list the minimum dependencies required for a single project? With the site packages directory full of packages from any and every project, these hurdles become difficult or impossible to address.

One way to solve these problems is to *isolate* the packages for each project. In isolation, you can keep a list of each project's minimum required dependencies. What's more, one project is free to use `requests==2.1.0` even though another project uses `requests==2.24.0`. You learned about the value of decoupling in chapter 1. Isolation of package dependencies decouples your projects from each other. You can achieve this isolation in Python using *virtual environments*.

DEFINITION   Python *virtual environments* are an isolated copy of Python with an isolated site packages directory. The copy of pip in the virtual environment's Python installs packages to its isolated site packages directory, keeping them separate from other environments.

A virtual environment isn't all that different conceptually from a normal Python installation. Instead of installing Python 3.7 and installing all your projects' dependencies into it, imagine installing Python 3.7 several times and giving each installation a unique name corresponding to each of your projects. You could then use each uniquely named Python installation for its corresponding project (see figure 2.1). This isn't far off from how virtual environments work in practice.

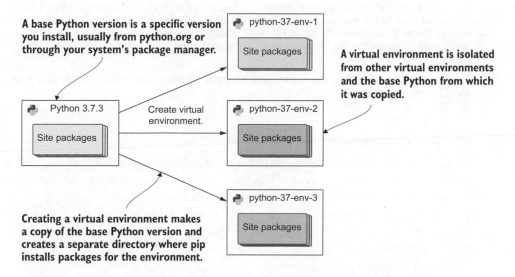

Figure 2.1   Virtual environments create isolated copies of Python and pip with their own installation directory for packages.

When you use Python within a virtual environment, you'll be using a *copy* of the base Python version that created the environment.

To test your package, you need to install packages not only in isolation from other projects but also across many base versions of Python. As the number of Python versions your project supports grows, it can become tedious to manage all the virtual environments and their Python installations manually (see figure 2.2).

You might be starting to see the value that tooling has in keeping all these things organized. Whereas asdf helps you install and manage base Python versions, venv helps you create virtual environments from those base Python versions.

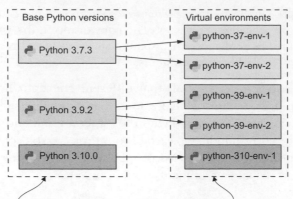

You should install the base Python versions you would need to run your code. If your code uses syntax or features from Python 3.10, you'll need a Python 3.10 base version.

You should create a virtual environment for each project to isolate its dependencies from other projects. This also ensures you don't rely on unspecified dependencies or run into dependency conflicts.

Figure 2.2   Many base Python versions, each with many virtual environments created from them, may exist on a single system.

2.1.1   Creating virtual environments with venv

To make a base Python version available on your system, you use asdf to install it from the source code on the internet. To create a virtual environment, you make a copy of an installed base Python version with a unique name.

To create a virtual environment, use the venv module from the base Python version, and pass it a name for the virtual environment's directory. It's a common convention to call this directory .venv/. Now create a virtual environment in your project by running the following commands:

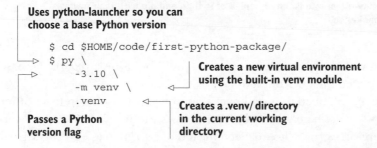

You won't see any output if the command is successful, but you should see a .venv/ directory created. python-launcher on Unix systems will pick up on the presence of this new virtual environment and use it by default whenever you're in this directory or its child directories. The Python launcher for Windows will pick up the virtual environment if that virtual environment is currently active. You can verify this by running the py command with no arguments. The interpreter that starts will match the base

Python version you used to create the virtual environment, and you can use the following code to be sure it's the virtual environment's copy of Python:

```
>>> import sys
>>> sys.executable
'/Users/<you>/code/first-python-package/.venv/bin/python'
```

If you pass a version flag to python-launcher, you'll still get the base version. As an example, you should see something similar to the following when using py -3.9:

```
>>> import sys
>>> sys.executable
'/Users/<you>/.asdf/installs/python/3.9.3/bin/python3.9'
```

To prove that your virtual environment is isolated from the base Python version from which it was created, first run the following commands from your project's directory to install the requests package in the virtual environment and check the resulting list of installed packages:

```
$ py -m pip install requests
$ py -m pip list
Package            Version
------------------ ---------
certifi            2022.6.15
charset-normalizer 2.0.12
idna               3.3
pip                21.2.4
requests           2.28.0
setuptools         58.1.0
urllib3            1.26.9
```

Now confirm that these packages aren't installed in the base Python version by explicitly passing the -3.10 version flag:

```
$ py -3.10 -m pip list
Package    Version
---------- -------
pip        21.1.2
setuptools 57.0.0
```

You can see that, by default, a virtual environment only has the pip and setuptools packages installed after you create it. These default packages and their versions are determined by the base Python installation. It's good to get into the habit of updating pip and Setuptools to their latest available versions and installing the wheel package so you can install packages that have been prebuilt for your system instead of compiling them yourself. Install these now:

```
$ py -m pip install --upgrade pip setuptools wheel
```

Going forward, you'll be able to use the `py` command in your project and be sure you're always getting the copy of Python from your project's virtual environment unless you explicitly ask for a different (base) Python. This can reduce your cognitive load, because you don't need to remember to activate or deactivate the virtual environment manually each time you start or stop work on the project.

> **TIP** If you're used to using your virtual environments automatically in an IDE like PyCharm (https://www.jetbrains.com/pycharm/) or Visual Studio Code (https://code.visualstudio.com/), you can still do so here even though you're using python-launcher at the command line; the .venv/ directory is still a standard virtual environment.

You've learned the ins and outs of managing Python versions and virtual environments with asdf and venv. You're ready to move on to creating the contents of your first Python package.

Summary

- Virtual environments decouple and isolate the dependencies of your different Python projects.
- Use python-launcher to reliably get the right version of Python.

The anatomy of a minimal Python package

3

This chapter covers

- The Python package build system
- Building a package using Setuptools
- The directory structure of a Python package
- Building a package for multiple targets

Python package builds are the product of coordination between a few different tools driven by a standardized process. One of the biggest choices you have as a package author is which set of tools to use. It can be difficult to assess the nuances of each, especially if you're new to packaging. Fortunately, tools are standardizing around the same core workflow, so once you learn it, you've got the agility to switch between tools with minimal effort. This chapter covers what each category of these tools accomplishes and how they work together to produce a package, as well as how package builds vary for different systems.

> **IMPORTANT** Before reading on, visit appendix B to install the tools you'll need for this chapter.

You can use the code companion (http://mng.bz/69A5) to check your work for the exercises in this chapter.

3.1   *The Python build workflow*

The following sections cover what happens when you build a package and what you need to do to build a package successfully. You first need to learn about the pieces of the Python build system itself.

3.1.1   *Parts of the Python build system*

In the root directory for your project, start by running `build` using the following command:

```
$ pyproject-build
```

Because your package has no content yet, you should see an error like the following:

```
ERROR Source /Users/<you>/code/first-python-package does not appear to be
➥ a Python project: no pyproject.toml or setup.py
```

The output makes two file suggestions. pyproject.toml is the newer standard file for configuring Python packaging introduced in PEP 518 (https://www.python.org/dev/peps/pep-0518/) and should be preferred unless a third-party tool you want to use is only compatible with setup.py. The file uses TOML (https://toml.io/en/), an INI-like language, to split configuration into relevant sections.

> **TIP** If you're following the practices in this book on one of your existing packages and it uses the setup.py file, you should consider migrating to the pyproject.toml file and the setup.cfg file covered later in this chapter if your project uses static metadata (http://mng.bz/ZAdZ). Some features of Setuptools still require setup.py; see chapter 4.

Teaching TOML is beyond the scope of this book, but the pieces you need for your packaging will be included and explained where needed in this book. Create the pyproject.toml file using the following command to correct the error:

```
$ touch pyproject.toml
```

Run the `pyproject-build` command again. This time the build should run successfully, and you should see a large amount of output with a few notable lines, as shown in listing 3.1. What's happening here? At a high level, the build command consumes your source code and the metadata you supply, along with some files it generates, to create the following:

- *A source distribution package*—A Python source distribution, or sdist, is a compressed archive file of the source code with a .tgz extension.
- *A binary distribution package*—A Python built distribution package is a binary file. The current standard for built distributions is what's known as a wheel or bdist_wheel, a file with a .whl extension.

Whereas a source distribution allows almost anyone to build your code on their platform, a binary distribution is prebuilt for a given platform and saves users the work of building it themselves. The importance of these two distribution types will be covered in depth in chapter 4.

Listing 3.1 The result of building an empty Python package

The source distribution package is built by the build_sdist hook.

Setuptools and the wheel package are used for the build backend.

```
...
Successfully installed setuptools-57.0.0 wheel-0.36.2
...
running sdist
...
warning: sdist: standard file not found:
➥ should have one of README, README.rst, README.txt, README.md

running check
warning: check: missing required meta-data: name, url

warning: check: missing meta-data: either (author
➥ and author_email)
➥ or (maintainer and maintainer_email) should be supplied

creating UNKNOWN-0.0.0
...
Creating tar archive
...
Successfully installed setuptools-57.0.0 wheel-0.36.2
...
running bdist_wheel
...
creating '/Users/<you>/code/first-python-
➥ package/dist/tmpgdfzly_7/
➥ UNKNOWN-0.0.0-py3-none-any.whl' and adding
➥ 'build/bdist.macosx-11.2-x86_64/wheel' to it
```

The build process expects a README file in one of a few formats.

The build process expects a name and a URL for the package.

The package is called UNKNOWN because no name was specified.

The binary wheel distribution package is built by the build_wheel hook.

The source distribution is a compressed archive file.

The binary wheel distribution is a .whl file.

The build process expects an author or maintainer of the package.

Because you haven't supplied any metadata yet, the build process alerts you to the fact that it's missing some important information like a README file, the author, and so on. Adding this information is covered later in this chapter.

Notice that the build process installs the setuptools and wheel packages. Setuptools (https://setuptools.readthedocs.io) is a library that was, for a long time, one of the only ways to create Python packages. Now, Setuptools is one of a variety of available *build backends* for Python package builds.

> **DEFINITION**   A *build backend* is a Python object that provides several required and optional hooks that implement packaging behavior. The core build backend interface is defined in PEP 517 (http://mng.bz/o5Rj).

A build backend does the logistical work of creating package artifacts during the build process, namely through the `build_sdist` and `build_wheel` hooks. Setuptools uses the `wheel` package to build the wheel during the `build_wheel` step. The `build` tool uses Setuptools as a build backend by default when you don't specify one.

   The presence of build *backends* may leave you wondering if there may be build *frontends* as well. As it turns out, you've been using a build frontend already. The `build` tool is a build frontend!

> **DEFINITION**   A *build frontend* is a tool you run to initiate building a package from source code. The build frontend provides a user interface and integrates with the build backend via the hook interface.

To recap, you use a build frontend tool like `build` to trigger a build backend like Setuptools to create package artifacts from your source code and metadata (see figure 3.1).

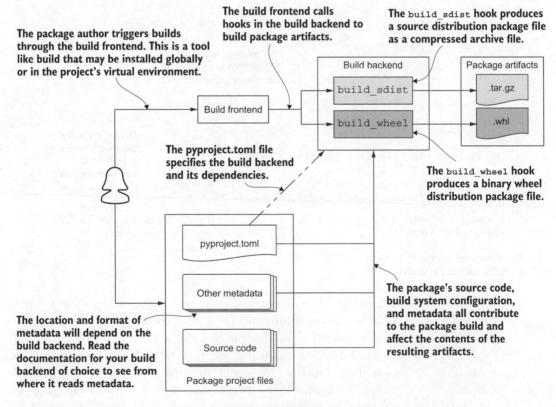

Figure 3.1   **The Python build system consists of a frontend user interface that integrates with a backend to build package artifacts.**

Because the build process creates package artifacts, you can now check the effect of running the build. List the contents of the root directory for your project now. You should see the following:

```
$ ls -al $HOME/code/first-python-package/
.
..
.venv/
UNKNOWN.egg-info/
build/
dist/
pyproject.toml
```

The UKNOWN.egg-info/ and build/ directories are intermediate artifacts. List the contents of the dist/ directory, where you should see the source and binary wheel package files, as shown here:

```
$ ls -al $HOME/code/first-python-package/dist/
UNKNOWN-0.0.0-py3-none-any.whl
UNKNOWN-0.0.0.tar.gz
```

Other build system tools

As I mentioned earlier, other options exist for both build frontends and backends. Some packages provide both a frontend and a backend. Through the rest of this book, continue using `build` and Setuptools as the frontend and backend for your builds.

If you want to explore some alternative build tools, check out Poetry (https://python-poetry.org/), flit (https://flit.readthedocs.io), and hatch (https://hatch.pypa.io). Each build system makes different trade-offs between ease of configuration, capability, and user interface. As an example, flit and poetry are geared toward pure-Python packages, whereas Setuptools can support extensions in other languages. Chapter 4 covers this in more detail.

You can switch to another build system in a few steps, shown here:

1 Install the new build frontend package.
2 Update pyproject.toml to specify the new build backend and its requirements.
3 Move the metadata about the package to the location expected by the new build backend.

Recall that `build` used Setuptools as the fallback build backend because you didn't specify one. You can specify Setuptools as the build backend for your package by adding the lines in listing 3.2 to pyproject.toml. These lines specify the following:

1 *build-system*—This section describes the package build system.
2 *requires*—These are a list of dependencies, as strings, which must be installed for the build system to work. A Setuptools build system needs Setuptools and wheel, as you saw earlier in this chapter.

3 *build-backend*—This identifies the entry point to the build backend object, using the dotted path as a string. The Setuptools build backend object is available at `setuptools.build_meta`.

These represent the complete configuration you need to specify the build backend.

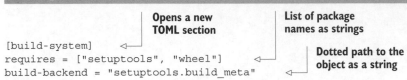

```
[build-system]
requires = ["setuptools", "wheel"]
build-backend = "setuptools.build_meta"
```

Once you've added the build system information, run the build again. Nothing should change in the output: you've just locked in Setuptools as the explicit backend instead of letting `build` fall back to it as a default. Now that you've got a handle on the Python package build system, you need to add some metadata about your package.

3.2   *Authoring package metadata*

You learned that each build backend may look for package metadata in different places and formats. For the Setuptools backend, you can specify static metadata in an INI-style file called setup.cfg in the root directory of your project. You'll add sections of key-value pairs to this file that provide information about the package and its contents.

Some metadata is essential to build a package that can be identified properly. When you ran the build, it resulted in files with "UNKNOWN-0.0.0" in the name, which is the result of some missing core metadata. Start by fixing these core metadata issues first.

3.2.1   *Required core metadata*

To fix the names of your package files, start by creating the setup.cfg file in the root directory of your project.

> **NOTE** PEP 621 (https://www.python.org/dev/peps/pep-0621/) describes a standard for declaring static metadata in the pyproject.toml file. Although it's been accepted, the standard is not yet widely adopted. In particular, as of the time of writing, Setuptools does not yet support it (https://github.com/pypa/setuptools/issues/ 1688), though some alternatives may. This and future chapters attempt to balance the developer experience for packaging, testing, code quality, and so on across setup.py, setup.cfg, and pyproject.toml accordingly.

Two fields are minimally required for a package: `name` and `version`. These distinguish a distributed version of your package from other packages and other versions of your own package. Add the fields to `setup.cfg` in a section called `metadata`. It should look like the following:

```
[metadata]
name = first-python-package
version = 0.0.1
```

This is the "metadata" section.

Sections contain one or more key-value pairs.

After you save the file, remove the dist/ directory and run the build process again. List the contents of the newly generated dist/ directory, where you should see the following:

```
$ ls -al dist/
.
..
first-python-package-0.0.1.tar.gz
first_python_package-0.0.1-py3-none-any.whl
```

This confirms that you've supplied the name and version correctly. The build process recognized the values you supplied and used them to populate the filenames of the package artifacts. "UNKNOWN" has been replaced by a normalized version of "first-python-package," and "0.0.0" has been replaced by "0.0.1" (see table 3.1).

Table 3.1 Filename comparison

Before	After
UNKNOWN-0.0.0.tar.gz	first-python-package-0.0.1.tar.gz
UNKNOWN-0.0.0-py3-none-any.whl	first-python-package-0.0.1-py3-none-any.whl

To confirm that the package contains the intended files, you can manually inspect its contents. Change to the dist/ directory and unpack the source distribution package using the following commands:

```
$ cd $HOME/code/first-python-package/dist/
$ tar -xzf first-python-package-0.0.1.tar.gz
```

This creates a first-python-package-0.0.1/ directory next to the package file, containing the files packaged from your project along with a few generated files. You should see the following:

```
$ ls -1R first-python-package-0.0.1/
PKG-INFO
first_python_package.egg-info
pyproject.toml
setup.cfg
```

The source distribution contains several generated files.

The source distribution also contains files you created in your project.

```
first-python-package-0.0.1/first_python_package.egg-info:
PKG-INFO
SOURCES.txt
dependency_links.txt
top_level.txt
```

TIP   You can also use the `tree` command (https://linux.die.net/man/1/tree) for nicely formatted output. If you don't have `tree` installed, you may be able to get it from your platform's system package manager.

You can also confirm that the metadata you specified has been faithfully reproduced in the package. Open either of the PKG-INFO files and take a look at the contents. The PKG-INFO file contains a normalized version of the metadata. You should see the following:

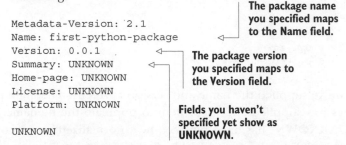

```
Metadata-Version: 2.1
Name: first-python-package
Version: 0.0.1
Summary: UNKNOWN
Home-page: UNKNOWN
License: UNKNOWN
Platform: UNKNOWN

UNKNOWN
```

The package name you specified maps to the Name field.

The package version you specified maps to the Version field.

Fields you haven't specified yet show as **UNKNOWN.**

The package name and version you specified show up here, but there are several other fields that are still UNKNOWN. The build process is still alerting you to a missing URL, README, and author information as well. Next, you'll fix these issues and flesh out the metadata a bit further to tell people about the package.

3.2.2   *Optional core metadata*

The name and version are the only two strictly required fields, per the core metadata specification (http://mng.bz/nez8), but several other fields are indexed by search engines or surfaced in highly visible ways on sites like PyPI. If you want others to find and use your package, it's a good idea to supply information for as many of the fields as possible.

A rundown on package metadata

If you want to learn all the different fields available and how they've evolved over time, the following PEPs (https://www.python.org/dev/peps/) deal with the package metadata specification:

- *PEP 241: Metadata for Python Software Packages* (https://www.python.org/dev/peps/pep-0241/) introduces the PKG-INFO file.
- *PEP 301: Package Index and Metadata for Distutils* (https://www.python.org/dev/peps/pep-0301/) introduces the idea of a centralized Python package index as well as classifiers to better distinguish Python packages.
- *PEP 314: Metadata for Python Software Packages v1.1* (https://www.python.org/dev/peps/pep-0314/) augments PEP 241 with additional fields.
- *PEP 345: Metadata for Python Software Packages 1.2* (https://www.python.org/dev/peps/pep-0345/) augments PEP 314 with additional fields, changed fields, and deprecated fields.

- *PEP 566: Metadata for Python Software Packages 2.1* (https://www.python .org/dev/peps/pep-0566/) augments PEP 345 with the core metadata specification, stricter allowable values for package names, additional fields, and a canonical transform of package metadata to JSON.
- *PEP 621: Storing project metadata in pyproject.toml* (https://www.python.org/ dev/peps/pep-0621/) defines a standard for providing package metadata in the pyproject.toml file as opposed to files like setup.py or setup.cfg. This has been accepted but doesn't yet have wide adoption by packaging tools.
- *PEP 639: Metadata for Python Software Packages 2.2* (https://www.python .org/dev/peps/pep-0639/) proposes an approach to standardizing how licenses are specified for packages.

The core metadata specification provides the most current list of available fields and their format.

The build process is still alerting you to a missing URL and author information. Add the following fields to the [metadata] section in the setup.cfg file, filling in your personal information where appropriate:

```
...
url = https://github.com/<username>/<package repo name>
author = Given Family
author_email = "Given Family" <given.family@example.com>
```

Run the build again, and you should no longer see the alerts about a missing URL and author. Unpack the source distribution file and view the PKG-INFO file again. You should see the following, with the new values you've added:

```
Metadata-Version: 2.1
Name: first-python-package
Version: 0.0.1
Summary: UNKNOWN
Home-page: https://github.com/<username>/           The url field maps
   <package repo name>                              to Home-page.
Author: Given Family
Author-email: "Given Family" <given.family@example.com>
License: UNKNOWN
Platform: UNKNOWN                                    The author and author_email
                                                     fields map to Author and
UNKNOWN                                              Author-email.
```

The summary is still showing as UNKNOWN. The summary is a short description of the package's purpose. You can think of this as an elevator pitch for your package: it's what people will see most often when they're searching for packages to use. If you're reading this book, chances are that you want to learn how to share your code. If you skimp on the metadata, it's likely that no one will find it. Metadata ensures that your package will be as discoverable as possible further down the line. In Setuptools, the summary is called `description`. Add the `description` field to your metadata now, like so:

```
...
description = This package does amazing things.
```

There's also that unlabeled UNKNOWN lurking at the end of the file. That space is for the package's long description, which can provide more details about how to install and use the package or what problems it solves. Recall that the build process is still complaining about a missing README file. You can fix both these issues in one pass by creating a README file and referencing it in the metadata. Create a README.md file now, with content something like the following:

```
# first-python-package

This package does amazing things.

## Installation

```shell
$ python -m pip install first-python-package
```
```

In setup.cfg, you can now use the `long_description` field to reference your README file using the special `file:` directive. The `file:` directive accepts the path to a file, relative to setup.cfg, whose contents should be taken as the value for the field. In addition, you also need to specify the `long_description_content_type` field to indicate that your README is something other than plain text. Because your file is a Markdown file, you should specify the `text/markdown` content type. Add both of these fields to your metadata now:

```
...
long_description = file: README.md
long_description_content_type = text/markdown
```

Run the build, extract the source distribution, and inspect PKG-INFO again. You should see the following:

- The `Summary` field is populated with the short description.
- The file now contains a `Description-Content-Type` with a value of `text/markdown`.
- The UNKNOWN at the end of the file is now replaced with the contents of your README.md file.

When you update your README file, those changes will be pulled into the next version of the package you build. This automation reduces the issue of remembering to update your documentation in multiple places. The license is the last UNKNOWN field you'll address for now, and it requires some special attention.

3.2.3 Specifying a license

In most regions, software is protected by copyright by default. If you don't provide any license, you're not giving anyone permission to use your code—even if you publish it as open source software (see Tal Einat, "Over 10% of Python Packages on PyPI Are Distributed without Any License," *Snyk*, http://mng.bz/vX9q). Licenses are important because they help your users understand the conditions under which they're allowed to use your software. The detailed process of choosing a specific license is outside the scope of this book, but sites like Choose a License (https://choosealicense.com) guide you through the process by asking you what freedoms and restrictions you want to provide with your software.

> **License granularity**
>
> Most often, you need to specify the license that pertains to your entire package only once at the package metadata level. If you need to give a more permissive or restrictive license to a specific file or files, you can include the overriding license directly in those files. The Python packaging process doesn't provide a way to handle complex per-file license granularity within a project, but third-party tools may exist to help with this.

Once you choose a license, you need to declare that license alongside your code so that users can identify whether they can work with your software. Sites like GitHub automatically discover license information from a few files like LICENSE or LICENSE.txt. At the same time, you need to provide your license in your source and binary package distributions so people who install your package can view the license as well.

To properly identify your license of choice and to include the license information in your built package distributions, use a combination of the following three fields:

- `license`—Specifies the identifier from the SPDX license list (https://spdx.org/licenses/) that corresponds to your chosen license
- `license_files`—Specifies the path to one or more license files, relative to setup.cfg
- `classifiers`—Specifies any relevant trove classifiers (https://pypi.org/classifiers/) your package falls under for discovery purposes

As an example, if you were to choose the MIT License (https://mit-license.org/), you'd place a copy of the license text in a LICENSE file in the root directory of your project, and then add the following fields to your metadata:

```
...
license = MIT
license_files = LICENSE
classifiers =
    License :: OSI Approved :: MIT License
```

Now you've learned how to specify a variety of metadata about your package for the Setuptools build backend, and you've seen how the build system normalizes and uses that metadata when it builds distribution packages. The flow of metadata between input files and output files is summarized in figure 3.2.

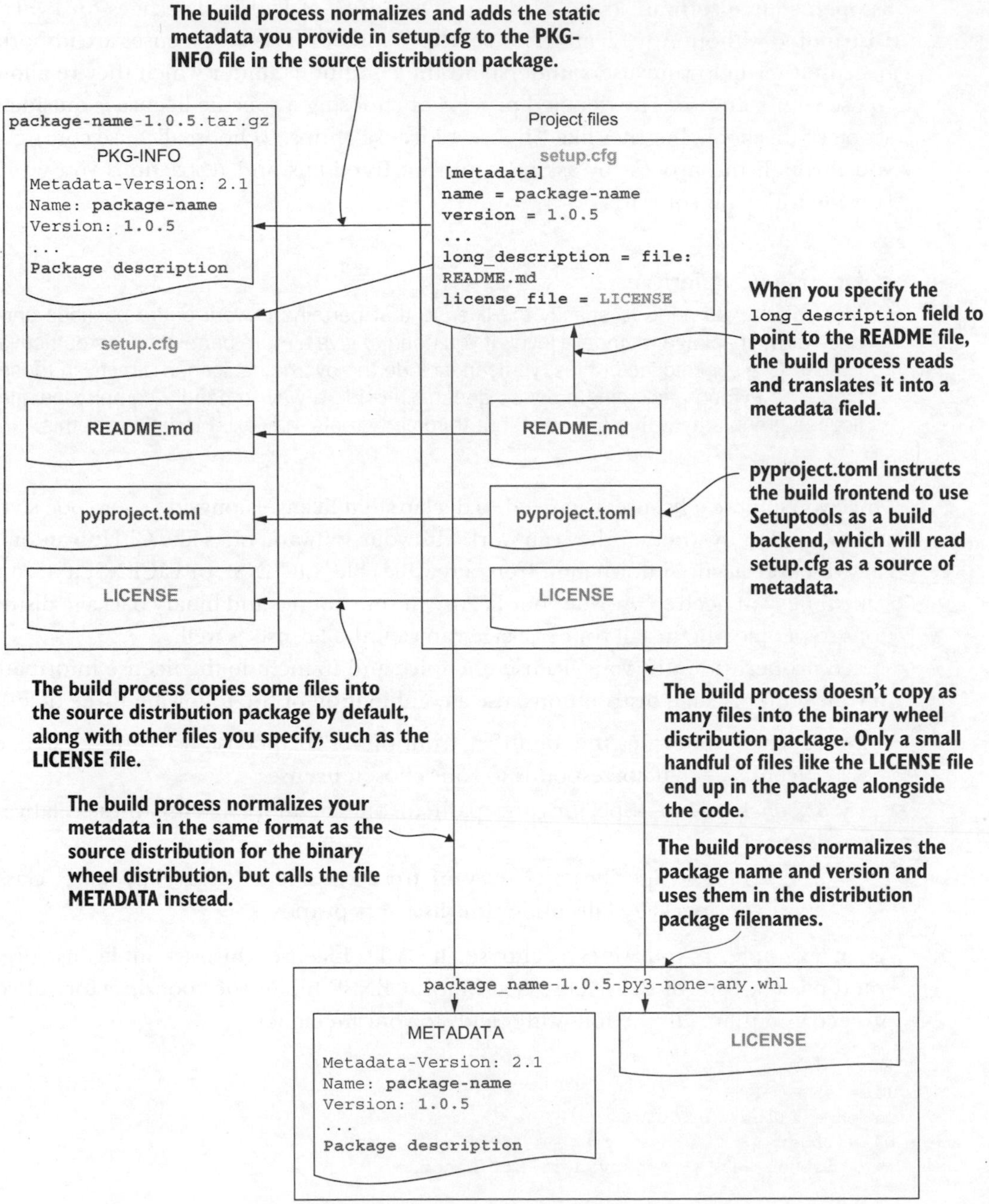

Figure 3.2   The flow of metadata between input project files and output distribution package files

Now that you understand how the metadata flows from your project into the distribution package files, it's time to learn how your source code does the same.

3.3 Controlling source code and file discovery

Imagine you've finally finished creating a package, complete with 100% unit test coverage. You publish it, only to start getting reports of a bug. It turns out that you ran your tests against the raw source code instead of the packaged code CarCorp actually received when they installed the package, and you packaged the code incorrectly.

Python doesn't impose a specific directory structure for your code and your tests. This flexibility can be helpful, but it also leads naturally to multiple conventions. Some conventions are open to practices that lead you to create broken packages due to missing files or incorrect imports. Use a convention that discourages these practices by forcing you to test the packaged code. Running the packaging manually often can become tedious as a result, but tools to remove that burden are covered in chapter 5.

Keeping your tests separate from your implementation code altogether limits the possibility of running the tests against the raw source accidentally. (See Ionel Cristian Mărieș, "Packaging a Python Library," http://mng.bz/49Bg.) In the following model, the implementation modules and the test modules are each nested in their own directory:

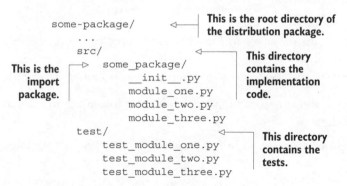

NOTE You'll learn more about testing the packaged code in chapter 5.

This approach also makes the purpose of each top-level directory clearer to someone who happens upon your project: the src/ directory likely contains the implementation, and the test/ directory likely contains code that tests the implementation. By separating the tests from the implementation, you've also decoupled the structure of the two areas. Although it can make sense for the tests and the implementation to share a similar hierarchy, you're not bound to that.

Exercise 3.1

Create the layout for your package. You should create the following structural pieces:

- An src/ directory
- A test/ directory
- An import package called `imppkg` containing an empty module called `hello.py`

After you're done, you should have the following directories and files in addition to the files you created earlier in this chapter:

```
first-python-package/
    ...
    src/
        imppkg/
            __init__.py
            hello.py
    test/
```

Run the build process and unpack the distribution file. Notice anything missing? The `imppkg` code files aren't there. Due to the flexibility of project layouts, and because you can distribute multiple import packages in a single distribution package, some build systems will require more specificity than you might think to discover your code. Setuptools needs to know the following:

- In which directories to look for packages
- The names of specific (sub)packages to look for, or a directive to recursively find them all automatically
- How to map any found package directories to different import names, if desired

For the layout you've created, you can accomplish this with the following additional sections and fields in setup.cfg:

- *[options]*—This section provides additional options for Setuptools package builds.
- *[options].package_dir*—This is a list of key-value pairs to map discovered directories to import paths. An empty key means the "root," such that any directory mapped to the root will be removed from the import path and only its child directories will be included.
- *[options].packages*—This is either an explicit list of packages or the special `find:` directive that tells Setuptools to recursively search for any packages. `find:` is often the best choice, because you won't need to update it if you add new packages later.
- *[options.packages.find]*—This section provides options to the Setuptools package discovery process triggered by the `find:` directive.
- *[options.packages.find].where*—This tells Setuptools which directory to look in for packages.

Add those options to your setup.cfg now. The configuration should look something like the next listing.

Listing 3.3 A configuration for discovering packages with Setuptools

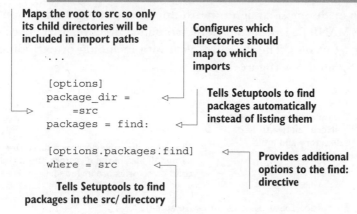

Maps the root to src so only its child directories will be included in import paths

Configures which directories should map to which imports

```
...

[options]
package_dir =
    =src
packages = find:

[options.packages.find]
where = src
```

Tells Setuptools to find packages automatically instead of listing them

Provides additional options to the find: directive

Tells Setuptools to find packages in the src/ directory

This configuration will cause Setuptools to search in the src/ directory, find the imp-pkg package there, map the src/imppkg/ directory to the imppkg import package, and include any modules within the imppkg/ directory in the distribution package.

Notably, this configuration does not include anything from the test/ directory. It's common to exclude tests from distribution packages to reduce the package size and also because users rarely run the tests for third-party packages.

> **TIP** You may wish to add a field in options.packages.find to explicitly exclude any test modules from the package in case any accidentally make their way outside the test/ directory in the future, as shown next:

```
...
exclude =
    test*
```

This will exclude any (sub)packages that begin with test from the distribution package.

Run the build process and unpack the distribution again. This time, it contains the imppkg package with its hello.py module faithfully reproduced there. You've got a working build! Although you've successfully packaged your Python files, there's still one configuration needed to ensure that non-Python files are included in your package.

3.4 *Including non-Python files in a package*

CarCorp has received your latest package, and the bug they'd been dealing with is fixed. Unfortunately, a new bug has reared its head—the JSON file containing input data seems to be missing!

You've successfully packaged up your Python code and your metadata, but you haven't accounted for non-Python files yet. Create a data.json file in the same directory as your `hello.py` module now. Run the build process and observe that the data.json file is not present in the distribution.

With Setuptools, one of the most straightforward approaches to including non-Python files is using the MANIFEST.in file. This file contains directives that specify how to treat a matching set of files. The directives deal with including or excluding and have varying levels of granularity (figure 3.3).

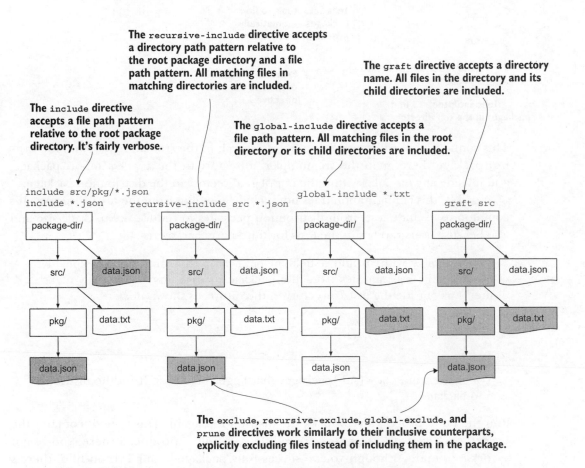

Figure 3.3   MANIFEST.in file directives to include non-Python files in packages

One of the quickest ways to start is by including all files in the src/ directory and recursively excluding some files generated by Python. You can achieve this by creating the MANIFEST.in file in the root directory of your project with the following content:

```
graft src
recursive-exclude __pycache__ *.py[cod]
```

← Includes all files from
the src/ directory . . .

. . . except __pycache__ directories or
files that end in .pyc, .pyo, or .pyd

Run the build process and check the source distribution for the data.json file. Now, check the binary wheel distribution using the following command:

```
$ unzip -l first_python_package-0.0.1-py3-none-any.whl
```

← Lists the contents of a ZIP
archive without unpacking it

The data.json file isn't present. You can tell Setuptools to include any non-Python files contained in the source distribution into the binary distribution as well by adding the following field to the [options] section of your setup.cfg file as follows:

```
...
include_package_data = True
```

The binary wheel distribution file is now configured such that the data.json file is included.

Exercise 3.2

Run the build process one more time and unpack both distributions. List the contents and confirm the presence of the data.json file. For reference, the file is located in the following places for each distribution:

```
$ ls <unpacked sdist>/src/imppkg/
__init__.py
data.json
hello.py

$ ls <unpacked bdist_wheel>/imppkg/
__init__.py
data.json
hello.py
```

You've learned how your source code, metadata, and supporting files can all be packaged together into single-file distributions. You've also learned the different pieces of the Python build system and how they interoperate to produce the package file. You're ready for chapter 4, where you'll get into the specifics of a project, installing third-party dependencies, and building for multiple target systems.

Summary

- A Python package build needs a build frontend and backend, your source code, and your metadata.
- Build frontends and backends can be swapped for alternatives but use the same core workflow.
- Packages rely on core required metadata to build properly, and systems rely on additional metadata to provide a rich discovery and browsing experience.
- Structure may differ from project to project, and build backends must be configured accordingly to package the right code.
- Build backends may need additional configuration to package non-Python files.

Part 2

Creating a viable package

Why are you building a package? You may want to share some code with your team to use in multiple projects. You may want to create a command-line interface that others can install and run. Or you may need to abstract performant code in a low-level language like C with an easy-to-use layer of interaction in Python. You might get dizzy thinking about the reasons to build a package and ways of doing so, but don't despair.

This part will help you think about your packaging project as a pipeline of moving pieces and build an orchestration process to manage it all. The project exercises real-world tools and activities that build your confidence and muscle memory, enabling you to change or add new activities to your pipeline later on. Although the possibilities are endless, you control the direction, and you should feel in control.

Handling package dependencies, entry points, and extensions

4

This chapter covers

- Defining dependencies for your package
- Making functionality available as command-line tools
- Packaging extensions written in C

You're just getting ready to start adding your groundbreaking functionality into your Python package for CarCorp when they call with a few last-minute requests. They want you to make sure it's *really fast* and that it can be run as a standalone command because their developers aren't as well-versed in Python as you are. You haven't even delivered the first version of your package yet, and already the requirements are growing! Before you panic, take a deep breath and read this chapter to learn more.

> **IMPORTANT** You can use the code companion (http://mng.bz/Xa0M) to check your work for the exercises in this chapter.

4.1 A package for calculating vehicle drift

Imagine that the software you've been working on for CarCorp will help them guide their vehicles on the road. During their testing they've observed that the vehicles tend to drift around the road more than they'd like, and they've started

41

measuring the drift. Although they have the raw data, they don't have a great way of measuring the impact of any potential improvements they make.

The package you're building will provide utilities for CarCorp to gain visibility into this issue. The first thing you'll do is provide a way to calculate the average drift in millimeters per second over a given distance. The vehicles measure their drift rate about one million times during each run through the five-kilometer testing course. Your package will consume these measurements as a list of floating-point numbers and calculate their *harmonic mean.*

> **Harmonic mean**
>
> The *harmonic mean* is different from the more common arithmetic mean and is the correct calculation to use when you want the average rate instead of the average *of* rates. Peter A. Lindstrom shows some examples in *The Average of Rates and the Average Rate* (http://mng.bz/19n1).

You can calculate the harmonic mean of the drift by dividing the total number of measurements by the sum of reciprocals of the measurements:

$$H = \frac{N_{measurements}}{\frac{1}{m_1} + \frac{1}{m_2} + \frac{1}{m_3} + \dots}$$

With one million inputs, this calculation might take some time. You can see why Car-Corp emphasized that they want speed. When examining code performance, it's best to profile the code instead of speculating about the impact of improvements (see Dane Hillard, "Designing for High Performance," *Practices of the Python Pro*, Manning Publications, 2020, pp. 72–76, http://mng.bz/m2N0). Before you go too much further, you must first observe how the Python version fares.

> **Exercise 4.1**
>
> In the root directory of your project, create a `harmonic_mean.py` module. In this module, write a `harmonic_mean` function that accepts an arbitrarily long list of floating-point numbers and returns their harmonic mean.

Now that you've written a Python implementation of the harmonic mean calculation, you can use the built-in `timeit` module (https://docs.python.org/3/library/timeit .html) to measure its performance. When you profile code, you should reduce it to the minimal portion for which you want to measure the performance to ensure an accurate picture when comparing solutions. The `timeit` module enables you to separate setup code from the code you want to measure by passing the setup code as a string to the `--setup` option. The setup code will run only once and will not be counted toward the measurement of your code. You can invoke the module directly with `py -m timeit` and any arguments you want to pass. You can use the `--setup` option multiple times to separate multiple expressions, or use it a single time by separating expressions with a semicolon, as shown in the following snippet:

```
$ py -m timeit \
    --setup '<SETUP EXPRESSION 1>' \         Multiple setup expressions
    --setup '<SETUP EXPRESSION 2>' \         can be separated into
    '<MEASURED CODE>`                        multiple arguments.

$ py -m timeit \                                  Setup expressions can
    --setup '<SETUP EXPRESSION 1>; <SETUP EXPRESSION 2>' \   also be separated by
    '<MEASURED CODE>'                             a semicolon in a
                                                  single argument.
```

To avoid setup overhead in your profile measurement, you should perform any imports and create data inputs in the setup step. Because you need the `harmonic_mean` function and the `random.randint` function, those should be imported as setup steps. You also want to measure the performance of `harmonic_mean` against a true-to-life set of data. You can create a list of random integers as a setup step as well and pass that list to the `harmonic_mean` function in the execution step. Your command should look something like the following snippet:

```
                                                  Imports the function
                                                  you want to measure
$ py -m timeit \
    --setup 'from harmonic_mean import harmonic_mean' \
    --setup 'from random import randint' \             Imports helper
    --setup 'nums = [randint(1, 1_000_000)              functions needed
➡ for _ in range(1_000_000)]' \                        for setup
    'harmonic_mean(nums)'                Creates data
                                         inputs ahead
    Uses only the function you want      of time
    to measure in the execution
```

Run the command now. The `timeit` module will print out the statistics of the profile, including

- How many times it ran the code to get an average execution time (the measurement loops)
- How many sets of measurement loops it ran
- The best execution time of all the sets of measurements loops

The following snippet shows the statistics of how the `harmonic_mean` function performed on my MacBook Pro with 16 GB of memory and a 2.2 GHz 6-core processor:

```
5 loops, best of 5: 52.8 msec per loop
```

The `timeit` module ran five sets of five-measurement loops and ultimately found that the call to `harmonic_mean` could run in as short a time as 52.8 milliseconds on average. You may see similar results, but they can vary based on what hardware you have and what else your computer is using it for at the time of measurement. The `timeit` module tries to account for some of these factors using the measurement loops. At the end of the day, it's important to remember that profiling should be used to compare one solution to another in a relative manner.

Save the results of your profiling somewhere for later reference, because now you're going to see how you can speed up this calculation to the level CarCorp is hoping for.

4.2 Creating a C extension for Python

When you write code or install third-party packages, you're extending the functionality of your software beyond what Python alone can provide. Typically, though, you're still using Python to achieve that extension. Just as you can use packages to extend functionality, you can also create and use extensions written in other languages to improve performance. Because the reference Python interpreter is written in the C programming language, C is a common choice for these extensions, but people also write extensions in C++ (http://mng.bz/M0om), Rust (http://mng.bz/aPwY), and even Fortran (http://mng.bz/gRgn).

You learned about Python build backends in chapter 3, and you used Setuptools to start building the skeleton of your package. Setuptools has strong capabilities for building extensions from other languages. Other build backends may offer differing levels of support for extensions. Any time you're considering switching your build backend, consider any candidate backend's ability to meet your needs in this area. For now, you'll continue using Setuptools to integrate a C extension into your package.

4.2.1 Creating C extension source code

Covering in depth the writing of C-level code for use in Python is beyond the scope of this book, but because extensions are a common need for numerical programming, it's important to learn how you can integrate them into a Python package. As with Python build backends and frontends, extensions and the tools to build them can be swapped in and out of your project as needed, and the details are left up to whichever tools you decide to invest in.

To expose you to one available option that also has a low barrier to entry, you'll convert your `harmonic_mean` function into a C extension using *Cython* (https://cython.org/). Not to be confused with CPython, the reference implementation of Python, Cython is a compiler and language for creating Python C extensions. The Cython language is a superset of Python and, at its most basic, can be used to speed up some Python code without requiring sweeping changes. The Cython compiler converts Cython source code to optimized C code, which will then be compiled during a package's build process (see figure 4.1).

Cython source files end with .pyx and can contain Python or Cython code. Because the Cython language is a superset of Python, a valid Python program is also a valid Cython program. Rename your `harmonic_mean.py` module to `harmonic_mean.pyx`

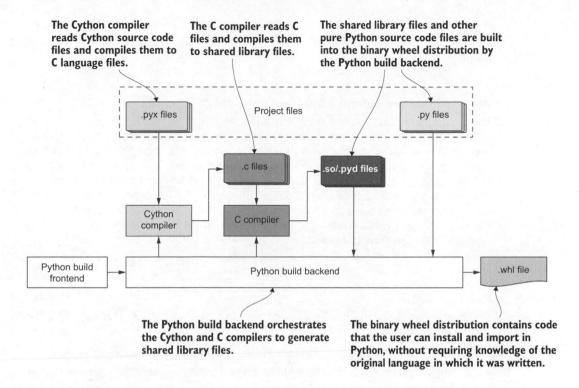

The Cython compiler reads Cython source code files and compiles them to C language files.

The C compiler reads C files and compiles them to shared library files.

The shared library files and other pure Python source code files are built into the binary wheel distribution by the Python build backend.

The Python build backend orchestrates the Cython and C compilers to generate shared library files.

The binary wheel distribution contains code that the user can install and import in Python, without requiring knowledge of the original language in which it was written.

Figure 4.1   Extensions are compiled into shared libraries that are included in binary wheel distributions.

and move it into the src/imppkg/ directory. Now that you have a Cython source code file, you need to integrate Cython into your package's build process.

4.2.2   *Integrating Cython into a Python package build*

You learned in chapter 3 that you can specify dependencies for a Python package's build process in the pyproject.toml file. Cython is a Python package itself, so you can add it to the list of build dependencies. This will ensure that Cython is installed before the build starts and is available to convert your Cython file to C code for compilation. Update the `requires` value in the `build-system` section of the pyproject.toml file to include `"cython"` now.

Next, you'll need to ensure that your Cython source files are included in your package. You also learned in chapter 3 that, when using Setuptools, you can include non-Python files in your package using the MANIFEST.in file. You used the `graft` directive to include all non-Python source files from the src/ directory. That expression also includes all .pyx files. Run the build process using the `pyproject-build` command, and confirm that your Cython file ends up in the package as expected.

Now that you've created and included your Cython code in the package, you need to tell Cython to convert it to C code so that it will be compiled. Without this step, your friends at CarCorp would only receive the raw .pyx file, which might leave them scratching their heads. To run Cython, you'll need to create one more file called setup.py.

Why do I see the setup.py file used so widely?

The setup.py file has been a part of the Python packaging ecosystem for ages—it even predates Setuptools. Introduced in PEP 229 (https://www.python.org/dev/peps/pep-0229/) in 2000, its goal was to centralize where packaging configuration happens. You'll likely see that a wide variety of packages still use it, and although it's still necessary for some use cases, the new build workflow and tools you learned in chapters 2 and 3 are intended to replace setup.py in the long term. For pure-Python packages that don't need to determine any dynamic information at build time, you can use pyproject.toml to define your build and setup.cfg for configuration when using Setuptools as your build backend.

Exercise 4.2

Create the `setup.py` module in the root directory of your project. The module must do the following:

1 Import the `setuptools.setup` function for hooking into the build process
2 Import the `Cython.Build.cythonize` function for identifying which Cython files need to be converted
3 Call `cythonize` with the path to your Cython file, relative to the root directory of the project
4 Call the `setup` function with the `ext_modules` keyword argument set to the result of the `cythonize` call

Now that you've created the `setup.py` module, you have a configuration that will convert your Cython files to C code and then compile it during the package build process. Run the build now. You should see the following new lines in the output that can help verify things are working as you expect:

- Cython is installed as a build dependency.
- Your Cython file is pulled into the source distribution.
- The `build_ext` process is triggered by your call to `setuptools.setup`.
- The extension is compiled to a binary file (.so for macOS and Linux, or .pyd for Windows) and added to the binary wheel distribution.

```
...
Collecting cython          ◁──┐  Cython is installed as
...                            │  a build dependency.
copying src/imppkg/harmonic_mean.pyx
➡ -> first-python-package-0.0.1/src/imppkg      ◁──┐  Your Cython file is
...                                                 │  copied into the
                                                    │  source distribution.
```

```
running build_ext          ⟵⎤ Setuptools builds
building 'harmonic_mean' extension  ⎦ your extension.
...
adding 'harmonic_mean.cpython-39-darwin.so'  ⟵⎤
```
**The created binary file is copied
into the binary wheel distribution.**

Additionally, you should see in the dist/ directory that your binary wheel distribution file has changed names. Before, it was first_python_package-0.0.1-py3-none-any.whl. Now, its name will depend on the system you're using and the Python version you used. On my MacBook Pro with Python 3.10, the file is named first_python_package-0.0.1-cp310-cp310-macosx_11_0_x86_64.whl. You'll learn more about why this is so later in this chapter. For now, continue to the next section where you'll install and profile the C extension version of your harmonic_mean function.

4.2.3 *Installing and profiling your C extension*

You've gone to all the work of building your package several times now, but you have yet to install it. In chapter 2, you created a virtual environment in the .venv/ directory, located in the root of your package directory. You can use this environment to test the installation of your package. Use the pip module to install it using the following command from the root directory of your project. The . indicates that pip should install the current directory as a package:

```
$ py -m pip install .   ⟵⎤ Installs the current
                          ⎦ directory as a package
```

After the command completes, your first-python-package package will be installed just as if it had been installed from PyPI! You should still be able to import your harmonic_mean module and use the harmonic_mean function, but this time, it will resolve to the installed package instead of directly from the source code. Try it in the Python interpreter, as shown in the following snippet:

```
$ py
...
>>> from imppkg.harmonic_mean import harmonic_mean
>>> harmonic_mean([0.65, 0.7])
0.674074074074074
```

Because your pure-Python version was importable as harmonic_mean.harmonic_mean but the C extension is imported from imppkg.harmonic_mean.harmonic_mean, you need to update the setup step to profile this new implementation.

> **Exercise 4.3**
>
> Run the command to measure the performance of the C extension version of your `harmonic_mean` function. As before, your setup step should do the following:
>
> - Import the `harmonic_mean` function
> - Import `random.randint`
> - Create a list of one million random numbers with values between 1 and 1,000 using the built-in `random.randint` function
>
> The code you measure should only be the call to your `harmonic_mean` function with the list of random numbers as input.

What do you see? Compare the results to your earlier measurement of the pure-Python implementation. Remember that you haven't changed the code you had to write—you changed only the filename and told Cython how to handle it. On my system, this change alone resulted in the following statistics:

```
20 loops, best of 5: 18.5 msec per loop
```

You read that correctly—the C extension version of the code can run as quickly as 18.5 milliseconds, nearly *three times* faster than the pure-Python implementation. And Cython did all the heavy lifting! Now, what about that binary wheel distribution file?

4.2.4   *Build targets for binary wheel distributions*

Although the performance you gained using Cython could be considered an easy win, it isn't without its trade-offs. When you write packages using Python alone, they're extremely portable—any system running a compatible Python version can run your code. As soon as you introduce code that must be compiled, everything changes.

Some of the most performant programming languages are able to achieve their speed through static typing, predefined memory allocation, and a compilation step prior to runtime. These features are valuable in computation-heavy contexts. Unfortunately, many of these same features also rely on knowledge of the computer architecture and operating system on which they're running. Performance is often gained by exploiting features and behavior of these systems, so what works in one place won't necessarily work in another. In the worst cases, it can actually cause memory corruption and failed execution if run in the wrong context.

Because of the nuances of execution, source code for these languages must typically be compiled separately for each of the architectures and operating systems where it will be used. Take another look at the binary wheel distribution file in the dist/ directory. Its filename is divided into several important sections (see figure 4.2). The first two are the normalized package name and version. These may be followed by an optional build number. The last three parts are tags that identify the compatibility of the binary wheel as follows:

- *Python version*—Which implementation of Python the code must execute on
- *Application binary interface (ABI)*—How the binary of the compiled code is organized
- *Platform*—Which operating system and CPU architecture the code must execute on

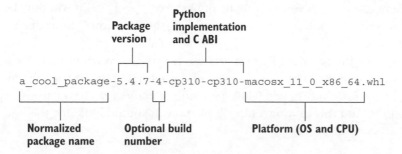

Figure 4.2 The anatomy of a binary wheel distribution filename

When you install packages, your package manager will determine which binary wheel distributions are available and use these tags to identify which of those it should download for your system. As an example, the binary wheel distribution file first_python _package-0.0.1-cp310-cp310-macosx_11_0_x86_64.whl is compatible with the CPython 3.10 implementation, the CPython 3.10 API, and the macOS 11 operating system running on an x86 64-bit CPU architecture.

You might notice that three of these filename segments relate to the number of binary wheel distributions you would need to build to cover all possible targets. Fortunately, the first two segments—the Python implementation and ABI version—are usually identical. On the other hand, some operating systems can run on different CPU architectures, so that single tag is really two pieces of information. This all boils down to the Python implementations, operating systems, and CPU architectures you want to support. That means the number of binary wheel distributions you need to build is roughly the following:

$$N_{\text{Python implementations}} \cdot N_{\text{Operating systems}} \cdot N_{\text{CPU architectures}}$$

As an example, at the time of this writing, the NumPy project (https://numpy.org/) supports CPython 3.7, 3.8, and 3.9 as well as PyPy 3.7. It supports these across different architectures for each of macOS, Linux, and Windows. In all, each release of NumPy makes twenty-seven wheels available. This sounds like a lot of work, and as a lone maintainer, that's probably true. But because NumPy is so central to the scientific community for building performant numerical software, the project maintainers are willing to put in this effort on an infrequent basis to deliver the performance their users need all the time.

4.2.5   *Specifying required Python versions*

You may build packages that are only compatible with features or syntax available since a specific Python version. When this is the case, it's best to specify this in your setup.cfg file because when you eventually publish your package, it will only be available when users try to install it using a compatible Python version. This reduces confusion and surprise.

You can specify the required Python version or range of versions with the `python _requires` keyword in the `[options]` section of the setup.cfg file, using the same PEP 440 (https://peps.python.org/pep-0440/) version specifiers that you use to specify package versions. Add this to your setup.cfg file now. It should look like the following:

```
[options]
...
python_requires = >=3.9
```

When users try to install your package using Python 3.8 or earlier, they'll see a message that no compatible versions of the package are available.

So far, you've built one pure-Python wheel and one wheel specific to your Python implementation and platform. This might seem like a far cry from the scale at which projects like NumPy are operating. Fortunately, some tools have emerged that can ease the burden of building these wheels, and you'll learn more about them in chapter 7. For the moment, rejoice that you've built a working Python package and get ready to handle that second request from CarCorp.

4.3   *Offering command-line tools from a Python package*

CarCorp wants to be able to run a standalone command to quickly calculate harmonic means. They're familiar with using a shell to run commands, but not as familiar with using Python to write and run scripts. Fortunately, most Python build systems also support this. You can tell these systems that, as part of the installation process, some part of the code should be exposed as a runnable command. In the following sections, you'll learn how Setuptools handles this use case.

4.3.1   *Creating commands with Setuptools entry points*

Setuptools enables you to provide commands to users through what it calls *entry points*. An entry point is like a door—a way in and out of a place. Setuptools entry points provide a way into a package's functionality in a discoverable way. Named commands are one such way of exposing those entry points.

You're likely familiar with the `if __name__ == "__main__":` syntax used in many Python scripts intended for command-line use. When you run `python some.py`, the

4.3   *Offering command-line tools from a Python package*   **51**

__name__ for some.py will be "__main__", and the code in the conditional will run. Commands are a more generalized and flexible version of this concept. At a high level, you create a command in Setuptools by mapping a name for the command to the dotted module path of a function. As an example, imagine you want a command named harmony that supplies the calculation behavior from the imppkg.harmonic_mean .harmonic_mean function. Instead of requiring you to run python harmonic_mean.py and respond with if __name__ == "__main__" in your code, an entry point enables you to run the harmony command and point to a function that calls imppkg.harmonic_ mean.harmonic_mean with the arguments from the command (see table 4.1).

Table 4.1   The different ways to execute code from a Python module

Approach	Command	Requires installation	Pros	Cons
Execute module directly	`$ py /path/to/ package/src/imppkg/ harmony.py [args]`	No		Imports within code may not work
Execute as importable module	`$ py -m imppkg.harmony [args]`	No (works for any importable code)	Imports within code work	Long command, requires knowledge of package structure
Execute as entry point	`$ harmony [args]`	Yes	Short command, no knowledge of package structure required	

To create a command entry point, you first need to create the handler function.

> **Exercise 4.4**
>
> Add a new Python module in your src/imppkg/ directory called harmony.py. Inside that module, create a main function that
>
> - Uses sys.argv to get the arguments from the command line
> - Converts the arguments to a list of floating-point numbers
> - Calls imppkg.harmonic_mean.harmonic_mean, passing in the list of numbers
> - Prints the calculated mean of the numbers
>
> Remember to import sys and imppkg.harmonic_mean.harmonic_mean.

With your handling function in place, you can now configure Setuptools to make it available as a command. You tell Setuptools where to look for the command using the [options.entry_points] section in the setup.cfg file. This section is a table mapping the entry point group to (command name, handler function) pairs. For commands, the entry point group is console_scripts. You've already used one console script in your packaging adventure so far: the `build` tool provides the `pyproject-build` command as a console script (http://mng.bz/2nBX).

> ### What other entry point types are there?
>
> The entry points system in Setuptools is quite flexible. The `console_scripts` group is the convention used for creating command-line tools, but a group can be any other valid string. This can be used to coordinate functionality *across* packages if they agree on a convention for an entry point, making plugin-based architectures possible. pytest, a popular testing package that you'll learn more about in chapter 5, uses this approach so others can write testing plugins (http://mng.bz/R4jP).
>
> Different packages can find each other's software without knowing specifics about it ahead of time, which is a powerful offering for extensibility (see Dane Hillard, "Extensibility and Flexibility," *Practices of the Python Pro,* Manning Publications, 2020, pp. 147–142, http://mng.bz/m2N0). If you want to build a package that others can extend without you needing to be involved, this is an area to look further into on your own.

Write the entry points section now. It should look like the following snippet:

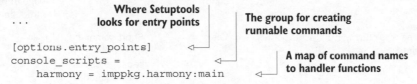

Now that you have a handler function and Setuptools knows to make it available through the `harmony` command, it's time to verify that it works. Reinstall your package into your virtual environment now. Once that completes, run the following command from the root directory of your project:

```
$ ./.venv/bin/harmony 0.65 0.7
```

You should see the following output:

```
0.674074074074074
```

> **TIP** Notice that you had to include the `.venv/bin/` prefix for the command. When a user installs your package into their active virtual environment or a base Python version, the installed command will automatically be added to their PATH, and the prefix won't be necessary.

You now have a buildable, installable Python package that delivers a fast calculation for harmonic means. Confident you've satisfied the functionality CarCorp asked for, you decide you want to wow them with something they didn't know they needed. Because working in a console often means finding lines of interest in a wall of text, you want the `harmony` output to really pop. You decide you want to add colorized text, but you don't have the time to learn ANSI escape sequences. You decide to install another package to handle this for you.

4.4 *Specifying dependencies for Python packages*

Up to now, your package has not depended on any third-party Python packages. Now that you want to add one, it might be tempting to install it directly into your virtual environment using pip. Unfortunately, this won't work for your users because they would also need to install the package themselves. Remember from chapter 1 that a major part of the value of package management systems is dependency resolution and installation. What you really want to do is specify to the Python package management tools that your package has a dependency and let them manage installation for you. This will help you get the dependency, but it will also help your users get it. A win all around!

Specifying dependencies for packages is similar to the familiar route of using something like a requirements.txt file to list your dependencies, but with the following two key differences:

- Dependencies need to be specified where your build system will see them so that the dependencies can be incorporated into the metadata package managers use to resolve and install dependencies.
- Dependencies should be specified as loosely as they can be to maximize compatibility for users.

> **IMPORTANT** To emphasize that last point: packages should avoid being pinned to an exact package version when they don't need to be. Imagine that you and I each create a package and they both depend on the `requests` package. Now imagine someone wants to use them both in their project. They install yours, but when they try to install mine, they get an error saying that my package depends on `requests==2.1.1`, but your package depends on `requests==2.1.2`. There's no way forward through this issue because solving the problem for one package creates a problem for the other.
>
> If instead we both make our packages depend on `requests>=2.1.1,<3`, any version of requests greater than 2.1.0 and less than 3.X will work for the user. As the user installs more packages with more dependency specifications, this ensures that we don't unnecessarily narrow the space of valid dependency combinations for them.

Another benefit to using looser dependency definitions for packages is that you can find issues caused by upstream packages sooner. If you pin to an exact version for six months and then try to upgrade later, you may find a cascade of issues and have to spend a whole day getting back up to speed. If you loosely define dependencies, you'll uncover those issues any time you reinstall dependencies for the package during development and testing. Dealing with new issues so frequently can feel daunting at first, but you'll appreciate iterating on these comparatively smaller changes regularly rather than having to put out a proverbial fire every few months.

Setuptools looks for package dependencies in the `install_requires` key of the [options] section in the setup.cfg file. The `install_requires` value is a list of dependencies specified using the same syntax you would use in a requirements.txt file. To add some color to the output of the `harmony` command, you'll use the `termcolor` package. As of this writing, the latest release of termcolor is 1.1.0. Because you aren't going to test earlier versions and you trust them to maintain existing features until at least the 2.0.0 release, you can specify `termcolor>=1.1.0,<2` as the version.

Add the `install_requires` key now. It should look like the following snippet:

```
[options]
...
install_requires =
    termcolor>=1.1.0,<2
```

Now, when your package is installed, pip will also download and install the latest 1.X version of `termcolor`. With this in place, you can make use of `termcolor` in your `harmony.py` module. Instead of using the built-in `print` function to print the result of the harmonic mean calculation, import and use the `termcolor.cprint` function. This function accepts additional arguments compared to `print`, described here:

- An optional foreground color specifier, like `'red'` or `'green'`
- An optional background color specifier, like `'on_cyan'` or `'on_red'`
- An `attrs` list for styles, like `['bold', 'italic']`

Exercise 4.5

Replace the `print` call in the `harmony.py` module with a call to `termcolor.cprint`. The text should be bold and red on a cyan background. Reinstall your package and rerun the `harmony` command to confirm that the output looks as you expect.

Looking spectacular? If not, play around with the values for `termcolor` and find a color scheme that you like.

You now have something fairly polished that you can think about shipping to Car-Corp. But you have a nagging feeling they'll be asking for more functionality soon. When you're ready, continue on to chapter 5 to see how you can integrate your test suite to verify your changes as your package grows.

Answer to exercises

4.1

```
def harmonic_mean(nums):
    return len(nums) / sum(1 / num for num in nums)
```

4.2

```
from setuptools import setup
from Cython.Build import cythonize

setup(
    ext_modules=cythonize("src/imppkg/harmonic_mean.pyx"),
)
```

4.3

```
$ py -m timeit \
    --setup 'from imppkg.harmonic_mean import harmonic_mean' \
    --setup 'from random import randint' \
    --setup 'nums = [randint(1, 1_000_000) for _ in range(1_000_000)]' \
    'harmonic_mean(nums)'
```

4.4

```
import sys

from imppkg.harmonic_mean import harmonic_mean


def main():
    nums = [float(arg) for arg in sys.argv[1:]]
    print(harmonic_mean(nums))
```

4.5

```
...

from termcolor import cprint

...

    cprint(harmonic_mean(nums), 'red', 'on_cyan', attrs=['bold'])
```

Summary

- Explore non-Python extensions by first using a high-level translation layer like Cython.
- Providing a non-Python extension gains runtime performance but adds build time complexity, either for you or your consumer.
- Entry points into your package offer more ways of interacting with its behavior than just importing the code.
- Leverage the power of package management systems to handle dependency resolution for you.

5

Building and maintaining a test suite

This chapter covers

- Running unit tests with pytest
- Creating test coverage reports with pytest-cov
- Reducing duplicated test code with parameterization
- Automating packaging for testing using tox
- Creating a test matrix

Tests are an important aspect of any project you plan to maintain. They can ensure that new functionality behaves as you expect and that existing functionality hasn't regressed. Tests are the guardrails for refactoring code—a common activity as projects mature.

With all this value that tests provide, you might think all open source packages would be thoroughly tested. But many projects pass on things like code coverage or testing for multiple target platforms because of the maintenance burden they present. Some maintainers even *create* maintenance burden without realizing it due to the way they design and run their test suite. In this chapter, you'll learn some beneficial aspects of testing and how to introduce them to your package's test suite, with an eye toward automation and scalability.

If you're still new to unit-testing concepts, you can learn all about them in Roy Osherove's *The Art of Unit Testing*, 3rd ed. (Manning Publications, anticipated 2023, http://mng.bz/YKGj).

> **IMPORTANT** You can use the code companion (http://mng.bz/69A5) to check your work for the exercises in this chapter.

5.1 Integrating a testing setup

The first step toward building a robust test suite is configuring a *test runner* to run any tests for the project. If you've used the built-in `unittest` module in the past, you've most likely used a command like `python -m unittest discover` as your test runner. `unittest` is a perfectly capable piece of software, but, like any Python built-in, it requires work on your part when you want to extend or change its behavior. Further, the framework `unittest` employs is inspired both functionally and semantically by the xUnit (https://xunit.net/) family of testing frameworks, which can feel awkward because its conventions don't always follow PEP 8 (https://www.python.org/dev/peps/pep-0008/) style.

For a testing experience that aligns more closely with Python runtime code and can scale in productivity with your test suite, pytest (https://docs.pytest.org) is a strong alternative. You'll use pytest throughout the rest of this chapter and learn some of the advantages it has over the `unittest` module.

5.1.1 The pytest testing framework

pytest aims to make it easier to write simple tests and support increasingly complex projects as they grow. It can run `unittest`-based test suites out of the box but also provides its own assertion syntax and a plugin-based architecture to extend and change its behavior to suit your needs. The framework also provides a number of utilities for designing scalable tests, such as

- *Test fixtures*—Functions that provide additional dependencies to a test, such as data or database connections
- *Parameterized tests*—The ability to write a single test function and multiple sets of input arguments to create a unique test for each set of inputs

> **TIP** For an in-depth look at pytest and all its features, check out Brian Okken's *Python Testing with pytest*, 2nd ed. (Pragmatic Bookshelf, 2022, http://mng.bz/1olg).

You *must* install pytest in the same virtual environment where your package and its dependencies are installed. Unit tests execute your real code, and that code must be importable. As an example, if you install pytest globally using pipx, pytest won't know where to find your project's dependencies and will fail to import them. Jump straight into pytest by installing it into your project's virtual environment using the following command:

```
$ py -m pip install pytest
```

Installing pytest makes the `pytest` module available. In chapter 4, you installed your package's code into the virtual environment so that it could be imported. pytest imports your code the same way when running tests. Run pytest now using the following command:

```
$ py -m pytest
```

This causes pytest to discover any tests it can and then execute them. Because you don't have any tests yet, you will see output like the following:

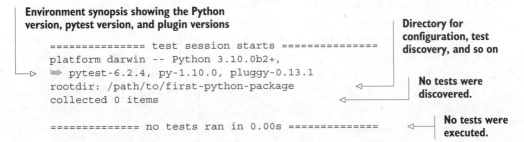

Environment synopsis showing the Python version, pytest version, and plugin versions

Directory for configuration, test discovery, and so on

```
=============== test session starts ===============
platform darwin -- Python 3.10.0b2+,
➡   pytest-6.2.4, py-1.10.0, pluggy-0.13.1
rootdir: /path/to/first-python-package
collected 0 items

=============== no tests ran in 0.00s ===============
```

No tests were discovered.

No tests were executed.

Remember that in chapter 3 you created a layout for your project that separates the source code from the test code. You added your implementation code to the src/ directory and created an empty test/ directory. To avoid including tests in the packaged code and to keep your tests in one easy-to-find place, you should place your tests in the test/ directory. By default, pytest discovers tests anywhere they might exist in your project. This includes tests in the root directory of the project or in the src/ directory, which isn't ideal. You'll configure pytest to ensure that it runs only tests placed in the proper location.

Exercise 5.1
Create a `test_harmonic_mean.py` module in the root directory of the project, and add one test function called `test_always_passes` that always passes. If you aren't familiar with pytest, you can use Python `assert` statements directly for your test assertions; a statement like `assert True` will always pass.

After you create the test module, run pytest again. This time you will see output like the following:

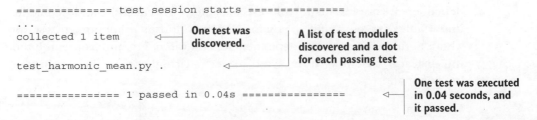

```
=============== test session starts ===============
...
collected 1 item

test_harmonic_mean.py .

=============== 1 passed in 0.04s ===============
```

One test was discovered.

A list of test modules discovered and a dot for each passing test

One test was executed in 0.04 seconds, and it passed.

This demonstrates that pytest is looking everywhere under the project's root directory for tests. To encourage the placement of tests in the appropriate location, you should configure pytest to look only in the test/ directory. You can add configuration for pytest into your package's setup.cfg file using a new section called `[tool:pytest]`. The `testpaths` key maps to a list of paths in which to look for tests. You need just one: `test`. After you add this configuration, pytest should confirm in its output both that it's using setup.cfg as the configuration file and that it found the `testpaths` configuration.

> **Exercise 5.2**
>
> Add the pytest configuration in `setup.cfg` to look only in the test/ directory for tests. After you add the configuration, do the following:
>
> - Run pytest again, and confirm that it discovers and runs no tests.
> - Move the `test_harmonic_mean.py` module into the test/ directory where it belongs.
> - Run pytest another time, and confirm that it discovers and runs the test you wrote.

Now you're in a good place to add more tests. pytest will pick up any new test modules you add to the test/ directory, according to its naming conventions, as follows (see figure 5.1):

1 Start in any directory in `testpaths`.
2 Find modules named `test_*.py`.
3 Find classes in those modules named `Test*`.
4 Find functions in those modules, or methods in those classes, named `test_*`.

Now that you've created a mechanism for writing and running tests, the next step is figuring out which tests to write. In the next section, you'll integrate test coverage and write more tests to ensure you're covering all the code paths for your package.

5.1.2   Adding test coverage measurement

Before starting into test coverage, you must first understand that it isn't a silver bullet. Test coverage tells you how much of your runtime code executed during test execution and can even measure how many conditional branches executed. But test coverage doesn't ensure that all those lines and branches have corresponding assertions that verify their behavior. A test that executes your entire code base but ends with an `assert True` will have 100% coverage but no value whatsoever.

That said, if you're diligent about designing your test cases properly, coverage is a useful tool to help you find areas of code that definitely *don't* have any assertions made about them. You can use this to add valuable tests and refactor your suite to get better

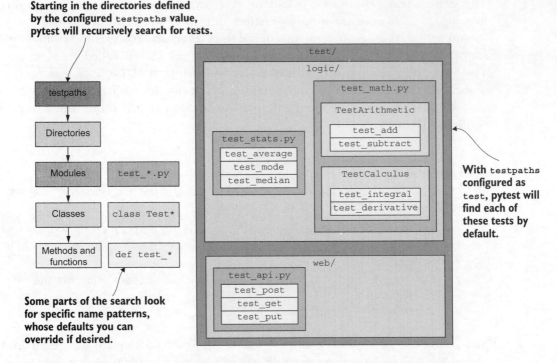

Figure 5.1   pytest discovers the unit tests in a project using recursive pattern matching.

coverage of your runtime code. To start measuring coverage, install the `pytest-cov` package in your project's virtual environment like so:

```
$ py -m pip install pytest-cov
```

This package provides a pytest plugin that integrates the Coverage.py project (https://coverage.readthedocs.io/) so that you can run it using pytest. Coverage.py is the de facto standard for measuring Python code coverage. With `pytest-cov` installed, run pytest with the `--cov` option to collect coverage measurements. You will see additional output at the end of the execution after the usual pytest report you've been seeing, listing a lot of files that you've never heard of, as shown here:

```
TOTAL
================ 1 passed in 0.04s ================
```
⬅ **The overall coverage of the entire code base**

Coverage.py measures the coverage of all the installed Python code it can find, which includes code for your package's dependencies and even pytest itself. To only measure coverage of your package, you can specify your import package's name as the value for the --cov option. Your tests don't even import your package yet, so you should expect the coverage to be zero. Run pytest again with your package specified for coverage and confirm this is the case. Coverage.py will produce output like the following:

```
$ py -m pytest --cov=imppkg
=============== test session starts ===============
...

Coverage.py warning: Module imppkg was never imported.
➡ (module-not-imported)
Coverage.py warning: No data was collected.
➡ (no-data-collected)
WARNING: Failed to generate report: No data to report.

/path/to/first-python-package/.venv/lib/python3.10/
➡ site-packages/pytest_cov/plugin.py:285:
➡ PytestWarning: Failed to generate report:
➡ No data to report.

  warnings.warn(pytest.PytestWarning(message))


-- coverage: platform darwin, python 3.10.0-beta-2 --


================ 1 passed in 0.04s ================
```

A confirmation that your package isn't imported in the tests

A confirmation that your runtime code is not covered at all

You can quickly fix the module-not-imported issue by importing your code in your tests. At the top of the test_harmonic_mean.py module, import the harmonic_mean function and the main function that supports the harmony command. After you add the imports, run pytest with coverage again. This time, you will see the __init__.py and harmony.py modules in the coverage output, similar to the following:

```
$ py -m pytest --cov=imppkg
...


-- coverage: platform darwin, python 3.10.0-beta-2 --
Name                    Stmts   Miss   Cover
--------------------------------------------
.../__init__.py             0      0    100%
.../harmony.py              6      2     67%
--------------------------------------------
TOTAL                       6      2     67%
```

There's no code in this module, so it's fully covered.

There are six statements in this module, two of which aren't executed by tests.

You should be able to see clearly now that test coverage doesn't necessarily correlate with test value. You've written one test that doesn't exercise any code, and you already have 67% coverage of your Python modules.

Coverage for non-Python extensions

Coverage.py typically covers Python source code, but for some non-Python extensions, it may be possible to cover their source code by enabling line tracing during compilation and using Coverage.py plugins that understand the line trace information. As an example, you can specify additional directives in your Cython .pyx files to enable line tracing and use the `Cython.Coverage` plugin to measure coverage.

ENABLING BRANCH COVERAGE

In addition to line coverage, an important aspect of testing is understanding how many alternative execution paths are possible and which of those paths are untested. A piece of code's *cyclomatic complexity* (Thomas J. McCabe, "A Complexity Measure." *IEEE Transactions on Software Engineering* 4 [1976]: 308–20., doi:10.1109/tse.1976.233837) measures the number of paths through the code, and for full coverage of your code's behavior, you need a test for each path. In Coverage.py, this is known as *branch coverage*.

To configure branch coverage for your tests, add a new section to setup.cfg called `[coverage:run]`. In this section, add a `branch` key with a value of `True` (see listing 5.1). This produces two new columns in the coverage output:

- *Branch*—How many branches exist throughout the code
- *BrPart*—How many branches are only partially covered by tests

---

Exercise 5.3

While you're adding the `[coverage:run]` section, add a `source` key with a value of `imppkg`. This is a handy way to stop specifying `imppkg` to the `--cov` option for pytest each time and ensures that anyone running tests with coverage will see the same output. You can also avoid specifying `--cov` altogether by adding an `addopts` key to the `[tool:pytest]` section with a value of `--cov`. You can override this at the command line later as desired using the corresponding `--no-cov` option.

After adding those configurations, what command should you run to get the same behavior you have been so far?

    A `pytest`
    B `pytest --cov`
    C `py -m pytest --cov`
    D `py -m pytest --no-cov`
    E `py -m pytest`
    F `py -m pytest --cov=imppkg`

Listing 5.1 Configuring coverage to measure branches

```
[coverage:run]
branch = True
```

With branch coverage enabled, possible branches are added to the statement count to determine total coverage. Run pytest again. Notice that the coverage for your code dropped from 67% to 50%, as shown next:

```
$ py -m pytest
...

-- coverage: platform darwin, python 3.10.0-beta-2 --
Name                 Stmts   Miss Branch BrPart  Cover
------------------------------------------------------
.../__init__.py          0      0      0      0   100%
.../harmony.py           6      2      2      0    50%      ◁──┐   Two branches were
------------------------------------------------------           found, and none were
TOTAL                    6      2      2      0    50%           partially covered.
```

> **NOTE** When branches are considered in coverage, the total coverage will be strictly less than or equal to the coverage without branching considered. The coverage percentage with branches considered can be difficult to calculate by hand because it considers all the different paths code may take during execution. You can read more about the specifics of branch measurement in the Coverage.py documentation (http://mng.bz/G1EA).

Now that you have a clearer picture of how well your tests cover your code and its execution paths, it's useful to know exactly which paths aren't covered.

ENABLING MISSING COVERAGE

Coverage.py can keep track of exactly which lines and branches aren't covered by tests, which is a big help as you try to write tests that increase the coverage of your code. You can turn this on by adding a new section to setup.cfg called [coverage :report], with a new key called show_missing set to a value of True (see listing 5.2). This will produce one new Missing column in the coverage output. The Missing column lists the following:

- Lines or ranges of lines that aren't covered. As an example, 9 means line 9 is uncovered, and 10-12 means lines 10, 11, and 12 are uncovered.
- Logic flow from one line to another that represents a branch that isn't covered. As an example, 13->19 means the execution path that starts at line 13 that would next execute line 19 is uncovered.

Listing 5.2 Configuring coverage to show uncovered code

```
[coverage:report]
show_missing = True
```

Run pytest again to see what the coverage report says you're missing. The lines listed in the report will correspond to the lines of the main function body in the harmony.py module, as shown here:

```
$ py -m pytest
...

-- coverage: platform darwin, python 3.10.0-beta-2 --
Name                   Stmts Miss Branch BrPart Cover Missing
--------------------------------------------------------------
.../__init__.py           0     0      0      0   100%
.../harmony.py            6     2      2      0    50%    9-10
--------------------------------------------------------------
TOTAL                     6     2      2      0    50%
```

Lines 9 and 10 are uncovered.

You can use the report of missing lines to quickly identify areas of focus for writing more tests.

Take a close look at the file paths in the Coverage.py output. They point to the files created in the virtual environment when you installed your package, with a prefix like .venv/lib/python3.10/site-packages/imppkg/. This is perfectly correct but can sometimes be difficult to read with the long prefix in front of each file. To simplify these paths and map the coverage back to the related source code, you can tell Coverage.py which file paths it should consider equivalent.

SIMPLIFYING COVERAGE REPORT OUTPUT

In your project, the .venv/lib/python3.10/site-packages/imppkg/ directory of your installed package is roughly equivalent to the src/imppkg/ directory of the package's source code. Tell Coverage.py this is the case with a new section in setup.cfg called [coverage:paths]. Add a source key to this section, with a list value of equivalent file paths. Coverage.py will use the first entry to replace any subsequent entries in the output. Paths in this list can contain wildcard characters (*) to allow any name in that portion of the path to match. The new section should look like the next listing when you finish.

Listing 5.3   Configuring coverage to output paths related to the source code

```
[coverage:paths]
source =
    src/imppkg/
    */site-packages/imppkg/
```

Run pytest again. The file paths in the output will be prefixed with src/imppkg instead of .venv/lib/python3.10/site-packages/imppkg, as shown next:

```
$ py -m pytest
...
```

```
-- coverage: platform darwin, python 3.10.0-beta-2 --
Name                        Stmts Miss Branch BrPart Cover Missing
------------------------------------------------------------------
src/imppkg/__init__.py          0    0      0      0  100%
src/imppkg/harmony.py           6    2      2      0   50%  9-10
------------------------------------------------------------------
TOTAL                           6    2      2      0   50%
```

As your project grows and you spend more time testing, it might become harder to pick out uncovered modules from the coverage report. If you're reaching 100% coverage for several files, it can be helpful to ignore them in the report output. You can add a skip_covered key with a value of True to the [coverage:report] section to filter those out (see the next listing). Files that are filtered out are only removed from the list; their coverage is still considered in the total coverage calculation for your code.

> **Listing 5.4 Configuring coverage to skip covered files**

```
[coverage:report]
...
skip_covered = True
```

Run pytest again. The __init__.py module will be filtered out of the report, with a message confirming that's the case, as follows:

```
$ py -m pytest
...

-- coverage: platform darwin, python 3.10.0-beta-2 --
Name                        Stmts Miss Branch BrPart Cover Missing
------------------------------------------------------------------
src/imppkg/harmony.py           6    2      2      0   50%  9-10
------------------------------------------------------------------
TOTAL                           6    2    . 2      0   50%

1 file skipped due to complete coverage.    ⟵——| **This confirms that fully
                                                covered files are filtered out.**
```

Now the coverage report shows you only those files that require your attention when your aim is to increase your test coverage.

5.1.3 *Increasing test coverage*

You've now got a trimmed-down way to see which files in your project may need testing attention with a report that can quickly let you know how changes you make impact the coverage. It's a great time to get a real test written to replace the assert True you wrote earlier.

In the test_harmonic_mean.py module, you need to write a test that exercises the code in the harmony.py module. The code there consists of the main function, which does the following:

1 Reads arguments from `sys.argv`
2 Converts those arguments to floating-point numbers
3 Calculates the harmonic mean of the numbers using the `harmonic_mean` function
4 Prints the result in colored text

You can write a test that will facilitate all these actions by patching `sys.argv` to a controlled value and asserting that the output is what you expect. This will also result in 100% coverage of the `harmony.py` module. However, this is what's known as a *happy path test*.

UNCOVERING UNHAPPY PATHS

Unhappy path tests exercise the less-frequent, error-prone ways through the code under test. When you want to make your code more robust, you should venture outside happy path tests to find these edge cases that may break your code (see figure 5.2).

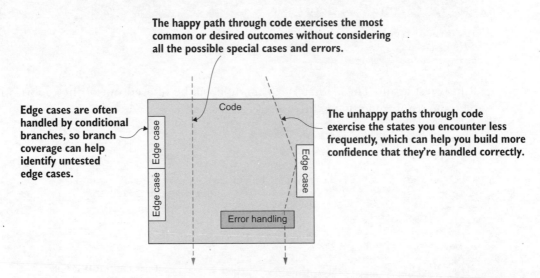

Figure 5.2   Tests may cover the common, desired execution paths or the less common edge and error cases.

You might be wondering how you can write tests with 100% line *and* branch coverage that can still miss code failures. If you have tests for every execution path that all pass, how can there be a way for the code to fail? The reason often comes down to the inputs that a piece of code accepts, especially if that input can come directly from a user. In the case of the `harmony` console script, it accepts input directly from the user at the command line and passes it into the `harmony.py` module's `main` function. If that input is invalid, your code may handle it in an unexpected way. This serves as a good reminder that full test coverage still isn't a perfect protection against errors.

Try running the installed `harmony` command. Note that you'll need to run it using `.venv/bin/harmony` because you haven't installed your package globally and the harmony command isn't on your $PATH. What happens when you pass it arguments that can't be converted to numbers? What happens when you don't pass it any arguments at all? You can produce a ZeroDivisionError or a ValueError. So even though a happy path where you pass in numbers works correctly, it's still possible to produce undesired outcomes with carefully chosen inputs. It's up to you in these cases to choose between documenting the proper usage and ignoring the edge cases, or updating your code to accommodate.

For the moment, assume that any inputs that result in a division by zero or that can't be converted to numbers should result in an output of 0.0. One way to accommodate this in the code is with a try for each potentially dangerous operation and a catch to handle the corresponding exception (see listing 5.5). This can start to feel like *defensive programming*, where you guard against all possible risks, no matter how unlikely they might be. But for some applications, you want to provide an error-free outcome, either for user experience or safety. You want CarCorp to be happy, and with the back and forth you've already had with them, it seems worth covering your bases.

Listing 5.5   A safer version of the main function that handles poor inputs

```
def main():
    result = 0.0          ◁───  The result will be zero unless
                                successfully calculated later.

    try:
        nums = [float(num) for num in sys.argv[1:]]
    except ValueError:       ◁───┐  If any input can't be converted
        nums = []                │  to a number, proceed as if
                                 │  there's no input.

    try:
        result = harmonic_mean(nums)
    except ZeroDivisionError:   ◁───┐  If there's no input or the input
        pass                         │  is only zero, proceed with the
                                     │  default result.

    cprint(result, 'red', 'on_cyan', attrs=['bold'])
```

This creates more lines and branches in the code, so you can expect the coverage to drop further. But now your coverage measurement can guide you to writing tests that assert the proper behavior for a wider variety of inputs. Update the source code in the harmony.py module to catch the ValueError and ZeroDivisionError cases. Then reinstall your package into your virtual environment using the py -m pip install . command.

Exercise 5.4

The following test covers the happy path of the main function, faking a user input and making an assertion about the printed output:

```
import sys

from termcolor import colored
```

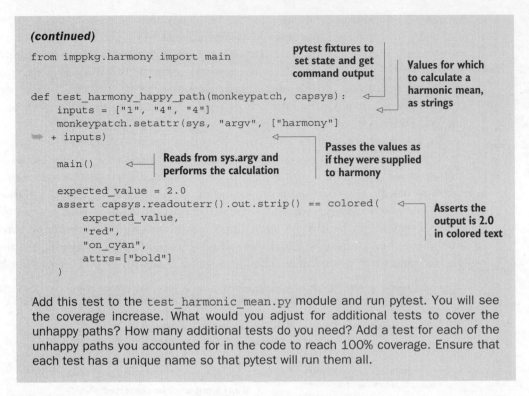

(continued)

```
from imppkg.harmony import main
```

pytest fixtures to set state and get command output

```
def test_harmony_happy_path(monkeypatch, capsys):
    inputs = ["1", "4", "4"]
    monkeypatch.setattr(sys, "argv", ["harmony"]
➡️  + inputs)
```

Values for which to calculate a harmonic mean, as strings

Passes the values as if they were supplied to harmony

```
    main()
```

Reads from sys.argv and performs the calculation

```
    expected_value = 2.0
    assert capsys.readouterr().out.strip() == colored(
        expected_value,
        "red",
        "on_cyan",
        attrs=["bold"]
    )
```

Asserts the output is 2.0 in colored text

Add this test to the `test_harmonic_mean.py` module and run pytest. You will see the coverage increase. What would you adjust for additional tests to cover the unhappy paths? How many additional tests do you need? Add a test for each of the unhappy paths you accounted for in the code to reach 100% coverage. Ensure that each test has a unique name so that pytest will run them all.

Earlier in this chapter, you configured Coverage.py to skip listing fully covered files. When you reach 100% coverage, all your files will disappear from the output because they're fully covered. The Coverage.py output shows an indication of 100% coverage as well, as shown next:

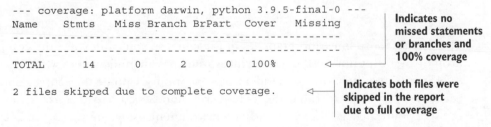

```
--- coverage: platform darwin, python 3.9.5-final-0 ---
Name    Stmts    Miss Branch BrPart  Cover   Missing
-----------------------------------------------------
-----------------------------------------------------
TOTAL     14       0      2      0    100%
```

Indicates no missed statements or branches and 100% coverage

```
2 files skipped due to complete coverage.
```

Indicates both files were skipped in the report due to full coverage

Now that you've reached 100% coverage, including some unhappy paths, you're in great shape. pytest will tell you if the behavior of your code regresses in the form of failing tests, and Coverage.py will tell you if there are any obvious opportunities for additional tests lurking. This leaves you free to get into the testing mindset and uncover unhappy paths that only you can identify. Now that you've got that out of the way, you'll take a few additional measures to further reduce the effort of testing going forward.

5.2 Addressing testing tedium

When you're new to testing, it can feel like a big thing standing in the way of getting things done. When you just want to deliver new features and value, tests can feel like a tangential effort. Reducing the effort of testing is a good way to encourage its adoption, and the investment will pay dividends in the future as your test suite grows.

5.2.1 Addressing repetitive, data-driven tests

You might have noticed that the tests you wrote to cover the `main` function all looked eerily similar. They each have the same basic shape, with just a few values altered. pytest has a great tool to address this kind of repeated, data-driven test. The `@pytest.mark.parametrize` decorator maps a list of values to arguments for the decorated test function, creating a separate test for each set of values. You can then use these arguments to construct a single test function that will properly assert the behavior for all the different values.

The `@pytest.mark.parametrize` decorator accepts the following arguments:

1 The argument names to map values to as a comma-separated string
2 A list, where each item is a tuple of values to map to the arguments

The decorated test function must accept arguments that correspond to the first `parametrize` argument, but it can accept additional arguments in any order. It's a common practice to place the parameterized arguments first and any additional arguments like fixtures last.

Imagine you've written a `mul` function that accepts two numeric arguments and returns their product. You want to write some tests that ensure it works properly when an input is positive, zero, and negative. You can use pytest's parameterization to do so, as shown in the following snippet:

```python
import pytest

from ... import mul


@pytest.mark.parametrize(          # The argument names to which values are mapped
    "input_one, input_two, expected",
    [                              # A list of tuples, each of which gets mapped
        (2, 3, 6),
        (-2, 3, -6),
        (-2, -3, 6),
        (0, 3, 0),
    ]
)                                  # Argument names that match the specification to parametrize
def test_mul(input_one, input_two, expected):   # A test constructed using the mapped arguments
    assert mul(input_one, input_two) == expected
```

This parameterized test function will result in four tests; each will have its own status in the pytest output. If one fails, the others can still pass. If you want to add more cases, it's a matter of adding a new tuple to the list of parameters. This can make it much faster to deal with data-heavy test suites with repetitive tests.

> **Exercise 5.5**
>
> Using `@pytest.mark.parametrize`, convert your tests for the `harmony.py` module's `main` function into a single, parameterized test. Don't forget to import `pytest`. After you finish, you should still have 100% coverage and the same number of passing tests.

Now that you've made your tests a bit leaner, you'll take a closer look at the testing process itself.

5.2.2 *Addressing frequent package installation*

You've installed your package into your virtual environment at least twice now. Because you set up your package to ensure you're always testing against the installed package, you need to reinstall the package each time you make any functional changes. This ensures that what you see matches what others see, but it also creates this manual work for you. You've only made one or two small changes to your source code so far, but imagine how you'll feel after your tenth feature request from CarCorp.

You also learned that making your package compatible with multiple dependencies and systems helps more people use it successfully. If you want to test your package with those different dependencies, that multiplies your manual work; each new dependency range causes further *combinatorial* growth (see figure 5.3). Combinatorial growth happens in a system where the number of possible states increases significantly with each new dimension added to the system. In your testing system, with only a few dependency variables, you can quickly reach tens of combinations to test.

tox (https://tox.readthedocs.io) automates the installation of packages for testing and the creation of a test matrix for dependency combinations. It significantly reduces the manual work you need to do, and as a result, it reduces the chance of human error in your testing.

GETTING STARTED WITH TOX

tox builds a fresh virtual environment for each combination of dependencies you test. Because of this isolated approach, you can make tox available globally and use it across projects instead of installing it separately in each.

> **NOTE** If you haven't installed tox yet, head over to appendix B and return to this section when you're done.

From the root directory of your project, run the `tox` command. Because you haven't configured tox yet, you will see the following output:

```
$ tox

ERROR: tox config file (either pyproject.toml, tox.ini, setup.cfg) not found
```

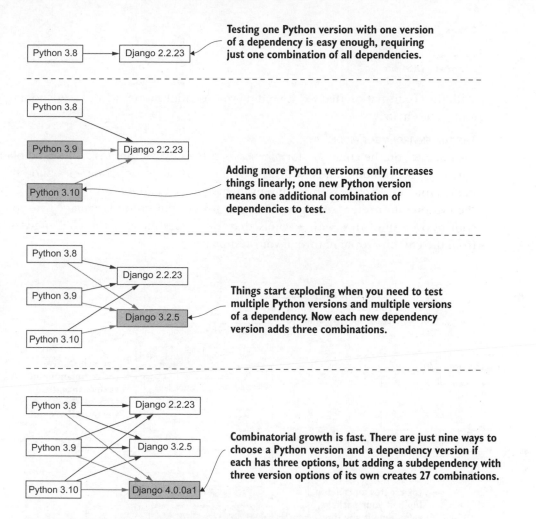

Figure 5.3   Testing across a range of versions for multiple dependencies grows very quickly.

Now add a new section to the setup.cfg file called [tox:tox]. This section is where you'll put the high-level configuration for your test matrix, as well as for tox itself. Start by adding an isolated_build key with a value of True as follows:

```
...

[tox:tox]
isolated_build = True
```

This tells tox to use the PEP 517 and PEP 518 standards you learned about in chapter 3 to build your package. Run tox again to confirm that it sees the configuration. tox produces the following friendly output:

```
$ tox

------------------
congratulations :)
```

With the confirmation that tox is reading your configuration, you're ready to start creating a test matrix.

THE TOX ENVIRONMENT MODEL

tox operates on the concept of *environments*. A tox environment is an isolated place to perform a set of commands, with its own set of installed dependencies and environment variables. Each tox environment includes a virtual environment with a copy of the Python interpreter (see figure 5.4). The tox configuration language gives you fine control over all of this, with a syntax that overcomes most of the challenges arising from the combinatorial nature of your test matrix.

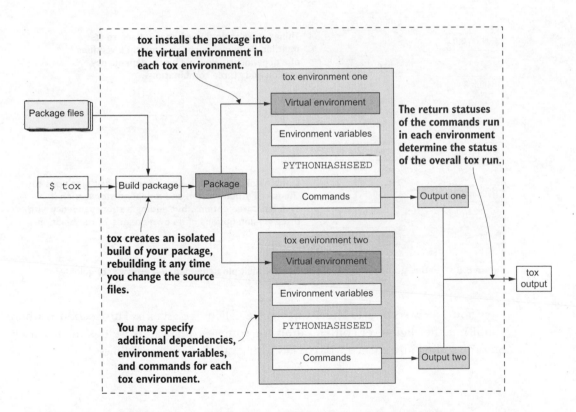

Figure 5.4   tox environments are an isolated place to build, install, and test your code.

You can create any arbitrary environments that you wish, but tox treats a few environment names specially. Environments with names like py37 or py310 will create a virtual environment with a copy of the corresponding version of the Python interpreter.

The envlist key in the tox configuration defines which environments tox should create and execute by default when running the tox command. The environments in the envlist can also be run individually as desired by using the -e argument to the tox command and specifying the environment name.

To get started, add an envlist key to the tox:tox section in your setup.cfg file with a value of py310 as follows:

```
[tox:tox]               The list of tox
...                     environments is
envlist = py310    ←——— your test matrix.
```

The next time you run tox, it will

1 Create an isolated build of your package
2 Create a virtual environment with a copy of Python 3.10
3 Install your package in the virtual environment
4 Set PYTHONHASHSEED to a new value to create more randomness for tests

Run the tox command again. You will see output similar to the following:

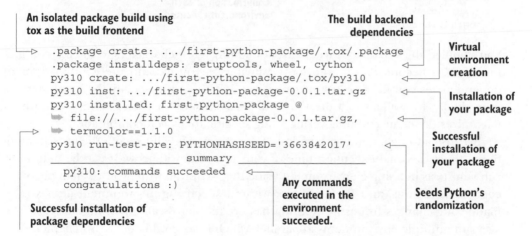

With only a small amount of configuration, tox is able to do all this work for you. You haven't told tox what commands to run in the environment yet, but your environment is there and ready. What if you want to do the same thing for multiple versions of Python? The envlist key accepts a comma-separated list of environments. As an example, you can specify py39,py310 to create both a Python 3.9 and Python 3.10 environment.

Update your envlist value to include an environment for an additional Python version. Although you've specified a new environment to create, tox will skip building your package because it knows the source code hasn't changed since the last build. Similar to the py310 environment you already created, in the py39 environment, tox will

1 Create the virtual environment
2 Install your package into it
3 Set `PYTHONHASHSEED`

tox will then execute the `py310` environment again. Because it already existed, tox won't recreate it or reinstall dependencies unless it detects that the dependencies have changed. Run tox again. You will see output similar to the following:

```
py39 create: .../first-python-package/.tox/py39            ◁──   The py39 environment
py39 inst: .../first-python-package-0.0.1.tar.gz                 is added.
py39 installed: first-python-package @
➥ file://.../first-python-package-0.0.1.tar.gz,
➥ termcolor==1.1.0
py39 run-test-pre: PYTHONHASHSEED='973215353'
py310 inst-nodeps: .../first-python-package-0.0.1.tar.gz   ◁──   The inst-nodeps
py310 installed: first-python-package @                          skips installing
➥ file://.../first-python-package-0.0.1.tar.gz,                 dependencies.
➥ termcolor==1.1.0
py310 run-test-pre: PYTHONHASHSEED='973215353'
_____ summary _____
  py39: commands succeeded        ◁──   Confirmation of each
  py310: commands succeeded              environment executed
  congratulations :)
```

You doubled the size of your test matrix by adding a few characters to the tox configuration. This becomes more and more valuable as you expand the combinations of dependencies you need to test, because you don't need to specify the combinations individually. tox will also ensure that your tests execute for each combination, which maximizes the chance of uncovering a bug specific to a given combination.

Because adding a new combination of dependencies will execute the tests an additional time, the total execution time of your test suite will grow. It can be helpful to run your tests in a single environment using the `-e` option while you're changing your code or your tests, and then run `tox` without specifying an argument after you've made your changes to ensure nothing has broken across all environments. You can also run multiple environments in parallel, which is covered later in this chapter.

Now you have two testing environments, but neither one does anything yet. The next step is to tell tox what to do within each environment.

5.2.3   *Configuring test environments*

So far you've configured tox in the `[tox:tox]` section to indicate how to build your package and which environments to create. To configure the test environments themselves, add a new `[testenv]` section. This section is used by default for any configured test environment. In this section, you tell tox what commands to run using the `commands` key. This key accepts a list of commands to run, with some special syntax available to pass arguments to the commands.

Within each command, you can use the `{posargs}` placeholder, which will pass any arguments to specify to the `tox` command along to the test environment commands.

As an example, if you specify python -c 'print("{posargs}")' as a command, running tox hello world will execute python -c 'print("hello world")' in the environment.

You can also pass options to a test command by separating them from the tox command and any of its options with two dashes (--). As an example, if you specify python as a command, running tox -- -V will execute python -V in the environment.

Exercise 5.6

Your test environments should execute the pytest command, with the ability to pass it additional arguments when running tox. Which of the following show a valid test command and corresponding tox command?

- **A** pytest {posargs}, tox
- **B** pytest {posargs}, tox --no-cov
- **C** pytest {posargs}, tox -- --no-cov
- **D** pytest --no-cov {posargs}, tox
- **E** pytest {posargs} --no-cov, tox
- **F** {posargs} pytest, tox -- --no-cov

After you add the pytest command to the commands list, run tox again. You'll see that after the steps you saw previously, tox tries to execute pytest and fails, as shown in the following output:

```
py39 run-test: commands[0] | pytest          ◁───┐  Attempted execution of
ERROR: InvocationError for command                │  the correct command
➥ could not find executable pytest           ◁───┐
                                                  │  The command can't be found
                                                  │  in the test environment.
```

Even though you installed pytest into the virtual environment for your project earlier, recall that tox creates and uses an isolated virtual environment for each test environment. This means that tox won't use the copy of pytest that you've been running. You haven't told tox to install pytest in those environments, so it can't find a copy there either. You can specify dependencies in the [testenv] section using the deps key. The value for deps is a list of Python packages to install, with syntax similar to requirements.txt or install_requires. For now, add pytest and pytest-cov as dependencies like so:

```
[testenv]
...
deps =
    pytest
    pytest-cov
```

Run tox again. This time it will install the additional dependencies, and the pytest command will successfully run the tests and the coverage report, with output similar to the following:

```
...
py39 installdeps: pytest, pytest-cov
...
py39 run-test: commands[0] | pytest
<PYTEST OUTPUT>
<COVERAGE OUTPUT>
...
py310 installdeps: pytest, pytest-cov
...
py310 run-test: commands[0] | pytest
<PYTEST OUTPUT>
<COVERAGE OUTPUT>
_____ summary _____
  py39: commands succeeded
  py310: commands succeeded
  congratulations :)
```

You've now got pytest and coverage running successfully in isolated environments on two different Python versions, without having to install your package manually. Any time you make a change to your source code, dependencies, or tests, you can run tox to see if things are still working. This early investment in infrastructure—especially for those who prefer test-driven development—will pay dividends throughout the rest of a package's life.

Before you move on, read the next section for some additional testing and configuration tips.

5.2.4   *Tips for quicker and safer testing*

As your project grows, you run the risk that the time you spend testing will grow along with it. To keep your productivity up, you want to keep testing as fast as possible and to reduce human error as much as possible. The following sections discuss some tips to keep your test suite execution in check.

RUNNING TEST ENVIRONMENTS IN PARALLEL

You might have noticed that your Python 3.9 and Python 3.10 environments have been executing sequentially. They each take a few seconds, so it's not too big of a deal. Now imagine a project where you're testing three Python versions and three different versions of a dependency. Are you patient enough to wait for nine environments to run sequentially?

tox provides a parallel mode (http://mng.bz/z546) that can execute multiple environments at a time. To run your two environments in parallel automatically, pass the -p option when running tox, as shown in the next code snippet. This mode will hide the output from each individual environment by default, showing only a progress indicator for the active environments and an overall pass or fail status for each environment:

```
$ tox -p
⠹ [2] py39 | py310

...
```

```
✓ OK py39 in 9.533 seconds
✓ OK py310 in 9.96 seconds
_____ summary _____
  py39: commands succeeded
  py310: commands succeeded
  congratulations :)
```

UNCOVERING STATEFUL TESTS

Consider the following snippet with two tests that make assertions about how Python lists work:

```
FRUITS = ["apple"]

def test_len():
    assert len(FRUITS) == 1

def test_append():
    FRUITS.append("banana")
    assert FRUITS == ["apple", "banana"]
```

Can you spot the issue? It might be subtle, but the second test alters the state of the system. Although FRUITS starts out containing one item, "apple", the test alters the list by adding "banana". These tests will pass as written, but they'll fail if you put them in reverse order (see figure 5.5):

```
FRUITS = ["apple"]

def test_append():
    FRUITS.append("banana")
    assert FRUITS == ["apple", "banana"]

def test_len():
    assert len(FRUITS) == 1
```

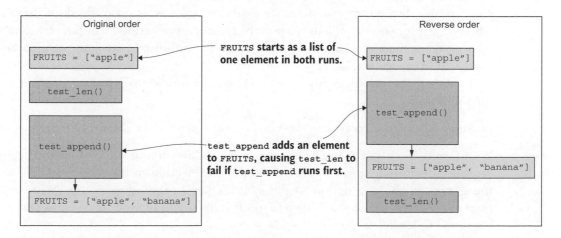

Figure 5.5 Tests that depend on state created by other tests may fail when reordered or moved.

Although it might be easy enough to spot and fix this example, stateful tests are often the result of several layers and interactions that you might not notice while writing the code. To increase the likelihood that you'll find and uncover these situations, you should run your tests in a random order. The `pytest-randomly` plugin (https://github .com/pytest-dev/pytest-randomly) does exactly this. It requires no configuration for the basic behavior of randomly ordered tests; add it to your `[testenv]` section's `deps` list, and you'll be all set.

By swapping the order of test modules, classes, methods, and functions, `pytest-randomly` uncovers tests that fail because of a dependency on state created in an earlier test (see figure 5.6). It does this by changing the random seed to a repeatable value for each run. This information is added to the pytest output shown here:

```
Using --randomly-seed=1966324489
```

When a test run produces a test failure, you can force future runs to execute in the same order that produced the failure by passing the `--randomly-seed` option to the `pytest` command with the same value output in the original run. Because pytest is being run by tox, you can pass the option to the underlying `pytest` command using a `--` to separate tox options from pytest options like this:

```
$ tox -- --randomly-seed=1966324489
```
⟵ **tox passes the argument to pytest.**

With `pytest-randomly` installed, your tests will run in a different order each time you run tox. If you notice that a test occasionally fails for no obvious reason, the test or the code under test may be stateful. You can use these hints as a good starting place to hunt down stateful issues.

ENSURING PYTEST MARKERS ARE VALID

Earlier in this chapter, you used the `@pytest.mark.parametrize` marker to parameterize a data-driven test. Although pytest provides built-in markers like `parametrize`, you can also devise your own arbitrary markers; in a way, you can think of them as labels or tags for your tests. This is a powerful feature, but because you can create arbitrary markers, there's a chance you'll misremember or misspell the name of a marker, which could cause silent issues down the road.

By default, pytest will gently warn you about an invalid marker, as you can see in the following:

```
... PytestUnknownMarkWarning: Unknown pytest.mark.fake - is this a typo?
```

If you want to ensure that all your markers are known and valid—that is, they're registered by a plugin or in your `[tool:pytest]` section in the `markers` key—add the `--strict-markers` option to the `addopts` key in the setup.cfg file. With strict markers enabled, pytest will fail a test run if it finds an unknown marker, as you can see in the following output:

```
'fake' not found in `markers` configuration option
```

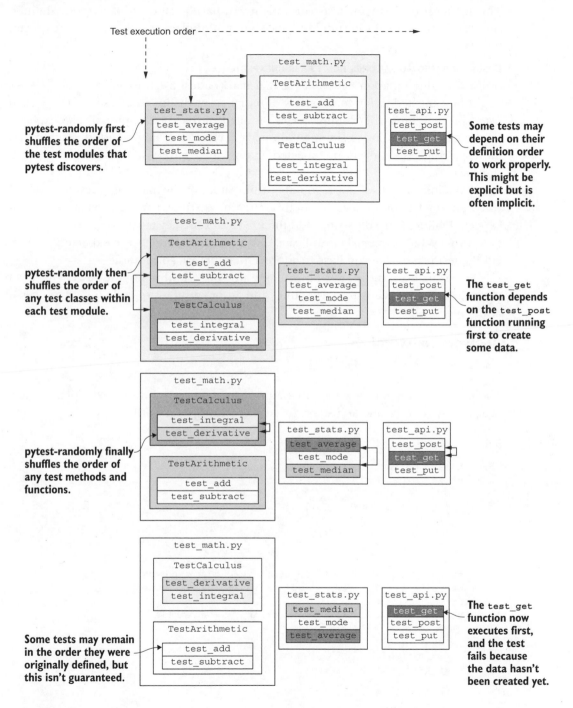

Figure 5.6 `pytest-randomly` runs your tests in a shuffled order on each run.

This will ensure that your tests run only if you have a valid set of markers defined. An invalid marker isn't harmful by itself, but it minimizes the chance of unexpected behavior.

ENSURING EXPECTED FAILURES DON'T PASS UNEXPECTEDLY

pytest provides a marker called `xfail` that marks a test as an expected failure. A test might be expected to fail for a variety of reasons—environmental issues, an upstream issue you're waiting on, or simply a lack of time to adress it. Occasionally, an expected failure can start passing again after you make a change. It might sound good to have more passing tests, but an unexpected change in behavior should always engender some scrutiny.

By default, pytest will warn you about this situation by marking a test as `XPASS`. If you want to be loudly alerted to this situation so that you can examine why an expected failure started passing, add the `xfail_strict` key to the `[tool:pytest]` section with a value of `True`. This will cause any passing tests that were expected to fail to fail the test run so that you have to address them before continuing.

With your lean, mean, testing machine well-oiled and ready for any changes you throw at it, you're ready to start adding and automating more code quality processes in the next chapter.

Answers to exercises

5.3—Answer: E

5.4—Answer: Add two new tests that adjust `inputs` to `[]` and, for example, `["foo", "bar"]` respectively, and adjust `expected_value` to `0.0` for both.

5.5

```
@pytest.mark.parametrize(
    "inputs, expected",
    [
        (["1", "4", "4"], 2.0),
        ([], 0.0),
        (['foo', 'bar'], 0.0),
    ]
)
def test_harmony_parametrized(inputs, expected, monkeypatch, capsys):
    monkeypatch.setattr(sys, 'argv', ['harmony'] + inputs)
    main()
    assert capsys.readouterr().out.strip() == colored(
        expected,
        'red',
        'on_cyan',
        attrs=['bold']
    )
```

5.6—Answer: A, C, D, E

B would pass the `--no-cov` option to tox itself instead of pytest. F would put any passed arguments before the command.

Summary

- The pytest framework has a rich plugin ecosystem that you can use to test more productively than using the built-in `unittest` module.
- Use test coverage to guide the tests you write by identifying areas of code that aren't executed by your existing tests.
- Test the uncommon paths through your code because coverage is useful, but not sufficient to understand how well your tests ensure the proper behavior.
- Testing many combinations of dependencies is tedious and error-prone, but tox reduces this effort and increases safety by automating most of the steps involved.
- To maximize safety, use plugins and tool options to your advantage to restrict your project to only valid configurations.

Automating code quality tooling

6

This chapter covers

- Using static analysis tools to find common issues early in the development process
- Automating dependency and command management for code quality tooling
- Enforcing standards as code is committed

As you continue marketing your tools to a variety of car manufacturers, you start to get the feeling you're going to need some help. You need to hire another developer to pick up a large share of the development work so you can continue developing the business. You also realize that you need to find a way to onboard your new partner effectively but quickly so they can be productive from day one. Looking at the latest code you're writing, you see that it would benefit from some basic quality standards and conventions to continue delivering value to CarCorp and your future additional clients.

If you were paying attention in the previous chapter, you're probably wondering how much code quality tooling you can automate instead of doing it all by hand. Reviewing code for quality and formatting issues distracts from the core value of what you're trying to deliver, and it can create tension between developers, especially when opinions differ. In the worst cases, arguments over unimportant details can cause you to overlook more pressing performance or security issues in a state of perceptual blindness (see Steven B. Most, "How Not to Be Seen: The Contribution of Similarity and Selective Ignoring to Sustained Inattentional Blindness," https://doi.org/10.1111/1467-9280.00303). It's often better for everyone involved to let a machine do the pedantic work and to reach an agreement that consistency is better than perfection for things that aren't directly creating impactful outcomes for your work. In this chapter, you'll learn the value of having an arsenal of code quality tools and how to integrate them effectively into your package.

> **IMPORTANT** You can use the code companion (http://mng.bz/69A5) to check your work for the exercises in this chapter.

6.1 *The true power of tox environments*

tox isn't just a testing tool. Through the course of this chapter, you'll use tox to manage several different code quality tools.

In the previous chapter, you learned how to use the `envlist` key and the `[testenv]` section to configure a list of environments for tox to create and run. The value of `envlist` defines the list of tox environments that should run by default when you run the `tox` command without specifying a particular environment, and the `[testenv]` section defines the default configuration for those environments. When you run the `tox` command, the environments in `envlist` are used by default. These are most useful for the things you'll check most often—typically, unit tests. If you're diligent about careful development and refactoring, you'll run your tests after almost every change. These test environments make a lot of sense as the default because of their speed and frequency of use.

You also saw that you can use the `-e` argument to specify a single environment. In addition to the environments in `envlist`, you can configure arbitrary environments for tasks other than testing: you can create an environment for building your project's documentation, formatting the code, and more. These activities aren't always as fast as unit tests, and they aren't something you need to verify after each and every change you make. Adding them to the default list of environments could slow down your feedback cycle when you're trying to move through some development quickly.

You need an approach that can be configured in a homogeneous way, enabling you to manage each of your different maintenance activities while keeping turnaround time as low as possible. Once again, tox proves to be an invaluable tool on this front. If you haven't already recognized the power of tox for automation, the following sections demonstrate the time it can save you.

6.1.1 *Creating nondefault tox environments*

In the previous chapter, you added a `[testenv]` section in the setup.cfg file that includes the dependencies to install and the commands to run. These are some of the basic ingredients for any environment you might want to create. The `[testenv]` section is used by default for any environment specified in envlist, but you can configure specific environments with their own section as well.

When configuring a tox environment that you don't want to run by default, you need to add a section to the setup.cfg file named [testenv:<name>], where name is the name you want for the environment. When you run tox -e <name>, tox uses the [testenv:<name>] section for that environment. This environment accepts all the same options as [testenv] does, including the deps and commands keys. You can provide explicit configuration for an environment that is in envlist as well; in this case, tox uses the [testenv] section as a base for configuration, adding to or overriding the base configuration with any keys it finds in [testenv:<name>] (see figure 6.1).

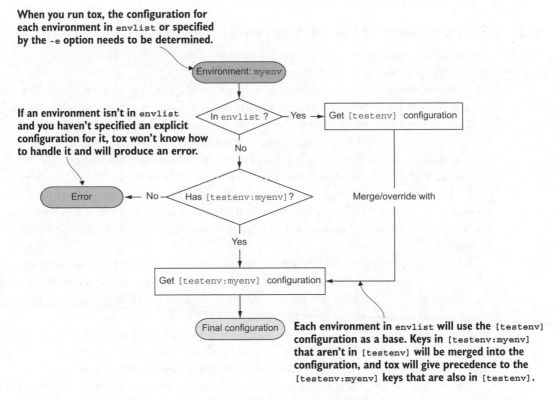

Figure 6.1   tox environments can be configured in a layered manner with default and explicit configuration sections.

Exercise 6.1

Add a new tox environment called get_my_ip that does the following:

1 Installs the requests package as a dependency
2 Runs a command that uses requests to get the IP address of the machine where tox is running and prints it

> You can use `requests.get("https://canhazip.com").text` to get the IP address, and you can use `python -c "# some python code here"` to run Python code as a command. When you're finished, the command `tox -e get_my_ip` should print your IP address.

Now you can run the `tox` command to use the environments listed in `envlist`, which uses the `[testenv]` section for configuration. You can also run `tox -e get_my_ip` to use the `get_my_ip` environment, which uses the `[testenv:get_my_ip]` section for configuration.

You might have noticed that the `get_my_ip` environment still performs the installation of your package, even though the environment doesn't need your package to perform its activities. In the future, you might also manage several environments that need the same base set of dependencies but that each need different additional dependencies. tox provides for these situations with some additional configuration options.

6.1.2 Managing dependencies across tox environments

Whereas unit tests execute your real code and need it to be installed in the environment to run, some maintenance that you do transcends the code and doesn't need it be installed to run successfully. Imagine that one of your maintenance activities focuses on generating a change log or printing some diagnostic stats about the project. These activities may not depend on your package's code at all, so installing the package only gets in the way of getting the task done. In these cases, you can skip installing your package into the relevant tox environment.

When you want to skip the installation step in a given tox environment, you must add the `skip_install` key to that environment's configuration section with a value of `True`. You may still install any additional dependencies needed for that environment's activities, but your package won't be installed into the environment. This provides a speed boost and also makes it clear which activities do or don't rely on your package being installed.

Whereas `skip_install` is all about reducing installed dependencies, you may also want to install additional dependencies in some environments without polluting others. Imagine that one of your maintenance activities uses a tool to verify that your import statements are all valid. The environment for analyzing imports should install your package so that it can validate code that imports it. The environment also needs to install the package for the analysis tool. If you want the tool to check your tests as well, it also needs to install any packages you import in your tests. How can you accomplish this without repeating yourself? You'll use a special tox syntax that allows you to reference other configuration sections and keys.

> **NOTE** You can find the full configuration specification in the tox documentation (https://tox.wiki/en/latest/config.html).

Imagine that the import analysis tool is in a package called shipyard (shipyards are where imports are checked). You could configure tox to install your package and the other packages imported in your tests, but this will result in a fair amount of duplication as your project grows. Notice how pytest and requests are repeated in the dependency list for the environments shown in listing 6.1. In large projects with many dependencies, this duplication can grow and lead you to add any new dependency to each of your environments "just in case" it's needed, because that's easier than determining the specific environments that need the dependency to run.

Listing 6.1   A naive configuration for dependencies with a fair amount of repetition

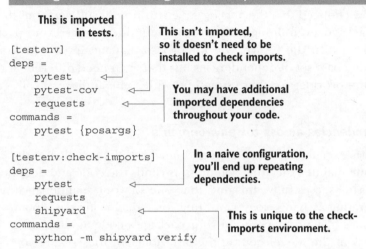

Instead of enumerating all dependencies in each environment, you can use tox to extract and give names to subsets of dependencies. This reduces repetition and centralizes dependency lists, making it more likely that each of your environments receives all the dependencies it needs each time you update a dependency list. To reference configuration from another section with tox, you specify the full section name—including square brackets—followed immediately by the key name, all in curly braces (see figure 6.2).

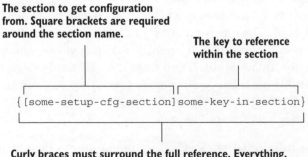

Figure 6.2   The tox syntax to reference a configuration key from another section in setup.cfg

You could reference the dependency list from the `testenv` environment in the `testenv:check-imports` environment, which would install all the necessary dependencies to check imports across your code and tests. But this would also install the `pytest-cov` package, which isn't imported anywhere and is, therefore, a bit of a waste. To maximize the efficiency of what you're installing, you can separate the minimal set of necessary dependencies into its own named section and reference that everywhere else instead. Listing 6.2 shows how you could update the configuration by extracting a `[testimports]` section.

The new section has a `deps` key with a list of dependencies, just like the previous sections did. It lists only the dependencies that are needed in all the other environments. Then, each section references the new section's dependencies using the `{[testimports]deps}` reference. This makes it clear that each environment needs `pytest` and `requests`, and that each environment needs additional, unique dependencies.

Listing 6.2 Extracting and referencing named configurations to reduce repetition

```
[testimports]                        ←⌐   This section lists
deps =                                     packages that are
    pytest                                 imported in tests.
    requests

[testenv]                                 This environment depends
deps =                                    on the same things listed
    {[testimports]deps}           ←       in testimports.
    pytest-cov               ←⌐   This environment also
commands =                             extends the list of
    pytest {posargs}                   dependencies further.

[testenv:check-imports]
deps =
    {[testimports]deps}           ←⌐   The list from
    shipyard                           testimports can be
commands =                             reused many places.
    python -m shipyard verify
```

This configuration is a few lines longer than the naive approach, but that may not always be true. If your tests import a large handful of packages, they'll be listed only in the `[testimports]` section, and the other sections don't need to change. As your package gains complexity over time, you continue to reap the savings.

Exercise 6.2
Given the following configuration, which are true?

```
[tox:tox]
envlist = py39,py310
isolated_build = True
```

(continued)

```
[testimports]
deps =
    pytest
    requests

[testenv]
deps =
    {[testimports]deps}
    pytest-cov
commands =
    pytest {posargs}

[testenv:myenv]
skip_install = True
deps =
    requests
commands =
    python -c "print(requests.get('https://canhazip.com').text)"

[testenv:check-imports]
deps =
    {[testimports]deps}
    shipyard
commands =
    python -m shipyard verify
```

   A Running the `tox` command uses two environments.
   B Running the `tox` command uses three environments.
   C Running the `tox` command uses four environments.
   D The `py39` environment has the `requests` package installed.
   E The `myenv` environment has the `requests` package installed.
   F The `check-imports` environment has the `requests` package installed.
   G The `myenv` environment is the only environment that skips installation of your package.
   H Adding a package to `[testimports]deps` impacts three environments.
   I Adding a package to `[testimports]deps` impacts four environments.

Now that you've got a handle on dependency management across a few tox environments, you're ready to dig into using it for code quality tasks.

6.2   *Analyzing type safety*

Python is a *dynamically typed language*—the type of an object is evaluated at run time, and as a result, it's possible for the object to be the wrong type for the intended operation. Further, Python has *duck typing*. If an object "looks like a duck and quacks like a duck, then it's a duck"—that is, if an object can perform the intended operation successfully, then it can be treated as if it were the type intended by the author of the operation.

This flexibility makes Python one of the most productive languages today. The type system stays out of your way a lot of the time, letting you focus on that quick thing you're trying to get done. Consider the following function, which returns True if the argument passed to it is too long:

```
def too_long(some_list):
    return len(some_list) > 100
```

The author of this function may have intended for callers to pass in a list, but the function also works without error on sets, dictionaries, strings, and more. In fact, any object that defines a __len__ method can be passed into a call to too_long without error.

This flexibility also presents challenges. As a code base scales, it becomes increasingly likely that someone somewhere will call a function, method, or initializer with an unintended data type. In the worst cases, this might even work at the time of writing, only to break later when you update the called code in a way that no longer accommodates the unexpected use case. When you're creating a package that you want others to use, their expectations of backward compatibility carry even more weight.

Type hinting, first proposed in 2014 and added to Python 3.5 (https://www.python .org/dev/peps/pep-0484/), provides a way to more strongly suggest types in signatures for functions, methods, and so on. With these hints, someone reading through the code base and trying to use a function is able to readily see what expectations the author of the function has about its use. Further, tooling like IDEs often use these hints to suggest to someone that they've used a function incorrectly when the type they use doesn't agree with the type hint given. Your new teammate would benefit a great deal from type hints and type checks, especially early on as they become familiar with the project.

A safer version of too_long might explicitly define the input argument as a list, like this:

```
def too_long(some_list: list) -> bool:
    return len(some_list) > 100
```

Or, if the author realizes that they really do want the function to be usable for any object that defines a __len__ method, they might choose to specify that any input argument of the Sized type is sufficient as follows:

```
from typing import Sized

def too_long(some_object: Sized) -> bool:
    return len(some_object) > 100
```

Then sets, dictionaries, and strings would be acceptable, but scalar values like integers or floats would not. Type checking tools can find situations where a call is made that doesn't match the type hints for the called function and presents an error to the developer to fix the calls.

These types of *static analysis*, or analysis that doesn't need to execute your code, are helpful because you can often run them quickly and frequently during development. They can also be integrated as part of your continuous integration pipeline, which you'll learn more about in chapter 7.

The Python Code Quality Authority

Code quality, and, in particular, static analysis tooling that doesn't need to run your code to perform checks on it, is a quickly growing space. The Python Code Quality Authority (PyCQA) (https://pycqa.org) adopts and maintains projects in this space to ensure they remain updated as Python and other areas of the ecosystem evolve. A few of the tools suggested in this chapter are maintained by the PyCQA.

To check your code's type hints, you'll use the mypy package.

6.2.1   *Creating a tox environment for type checking*

mypy (https://github.com/python/mypy) is one of a number of available static analysis tools for verifying type safety in your code base. mypy can detect common bugs in Python code without type hints and verifies that all calls agree with any type hints you or any of your dependencies have added. This makes for a fluid experience when adding it into an existing code base, because you can incrementally add and check type hints to make your code safer instead of trying to update it all at once.

Start by adding a section for a new tox environment called typecheck in the setup.cfg file. This environment needs to install the following:

- Your package, so imports of your code can be followed properly
- The pytest package, so imports in your tests can be followed properly
- The mypy package, so you can use it to check type safety
- The types-termcolor package, so mypy can better verify your usage of the termcolor package

Configure the environment to run the following command:

```
mypy --ignore-missing-imports {posargs:src test}
```

This tells mypy to follow as many imports as it can, ignoring the ones for which it can't analyze types. mypy defaults to analyzing all the code in your src/ and test/ directories, but you can pass specific files as positional arguments to the tox command if you want to check a subset of your project. Recall that you can use tox's -e flag followed by a tox environment name to run only that environment. Run the environment now using the following command:

```
$ tox -e typecheck
```

You should see something similar to the following at the end of the command output:

```
typecheck run-test: commands[0] | mypy --ignore-missing-imports src test
Success: no issues found in 4 source files
_____ summary _____
  typecheck: commands succeeded
  congratulations :)
```

This confirms that your code is currently safe with regard to types. From a test-driven development perspective, you're in a "green" state which you can use to refactor your code.

Exercise 6.3

The `main` function in the `src/imppkg/harmony.py` module is a bit long and handles a number of concerns, shown here:

- Parses the input from the command line into a list of floating-point numbers
- Calculates the harmonic mean if possible, defaulting to `0.0` otherwise
- Formats and prints the output

Right now, there's no good juncture for type checking either, because the `main` function doesn't accept any arguments or return a value. Split the body of the `main` function into three helper functions with the following signatures:

```
def _parse_nums(inputs: str) -> list[float]:
    ...

def _calculate_results(nums: list[float]) -> float:
    ...

def _format_output(result: float) -> str:
    ...
```

The `main` function should then use these three functions and print the final result. You can use the `termcolor.colored` instead of `termcolor.cprint` to get formatted text as a string without printing it.

When you're done, the `typecheck` environment should still run successfully. Your unit tests should remain unchanged and continue to pass. After you're done, change some of the type hints to disagree with each other, and rerun type checking to see how it behaves in response; mypy should raise an error for each type disagreement.

Now that you have mypy working, you'll configure it for some additional productivity.

6.2.2 *Configuring mypy*

You can configure mypy by adding a `[mypy]` section to your setup.cfg file. The mypy configuration documentation (http://mng.bz/096E) covers a wide variety of available configuration options. A few of the most important follow:

- *python_version*—Set this to the lowest version of Python your package supports. As an example, if you want to support Python 3.8, 3.9, and 3.10, set this to 3.8.
- *warn_unused_configs*—Set this to True so that mypy alerts you if you've added other configuration sections that have no effect.
- *show_error_context*—Set this to True for mypy to show you the code surrounding the line where it finds an issue; this can be helpful in understanding the issue without having to repeatedly switch between the command line and the file.
- *pretty*—Set this to True for mypy to output more human-readable error messages. In particular, mypy gives a visual indication of the column of your code where the error occurs, which can help you more quickly identify issues that arise.
- *namespace_packages*—Set this to True so mypy can find a wider array of potential package configurations—namely, it finds implicit namespace packages as defined in PEP 420 (https://www.python.org/dev/peps/pep-0420/). This future-proofs your type checking configuration as you install more packages that have the potential to be implicit namespace packages.
- *check_untyped_defs*—By default, mypy will only check the types of things to which you've explicitly added type hints. It can miss cases where you forgot to add type hints and used a function incorrectly. Set this to True so mypy will check type agreement in as many places as possible.

Add each of these keys to the [mypy] section in your setup.cfg file.

A case study in type safety

The urllib3 package is a widely used Python package; GitHub's dependency graph indicates that over 5,000 other packages depend on it (http://mng.bz/K0xg). The urllib3 team undertook an effort to introduce type hints as widely and strictly as possible in the project without breaking the code for its consumers. They found that adding type hints uncovered bugs and design flaws that their extensive test coverage hadn't. Read about the different kinds of improvements they were able to identify in a large project in the wild at http://mng.bz/82Ez.

At this point, you're set up to catch any type-related issues in your package as they arise. You can also help people who use your package to ensure they're using it with the right types. To do so, create an empty py.typed file in the src/imppkg/ directory. This file, when present in the contents of a package installed in a project, tells mypy to check usages of code from that package for type-related issues as well. This extends the type safety you add out to anyone who consumes your work in their applications.

NOTE   The py.typed file will be automatically included in your package because of the graft directive you added to the MANIFEST.in file in chapter 4.

Next, you'll create a tox environment to automatically check and update the formatting of your code.

Alternative type checkers

mypy, first developed at Dropbox, is one of the most widely used type checking tools, but many others are out there. If you'd like to explore the landscape further, check out these type checkers that each have their respective corporate backing:

- pyright (https://github.com/Microsoft/pyright) from Microsoft
- pyre (https://github.com/facebook/pyre-check) from Facebook
- pytype (https://google.github.io/pytype/) from Google

6.3 Creating a tox environment for code formatting

Code is read many more times than it's written, so it stands to reason that code should be *readable*. Often, what one developer believes is readable doesn't agree with what another developer believes. This can lead to wasting time during review discussing levels of indentation, where newlines should occur, whether to use single or double quotes, and so on. Although readability for a given piece of code can be fairly objective in some cases, even then you can waste time remembering to format the code that way as you're writing. PEP 8 (https://www.python.org/dev/peps/pep-0008/) defines a style guide for Python code. Most Python code formatting tools adhere to the suggestions laid out in PEP 8, but PEP 8 doesn't cover all formatting decisions a Python developer ever needs to make. Each formatter introduces its own additional rules, some of which can become burdensome to remember and address manually.

To alleviate these pressures, let an automated process do the formatting for you. Many developers use their IDE to perform this task. Some developers even have the IDE automatically format their code each time they save the file, tightening the loop on the code they're working in. The formatting style can differ between IDEs, or even between two developers using the same IDE with differing preferences set. Using a consistent formatting style ensures that your team's pull requests don't continually include reformatting code back and forth depending on which developer most recently updated the code.

The `black` package (https://black.readthedocs.io/en/stable/) seeks to format Python code uniformly, with few configuration options, such that the vast majority of Python project code is readable after formatting. It can automatically update code that doesn't adhere to the style, making it fast to reformat an entire codebase and any new code as it's added. `black` also prefers code that results in short diffs when changed, such as always using trailing commas in multiline lists or dictionaries. Consider the following code that assigns a list of strings to a variable:

```
a = [
    "one",
    "two",
    "three"
]
```

The last item doesn't include a trailing comma.

Because this code doesn't use a trailing comma for the last item in the list, adding a fourth string to the list results in a diff like the following:

```
--- before.py    ...
+++ after.py     ...
@@ -1,5 +1,6 @@          Because a comma
 a = [                   was added, this line
     "one",              shows as removed.
     "two",
-    "three"             The added line
+    "three",            includes the comma.
+    "four"
 ]                       The new line with the new
                         string shows as added.
```

Notice that the diff shows a removed line and two added lines, even though the spirit of the change was adding a single new item to the list. black prefers to use trailing commas so that diffs reflect this more faithfully. Now consider the case where a trailing comma is included after the third list item. When adding the fourth item with a trailing comma of its own, the diff would look like this instead:

```
--- before.py    ...
+++ after.py     ...
@@ -2,4 +2,5 @@          With an existing
     "one",              trailing comma, this
     "two",              line is unchanged.
     "three",
+    "four",             Only the new string
 ]                       shows as added.
```

Because the punctuation of the code didn't change, the diff is now simpler. When making larger changes to code, these small simplifications can add up to a much easier review for the team.

One of the best features of the black package is that, by default, it ensures that the code before and after formatting has the same *abstract syntax tree* (https://docs.python.org/3/library/ast.html). That is, the code before and after the change remains functionally equivalent. You can have high confidence that the changes black makes are strictly nonfunctional.

Exercise 6.4

In your setup.cfg file, configure a new tox environment called `format` for checking and formatting your code. This environment has one dependency—the `black` package. The environment should run one command, `black`, with the following default options, using tox's `posargs` syntax you learned earlier:

- `--check`—Checks the formatting of the code without actually changing the formatting
- `--diff`—Outputs the changes black would make if it formatted the code
- `src test`—The areas of code for which to check the formatting

When you're finished, you should be able to run `tox -e format` to check the formatting of your package code and `tox -e format src test` to reformat the code. Run the checks to determine whether `black` finds any opportunities to change the formatting of your code. If it does, use the environment to make the changes automatically.

6.3.1   Configuring black

You can configure the `black` package using the pyproject.toml file in a new section called `[tool.black]`. Note that `black` does not support using the setup.cfg file. As mentioned earlier in this chapter, `black` has very few options for configuration (http://mng.bz/9V5q). The two most notable follow:

- *line-length*—The maximum line length allowed, defaulting to `80`. Lines longer than this are reformatted to span two or more lines if possible.
- *target-version*—The list of Python versions your code should be compatible with. This stops `black` from using syntax that is too new for your supported Python versions.

You should set the `line-length` to whatever you find most readable for the majority of your code. As an example, I prefer to use a line length of 100 or 120 because the length of 80 results in a lot of multiline wrapping in big projects in which longer, descriptive variable and method names are used.

For consistency, the `target-version` list should match the list of Python versions you support and test against. In chapter 5, you specified an `envlist` with at least two Python versions. These same Python versions should be reflected in your `black` configuration as well. As an example, if you need to support Python 3.8 and 3.9, your black configuration might look like the following:

```
[tool.black]
line-length = 120
target-version = ["py38", "py39"]
```

Run the `format` environment again with this new configuration to see whether `black` should reformat anything with the new configuration, and reformat the code if so.

Finally, you can speed up the `format` environment by skipping the package installation step. Because `black` statically checks your code and doesn't perform any work based on `import` statements or other knowledge of the code's functionality, you can avoid installing the package in the tox environment. Add tox's `skip_install` key with a value of `True` in the `[testenv:format]` section you created earlier to skip the package installation.

Now you're able to keep your code in a consistent format with a single command. In the next section, you'll learn to configure automated checks for common bugs in your code.

> **Alternative code formatters**
>
> `black` is quickly becoming one of the most popular formatters, and has been adopted under the umbrella of the Python Software Foundation for further development. That being said, its opinionation and lack of configurability isn't for everyone. If you want to explore further, check out these other popular formatters:
>
> - autopep8 (https://github.com/hhatto/autopep8)
> - yapf (https://github.com/google/yapf), from Google

6.4   *Creating a tox environment for linting*

Some bugs and extraneous code in Python are incredibly common. Those that can be detected by their abstract syntax tree or other static analysis can be automatically scanned for. Consider the following function that uses an empty dictionary as the default value for an input argument, which is updated in the body of the function:

```
def remove_params(
        param_names: list[str],
        all_params: dict = {"default_key":       ← Uses a default
                                                    dictionary if one
  "default_value"}                                  isn't supplied
) -> dict:
    for param in param_names:
        all_params.pop(param)    ← The dictionary, whether
    return all_params              supplied or default, is
                                   updated and returned.
```

This may look innocuous enough, but it turns out that mutable default argument values are dangerous. A mutable default argument value is initialized once at module import time and then remains for the duration of the Python process. That means that you could call `remove_params(["default_key"])` once, removing the `"default_key"` key from the default dictionary argument. But subsequent calls to the `remove_params` function will fail with a `KeyError`, because the default argument doesn't get reinitialized and the `"default_key"` key has already been removed from the dictionary.

Like code formatting, checking for this kind of common issue is often the default behavior in IDEs, but depending on your IDE, it may be easy to overlook errors or warnings if they aren't currently causing runtime exceptions or test failures. To ensure these situations don't go unnoticed, you can incorporate a tool to do this kind of scanning—often called *linting*—into your tox setup. Linting keeps your project free of unused code, such as unused imports. Linting also identifies things that may not cause immediate bugs or exceptions but may do so later in ways that are difficult to identify, like using a duplicate key in a long dictionary.

The flake8 package (https://flake8.pycqa.org/en/latest/) is another project maintained by the PyCQA that combines several other smaller code quality tools into one command-line interface. flake8 has been praised for providing strong coverage without being too tedious to manage. flake8 combines the powers of the following:

- pyflakes (https://github.com/PyCQA/pyflakes)
- pycodestyle (https://github.com/PyCQA/pycodestyle)
- mccabe (https://github.com/PyCQA/mccabe)

TIP The mccabe package measures code complexity. Automating code complexity thresholds has proven finnicky for me at best. And when I do want to measure complexity, I like to use radon (https://radon.readthedocs.io/en/latest/) because it measures a wider variety of metrics in addition to the McCabe metrics. Although flake8 includes it, you don't need to deal with mccabe unless you'd like to.

flake8 is also built as a plugin-based architecture, with many extensions to the code behavior available from the community. As an example, flake8-bugbear (https://github.com/PyCQA/flake8-bugbear) catches a few common issues that flake8 doesn't by default, such as the use of mutable default arguments (see "Mutable Default Arguments," *Real Python*, http://mng.bz/jA28). flake8 uses flake8-bugbear's functionality so long as flake8-bugbear is installed. Together, flake8 and its extensions find a wide variety of common issues, listing them in an actionable format. Each issue flake8 identifies is printed with the following information:

- The name of the file where the error was found
- The line and column number in the file where the issue arose
- The error code for the issue
- A message indicating what went wrong, most often giving enough information for corrective action

Exercise 6.5

In your setup.cfg file, configure a new tox environment called lint for linting your project code. This environment has two dependencies—the flake8 and flake8-bugbear packages. The environment should run one command, flake8, using tox's posargs syntax you learned earlier, with the following default option: src test. This will indicate to flake8 which areas of code to lint.

When you're finished, you should be able to run tox -e lint to lint your package code. Run the checks to determine whether flake8 finds any issues with your code. If you see an issue related to line length, continue to the next section before fixing. Fix any other issues that flake8 identifies.

6.4.1 Configuring flake8

You can configure flake8 using a new [flake8] section in your setup.cfg file. The main configuration options for flake8 (http://mng.bz/WMxl) involve fine-tuning some of the checks it performs, as well as ignoring some of the checks altogether. You should start by running all checks and learning which of them aren't valuable to you.

For now, start by ensuring that flake8 is configured to allow the same maximum line length you set for `black`. Whereas the option for `black` was `line-length`, the option for flake8 is `max-line-length`. Once you've configured the line length, run flake8 again and ensure that it finds no remaining issues.

Alternative linters

You might find that flake8 is just right, but it can be extended a bit to get you what you want. If you're looking for something much more intensive, something that stays out of your way a bit more, or just something different, you can have a look at the following linters:

- pylint (https://github.com/PyCQA/pylint/)
- prospector (https://github.com/PyCQA/prospector)
- bandit (https://github.com/PyCQA/bandit), which has a specific eye toward security
- vulture (https://github.com/jendrikseipp/vulture), which has a specific eye toward cleaning out unused code

You can also use pyflakes, pycodestyle, or mccabe on their own as well.

By augmenting your unit tests with linting, you can develop high confidence that your code behaves as you expect, without any lurking issues waiting to jump out later down the line.

If you've made it here, you've successfully configured tox environments for checking the types, formatting, and linting of your code. Although you've put some important configuration in place that gives you a uniform way of performing static analysis, you might see that it can still be tedious to run these on a regular basis. With each change to your code, you'd need to run the following to fully exercise all the checks you've built:

- `tox` to test the code
- `tox -e typecheck` to type check the code
- `tox -e format` and sometimes `tox -e format src test` to format the code
- `tox -e lint` to check the code for common bugs

You can always speed up the process by running all the commands in parallel using a command like the following:

```
$ tox -p -e py39,py310,typecheck,format,lint
```

But even this can be tedious, and you may still forget a step on occasion. Continuous integration practices help address these gaps by running important checks on each change you make. Continue to the next chapter to jump in when you're ready.

Answers to exercises

6.1

```
[testenv:get_my_ip]
deps =
  requests
commands =
  python -c "import requests; print(requests.get('https://canhazip.com').text)"
```

6.2—Answer: A, D, E, F, G, I

- (A), B, and C: tox uses the environments in `envlist` by default. `envlist` lists two environments.
- (D): Yes, because it's in `[testimports]deps`, which `[testenv]deps` extends— and `py39` uses `[testenv]` for configuration.
- (E): Yes, because it's explicitly listed.
- (F): Yes, because it's in `[testimports]deps`, which `[testenv:check-imports]` deps extends.
- (G): Yes, because installation always happens unless you explicitly opt out.
- H and (I): There is a total of four environments—the two environments in `envlist` (that use `[testenv]deps`, which extends `[testimports]deps`), the `myenv` environment, and the `check-imports` environment. The `myenv` environment doesn't reference `[testimports]deps`, so it is unimpacted, leaving a total of three impacted environments.

6.3—Answer: See the code companion for this chapter.

6.4—Answer: See the code companion for this chapter.

6.5—Answer: See the code companion for this chapter.

Summary

- Although commonly used for testing, tox is a productive general-use task management tool.
- Type checking builds higher confidence that the intended interfaces for code are being used properly.
- Automate or obviate decisions unrelated to the core value of what you want to deliver.
- Leverage linting tools to find common issues your unit tests may not uncover.

Part 3

Going public

Regardless of your motivations for packaging your software, chances are good that you plan to share the work in at least one context outside your immediate day-to-day work. Whoever you share the code with is likely to find bugs or desire new features. As the requirements of your project shift and grow, your capacity shrinks surprisingly quickly. You need practices that maximize productivity and commodify contribution to the project, allowing you to take on help from anyone and everyone willing to give it.

This part brings your packaging project into collaborative mode. You'll enhance your pipeline to include automated checks whenever you or your team members introduce changes to the code, provide useful documentation so the team and your users can understand the project, and keep your project from going stale with regular updates to dependencies and syntax.

Automating work through continuous integration

This chapter covers

- Automating code quality checks on each change using GitHub Actions
- Building distributions for a variety of platforms
- Publishing distributions to PyPI

Throughout the course of the previous chapters, you've built up a repertoire of tasks you execute each time you change your package so that you can maintain functionality and code quality. This is a huge stride in building confidence in changes, but doing all this locally on your own computer is still a big limitation, as you've already seen when interacting with the team over at CarCorp. You may have trouble remembering all the steps that go into verifying a change, and people just starting to work on the project may struggle even more. Even when they perform their due diligence, you can't directly verify commands they run locally unless you're supervising them. This is difficult enough with a team of a few people, but it becomes impossible in the open source world, where you may not even know the person contributing code changes.

In this chapter, you'll create a pipeline for your package to bring automation to nearly every aspect of the packaging process—aside from writing the code, of course.

Before getting too deep into the details of setting up this pipeline, you first need to understand the high-level flow.

> **IMPORTANT**   You can use the code companion (http://mng.bz/69A5) to check your work for the exercises in this chapter.

7.1   *The continuous integration workflow*

Imagine you've onboarded several new developers to your project to continue taking on new vehicle clients. Your team has spent the last several weeks getting ready for the next release of your package, and you finally shipped the new version earlier in the day. As your team celebrates, the incessant vibration of your phone gives you the sinking feeling that something is wrong. It turns out that the developer who worked on the final changes before release forgot to run the unit tests, and the last change broke a core piece of functionality.

You need a system in place that can run the valuable checks you've developed on each change automatically in an environment where everyone working on the project can confirm their status. These *continuous integration* systems are another major stride in productivity and confidence in your project as it evolves.

> **DEFINITION**   Continuous integration (CI) is the practice of incorporating changes as often as possible into the main stream of development for a project to minimize the possibility of behavior that diverges from the desired or expected behavior. CI is diametrically opposed to the early practices of large software projects where development might go on for months or years before being merged and released. CI encourages small, incremental changes with the aim of delivering value earlier and more frequently.

> For in-depth coverage of continuous integration, check out *Grokking Continuous Delivery* (Manning, 2022, http://mng.bz/82M5) by Christie Wilson and *Pipeline as Code* (Manning, 2021, https://www.manning.com/books/pipeline-as-code) by Mohamed Labouardy.

Most continuous integration workflows consist of the same basic steps, as shown in figure 7.1. The automatic *build* and *test* steps are the gaps in your current process.

Because the automated building and testing steps are performed in a shared location, you and your team can verify that a given change works as expected, regardless of any testing steps the author of the change performed locally. This is a key shift: local testing can now focus on writing new tests or updating existing tests in quick iterations, and running the full test suite becomes an optional convenience. Developers have options during their implementation based on their capacity at the moment, instead of being forced to do things one very specific way.

Now that you're familiar with the basic flow of continuous integration, you can start working toward building one using freely available tools.

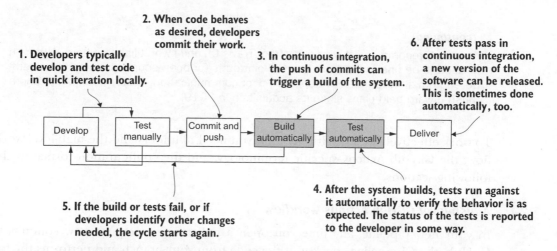

Figure 7.1   A basic continuous integration workflow gives developers an automated feedback loop about their changes.

7.2   *Continuous integration with GitHub Actions*

Before merging any new code, you decide each change to the project should be verified, recorded, and published using a CI pipeline in a shared environment. This removes any variability due to someone's local configuration and prevents the scenario where someone publishes a package version from their computer that never gets incorporated into the code base. Because your team has been using GitHub to host the code base and collaborate on changes, you decide to give GitHub Actions (https://github.com/features/actions) a try.

Other continuous integration solutions

Although I've chosen to cover GitHub Actions in this book, it's just one of a wide variety of options out there. Most continuous integration solutions have strong overlap in their concepts, so learning a different platform is often a matter of understanding their particular lingo.

Some widely used cloud-first CI solutions follow:

- GitLab CI/CD (https://docs.gitlab.com/ee/ci/)
- CircleCI (https://circleci.com/)
- Azure DevOps (https://azure.microsoft.com/en-us/services/devops)
- Google Cloud Build (https://cloud.google.com/build)

It can be useful to choose one of these if it aligns with your existing choice of cloud provider for personal or organizational work. Jenkins (https://www.jenkins.io/) is an open source solution that typically requires a bit more effort on your part but might be nice if you want full end-to-end control.

(continued)

I strongly recommend staying away from Travis CI, and I won't link to it here. Although it used to be one of the most beloved platforms for open source projects, it has suffered from slow feature development, poor communication, security concerns, and a push toward paid plans since its acquisition in 2019.

To work effectively with GitHub Actions, you need to understand the high-level workflow, the GitHub Actions–specific terminology, and the configuration format in the following sections.

7.2.1   *A high-level GitHub Actions workflow*

In your new pipeline, any time you open a pull request or push new commits to GitHub, the CI pipeline checks out the code from your branch and performs the following in parallel:

- Checks code formatting using `black` and the `format` tox environment
- Lints the code using flake8 and the `lint` tox environment
- Type checks the code using mypy and the `typecheck` tox environment
- Unit tests the code using pytest and the default tox environment
- Builds a source distribution using `build`
- Builds binary wheel distributions using `build` and cibuildwheel (more on this later in the chapter)

Whenever you tag a commit, the pipeline additionally publishes the distributions to PyPI. Figure 7.2 depicts this flow at a high level.

You're locking all the testing and code quality work you did into an automated pipeline. In the future, if you change how one of your tox environments works or add a new kind of check, you can add them to your pipeline as well. This investment will pay dividends with each new process you create.

7.2.2   *Understanding GitHub Actions terminology*

You need to make use of the following GitHub Actions concepts to build your CI pipeline:

- *Workflow*—The highest level of granularity for a CI pipeline. You can create multiple workflows that happen in response to different events.
- *Job*—A high-level phase you define for a workflow, such as building or testing something.
- *Step*—A specific task you define in a job, usually consisting of a single shell command. Steps can also reference other predefined actions, which is useful when building off of common tasks like checking out your code.

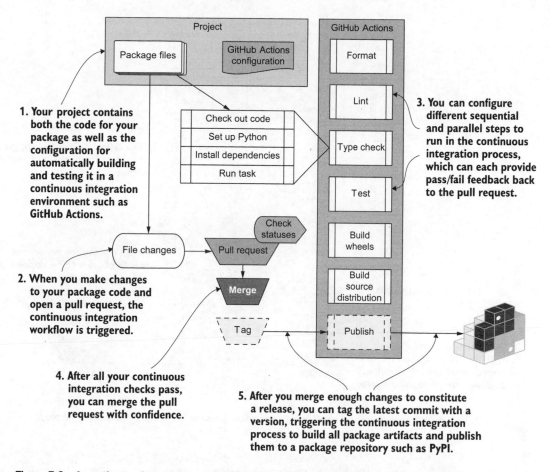

Figure 7.2 **A continuous integration pipeline flow for Python packaging using GitHub Actions**

- *Trigger*—An event or activity that causes a workflow to happen. Even when a workflow is triggered, you can skip jobs in that workflow conditionally with expressions.
- *Expression*—One of a set of GitHub-specific conditions and values that you can check to control your CI pipeline.

For now, you need just one workflow consisting of several jobs, some of which run conditionally based on the triggering event. Each job has several similar steps to install dependencies and tools and finally run a task. The workflow is triggered by pull requests and tags that you create. Figure 7.3 shows the same CI pipeline you saw earlier, this time pointing out how these different moving parts map to GitHub Actions concepts.

1. **The configuration you provide in your project repository defines the GitHub Actions workflows, jobs, steps, and triggers.**

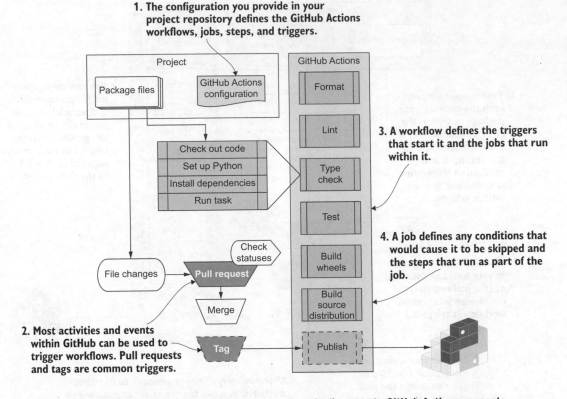

3. **A workflow defines the triggers that start it and the jobs that run within it.**

4. **A job defines any conditions that would cause it to be skipped and the steps that run as part of the job.**

2. **Most activities and events within GitHub can be used to trigger workflows. Pull requests and tags are common triggers.**

Figure 7.3   How different parts of a continuous integration pipeline map to GitHub Actions concepts

Understanding GitHub Actions in depth

Teaching all of what GitHub Actions has to offer is outside the scope of this book, but if you'd like to explore more features, you can follow GitHub's learning materials (http://mng.bz/EOWX).

With the terminology in hand, you're ready to start building a GitHub Actions workflow for your package.

IMPORTANT   If you haven't done so yet, now is a good time to bring your project under version control in a Git repository and push it to GitHub. If you aren't familiar with Git or GitHub, pause here and take some time to familiarize yourself. Their documentation (http://mng.bz/N56v) and *Git in Practice* by Mike McQuaid (Manning, 2014, https://www.manning.com/books/git-in-practice) are good resources.

7.2.3   Starting a GitHub Actions workflow configuration

You configure GitHub Actions workflows using YAML (https://yaml.org/). For your workflow, you can use a single YAML file to specify the jobs and steps. Start by creating a new branch in your repository. Create a .github/ directory in the root directory of your project if it doesn't already exist. Inside the .github/ directory, create a new directory called workflows/. GitHub automatically discovers files with a .yml extension in the .github/workflows/ directory and expects them to be valid workflow definitions.

You can give your workflow configuration file almost any name you like, but using the name main.yml is a common practice when a project has only one workflow configured. You can also use a name that indicates the purpose of the workflow, such as packaging.yml. Create an empty configuration file in the .github/workflows/ directory now.

Each GitHub Actions workflow must have at least the following few fields:

- `name`—A human-friendly string to display in a few parts of the GitHub interface
- `on`—A list of one or more events that trigger the workflow
- `jobs`—A map of one or more jobs to perform

In turn, a job must have at least a few fields as follows:

- *Key*—A machine-readable string by which to reference the job elsewhere in the pipeline. Often this is a version of the job name that uses only letters and hyphens.
- `name`—A human-friendly string to display in a few parts of the GitHub interface.
- `runs-on`—The type of GitHub Actions runner to use for the job. For your purposes, `ubuntu-latest` works well. You can see all the available runners in the `runs-on` documentation (http://mng.bz/PnKP).
- `steps`—A list of one or more steps to perform.

Finally, a step may be in one of the following two formats:

- A reference to a predefined action, such as the official checkout action (https://github.com/actions/checkout) provided by GitHub or by a third party. This format specifies a `uses` key whose value references the action's GitHub repository and an optional version string separated by an `@` character.
- A human-friendly `name` string to display in a few parts of the GitHub interface, and a `run` field that specifies the command to run.

The next listing shows how these pieces fit together into a sample workflow configuration.

Listing 7.1   A sample GitHub Actions workflow

```
name: My first workflow        ◁─────        A human-friendly
                                             name for the workflow

on:         ◁─┐   The workflow is triggered
  - push      └   by pushed code and tags.
```

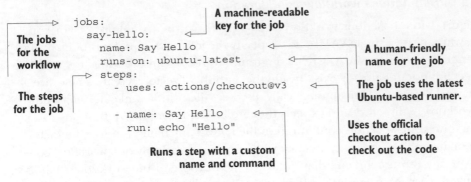

When run, the workflow checks out the code of the branch or tag that triggered the workflow and then runs an echo command to say hello. If the triggering push event is a pull request, GitHub Actions reports the pending status near the bottom of that pull request's page (see figure 7.4).

Figure 7.4   A pending GitHub Actions workflow displayed at the bottom of a pull request

After the workflow completes, GitHub Actions shows the completed status on the pull request page (see figure 7.5).

Figure 7.5   A successfully completed GitHub Actions workflow on a pull request

You can click the Details link on a workflow job to see the output of individual steps (as shown in figure 7.6). You can also find all previous job runs on the Actions tab of your repository. GitHub Actions performs some steps of its own before and after the steps you define.

Figure 7.6 The detailed steps and output for a GitHub Actions workflow job. Some steps are user-defined, and some are built into GitHub Actions.

You can click a step's name to expand and view its output, which can be useful in better understanding actions provided by GitHub or a third-party (see figure 7.7).

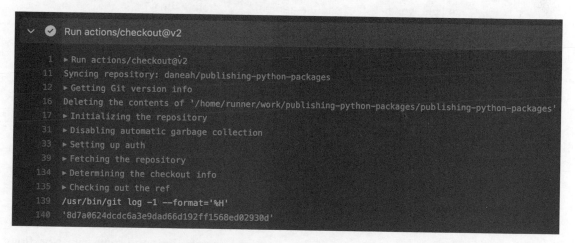

Figure 7.7 The output from the official checkout action shows all the steps involved in checking out the code from the triggering branch or tag.

You can also use the output to confirm or debug steps you create yourself, such as ensuring that a logged value is what you expect (as shown in figure 7.8).

Figure 7.8 Commands specified in a workflow job step are displayed along with their output.

When a workflow fails, browsing these different levels of the GitHub Actions interface becomes especially important in discovering how to fix the failure. These areas are where you'll see failing unit tests and messages about improperly formatted code or other code quality issues found by your tools.

Exercise 7.1

On a new branch in your repository, do the following:

1. Create a .github/ directory in the root directory of your project if it doesn't already exist.
2. Inside the .github/ directory, create a new directory called workflows/.
3. Create a YAML file for your workflow configuration in the .github/worfklows/ directory. You can name your workflow configuration file what you like, but using the name main.yml is a common practice when a project has only one workflow configured. You can also use a name that indicates the purpose of the workflow, such as packaging.yml.
4. In your workflow file, add the sample YAML from listing 7.1.
5. Commit and push your changes to GitHub.
6. Open a pull request.

After you complete these steps, you should see GitHub Actions trigger the workflow on your pull request. Confirm that the workflow succeeds and performs the steps you defined. Change the `echo` command to a new string, and push a new commit. The workflow should trigger again, and the output should reflect your updated string.

Now that you've created a working GitHub Actions workflow, you're ready to add your real tasks to it.

7.3 *Converting manual tasks to GitHub Actions*

Earlier you learned about the high-level flow of continuous integration in GitHub Actions. Zooming in a bit, your focus now is the specific jobs and steps your workflow needs to perform. Several correspond to the tox environments you created in chapters 5 and 6. Most of these jobs can also be run in parallel; the only exception is the publishing job, which should wait for all the other jobs to succeed before proceeding to ensure only verified changes get published. Figure 7.9 iterates what you need to implement.

You need to update your workflow config to use a clearer value for name, remove the say-hello job, and add the real jobs. Rename your workflow something like Packaging and remove the say-hello job now. To add the new jobs, start with the job for checking the formatting of the code. This job needs to do the following:

1. Check out the code using the `actions/checkout@v3` action.
2. Set up the most recent version of Python your package supports using the `actions/setup-python@v4.0.0` action. You can specify the Python version using

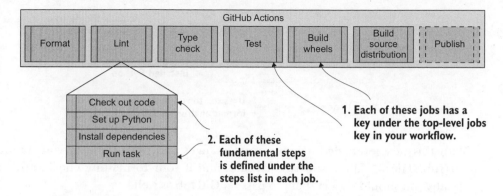

Figure 7.9 The jobs for a Python packaging workflow. Each job has a similar set of steps.

the `with` key and specify a value for the `python-version` key underneath it. Be sure to put the Python version in quotes; YAML will interpret the version as a floating-point number otherwise.

3 Install tox. By using the `setup-python` action, the version of Python you request will be available as the `python` command in the `run` value of the step.

4 Use tox to run the appropriate environment for the job. In this case, you'll use the `format` tox environment.

NOTE You may notice that the code companion (http://mng.bz/69A5) also includes a `working-directory` key in some steps, but this is only because the package directory isn't in the root of the Git repository. If your package is in the root of your repository—which is the case if you've been following along closely with this book—you should omit the `working-directory` key.

Add the new job now and return here when you're done. Make sure to give your job and custom steps human-friendly names using their respective `name` keys. Your workflow file should look something like the following listing.

Listing 7.2 A GitHub Actions job for checking Python code formatting

```
name: Packaging        ◁  Ensures the workflow
                          name always reflects
on:                       its purpose
  - push

jobs:                     A job to check the
  format:                 code formatting
    name: Check formatting    ◁
    runs-on: ubuntu-latest    Ensures job names
    steps:                    also reflect their
      - uses: actions/checkout@v3   purpose
```

```
  - uses: actions/setup-python@v4.0.0        ←┐   Installs the desired
    with:                                        Python version
        python-version: "3.10"

  - name: Install tox                        ←    Installs tox to the
    run: python -m pip install tox                installed Python

  - name: Run black          ←    Uses tox to run the
    run: tox -e format              format environment
```

With this new job added, commit your changes and push them to your branch on GitHub. The workflow will trigger again, and if your formatting checks are passing locally, you should expect them to pass on GitHub as well.

> ### Exercise 7.2
>
> The jobs for linting and type checking your code look nearly identical to the one for checking the code formatting; only the tox environment and the `name` values should differ. Add a job for linting and a job for type checking.
>
> Remember that multiple jobs run in parallel by default. After you push the changes to add these jobs, you should see your three jobs run in parallel.

You now have all of your code quality checks in place. You should feel a sense of calm washing over you. Before it takes over completely, you'll need to learn some additional GitHub Actions features before getting your testing and wheel-building jobs working.

7.3.1   *Running a job multiple times with a build matrix*

Remember from chapter 5 that tox can create a build matrix to run your tests across several configurations. GitHub Actions provides a rather similar feature. You can use the GitHub Actions matrix feature in tandem with tox's matrix feature to install the appropriate Python version for a particular tox testing environment.

> **NOTE**   You could also achieve this with distinct jobs, but much like tox, using the matrix feature saves you a fair amount of repetitive manual configuration, especially when you need to support many configuration variants.

You tell GitHub Actions that a particular job should be run for several combinations using the `strategy.matrix` key. Each key nested within the `strategy.matrix` key can have a name of your choosing and represents one set to choose from in the matrix expansion. The value for each key is a list of maps, with each map supplying variables that will be substituted into a particular job instance.

As an example, if you have four keys defined in `strategy.matrix` and each has a list of four variable maps, the matrix will have 16 combinations and the job will run across each of those 16 variants. You can reference the variable substitutions from the matrix using the `matrix` value from the GitHub Actions context (http://mng.bz/DDgA). The next listing shows an example of the syntax for defining a job with a matrix. For a full reference, you can also reference the GitHub documentation (http://mng.bz/J2pv).

Listing 7.3   A GitHub Actions job that uses a matrix build strategy

```
test-color-a11y:
  name: Test color accessibility
  runs-on: ubuntu-latest

  strategy:                                        Text color is
    matrix:                                        one factor of
      text-color:          ◁────────────────       the matrix.
        - value: "#000000"      ◁──────────
        - value: "#33A5F3"                  The text-color.value
        - value: "#59FFE9"                  variable has four
        - value: "#999999"                  options.
      background-color:        ◁──────       Background color is
        - value: "#000000"                  another matrix factor.
        - value: "#336633"
        - value: "#989A5F"
      standard:                             A matrix factor can
        - name: "WCAG"         ◁────────    have multiple variables
          level: "AA"                       per option.
        - name: "WCAG"
          level: "AAA"
                                            This step will be run for
  steps:                                    each of the 24 possible
    - name: Check accessibility  ◁────      combinations.
      run: |
        echo Checking ${{ matrix.text-color.value }}      ◁──   Values for each matrix
          on ${{ matrix.background-color.value }}               factor are available in
          for ${{ matrix.standard.name }}                       the context.
          level ${{ matrix.standard.level }}
```

Because you're using tox to run your unit tests on multiple Python versions, the main matrix factor you need is the Python version. But the string tox uses for the testing environments differs from the Python version string, so you need to specify both of these separately. You can model this in your configuration using a single `python` matrix factor where each option has both a `version` and `toxenv` variable. In your job, you can then reference the `matrix` context values for the Python version in the `actions/setup-python@v4.0.0` action and run only the relevant tox environment in the last step.

Add the new job for unit testing your code to your workflow file now and return here when you're done. It should look something like the following listing.

Listing 7.4   A job that runs different Python versions and tox environments

```
...

test:
  name: Test
  runs-on: ubuntu-latest
```

```
strategy:
  matrix:
    python:                  ◁────  A factor for the Python
      - version: "3.10"              version and tox environment
        toxenv: "py310"      ◁────
      - version: "3.9"       ◁────  The Python
        toxenv: "py39"               version to use for
                                     a particular job

  steps:                            The tox environment
    - uses: actions/checkout@v3     name to use for a
                                    particular job
    - uses: actions/setup-python@v4.0.0
      with:                                           A reference to a
        python-version: ${{ matrix.python.version }}  context value for
                                                  ◁─  a particular job
    - name: Install tox
      run: python -m pip install tox
                                              Another reference
    - name: Run pytest                        to a context value
      run: tox -e ${{ matrix.python.toxenv }}  ◁─  for a particular job
```

Commit and push your changes. GitHub Actions will show you the status of each job individually on your pull request (see figure 7.10).

Figure 7.10   GitHub Actions pull request feedback for jobs in a build matrix

In the Details view, you can see that it groups the related jobs from the matrix together (figure 7.11).

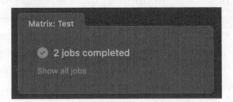

Figure 7.11   GitHub Actions build matrix in the detailed view on the Actions tab

You can expand them to see each individual job by clicking the aggregated summary (see figure 7.12).

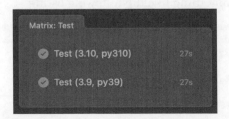

Figure 7.12   The expanded build matrix that shows each individual job in the Actions tab

In addition to the code quality checks, your unit tests are also fully automated in your continuous integration pipeline. Now you can move to the jobs that build the distributions of your package.

7.3.2 *Building Python package distributions for a variety of platforms*

You learned in chapter 4 how to build an extension in a language other than Python. You also learned that, unlike a pure Python package, packages with non-Python extensions need to be distributed either as source code that must be built by the user or as binary distributions for many different platforms. Whereas building all those different distributions is tedious and in some cases impossible on your local machine, for CI solutions with runners on a variety of operating systems and architectures, this becomes a matter of some additional configuration.

To achieve the building of binary wheel distributions across a broad swath of target platforms, you can make use of the fantastic cibuildwheel tool from the PyPA (https://github.com/pypa/cibuildwheel). This tool is intended to act as a convenient way to build wheels across as many platforms as possible. As of this writing, cibuildwheel also has the widest support on GitHub Actions over other popular continuous integration solutions.

You need to create a job rather similar to the others you've created so far, with only a few key differences, as shown next:

- Install the `cibuildwheel` package instead of the `tox` package.
- Run a command using cibuildwheel instead of a tox environment.
- Use the `actions/upload-artifact@v3` action (https://github.com/actions/upload-artifact) to store the files created by cibuildwheel when needed for publishing.

You can run cibuildwheel as a module using Python. You can pass it a directory in which to put the built wheels using the `--output-dir` flag. As an example, the following command builds wheels and puts them in a `wheels/` directory:

```
$ python -m cibuildwheel --output-dir wheels
```

When you have files you want to upload to GitHub Actions as artifacts for later use, you can pass a glob pattern of files to upload to the `actions/upload-artifact@v3` action using the `with.path` key. The following example uploads all files with a .whl extension from the `wheels/` directory:

```
...

    - uses: actions/upload-artifact@v3
      with:
        path: ./wheels/*.whl
```

Exercise 7.3

Add a new job for building wheels to your workflow file that does the following:

1 Uses a build matrix and the `runs-on` key to run the job on `ubuntu-20.04`, `windows-2019`, and `macOS-10.15`
2 Uses cibuildwheel to build wheels in a wheels/ directory
3 Uses the `actions/upload-artifact@v3` action

Reference the code companion (http://mng.bz/69A5) if you need to check your work. Commit and push your changes to confirm the wheels build successfully. Note that these jobs may take significantly longer than the tests and code quality checks because of the amount of work cibuildwheel needs to do.

Although the binary wheel distributions require a fair amount of heavy lifting, you need to build only a single source distribution. You can do this by using the `build` tool that you learned about in chapter 3. You can run `build` as a module using Python. Tell it to build a source distribution using the `--sdist` flag, and it will build the distribution to a dist/ directory by default.

Exercise 7.4

Add a new job for building a source distribution to your workflow file that does the following:

1 Installs the `build` package
2 Runs `build` to create a source distribution in the dist/ directory
3 Uses the `actions/upload-artifact@v3` action to upload all .tar.gz files from the dist/ directory for later use

Reference the code companion (http://mng.bz/69A5) if you need to check your work. Commit and push your changes to confirm the source distribution builds successfully.

You now have automation for each and every activity you've learned in the packaging workflow up to now. With these checks in place, you can feel confident that each change submitted to your project will pass muster. You can also do this without lifting so much as a finger, because GitHub Actions will give feedback to the author of a change on the pull request, letting them know they need to fix something if it breaks. You and your team can even start to develop a hypothesis-driven development model. You can run a subset of tests locally that pertain directly to your change, make a hypothesis that the full suite will pass, and see if the status of the full suite of checks confirms your expectations. This is a highly productive position to be in and can even give a bit of a rush with the confidence you may feel. The final step to automate is the publishing of the package.

7.4 Publishing a package

This book is called *Publishing Python Packages*, so you may have been wondering when it would actually get around to the publishing aspect. Although there's been a big lead-up to this moment, it's been in the name of learning the concepts so you can react to alternative tools, debug issues along the way, and generally explore the packaging landscape with confidence. I'm proud of you for making it this far, and I hope you are too!

> **IMPORTANT** Before you can publish a package to PyPI, you need a PyPI user account. Visit the registration page (https://pypi.org/account/register/) now to create an account if you don't already have one.

Before you can automate publishing your package properly, you first need to "claim" the package name you want to use on PyPI by manually uploading your package. I strongly urge you to use the format `pubpypack-harmony-<firstname>-<lastname>` for your package if you're following the exercises in this book closely so that you don't use up good package names on PyPI for your practice package. Update the name field in your setup.cfg file to use this format now. You should also check whether a package with that name already exists by searching for it from the PyPI home page (https://pypi.org) or visiting what would be the project's URL (https://pypi.org/project/pubpypack-harmony-<firstname>-<lastname>), in case you share your name with another reader. This will also help me find all your successes more easily! My version lives at https://pypi.org/project/pubpypack-harmony-dane-hillard.

> **TIP** You can also do all these same steps on the test PyPI instance (https://test.pypi.org/), which is helpful for trying new things out before doing them on the live instance. You need to create a separate account and any other credentials specific to the test instance if you decide to do so.

After you settle on a package name, you can use the twine (https://twine.readthedocs.io/en/stable/) tool to publish your package. To do so, you need to have your PyPI username and password handy. When you're ready, run the following commands from the root of your package to create a source distribution and upload it to PyPI. You'll be prompted to enter your PyPI credentials:

```
$ pipx install twine
$ pyproject-build --sdist
$ twine upload dist/*
```

> **TIP** You can create a tox environment for uploading the package using twine. This can be helpful for running repeatedly while debugging issues, and is especially helpful if you use a private package repository such as Artifactory that requires you to specify a nonstandard repository URL.

After you successfully upload the package, it becomes associated with your account. This allows you to create an API token specific to that package, which is very useful for automation purposes because you don't need to use your personal username and password directly. Create an API token specific to your package now using the following steps, also shown in figure 7.13:

1 Visit the API token creation page (https://pypi.org/manage/account/token/).
2 Give the token a name you'll recognize, such as pubpypack.
3 Select Project: pubpypack-harmony-<firstname>-<lastname> from the Scope dropdown menu.
4 Click Add Token.

Add API token

Token name (required)

> pubpypack

What is this token for?

Permissions
Upload packages

Scope (required)

> Project: pubpypack-harmony-dane-hillard ⌄

> Add token

Figure 7.13   The interface for adding a project-specific API token to a PyPI account

After you add the token, you'll be shown a page with the contents of the token (see figure 7.14). You should copy this token somewhere for safekeeping, because you'll be able to access it only this one time. You can always generate a new one later, but if you lose the token, you may need to update it in a variety of places, depending on where you used it.

Now you need to add your newly created PyPI API token as a *secret* in your GitHub repository. Secrets are sensitive information that GitHub Actions encrypts for storage. They can be injected into GitHub Actions but aren't viewable directly by anyone. Add your token using the following steps, starting from your repository's GitHub page:

1 Click Settings.
2 Click Secrets in the lower left. Make sure you end up on the Actions Secrets page, which is the default as of this writing.
3 Click New Repository Secret in the top right.
4 Name the secret PYPI_API_TOKEN.
5 Paste the value of the API token you saved from PyPI.
6 Click Add Secret.

Token for "pubpypack"

Permissions: Upload packages
Scope: Project "pubpypack-harmony-dane-hillard"

```
pypi-AgEIcHlwaS5vcmcCJDgwOGQxMzg3LWNmNDQtNGI2OS05YmZjLWMwOTk1YzI3Yzc1ZQACT3sicGVybWlzc2lvbn
MiOiB7InByb2plY3RzIjogWyJwdWJweXBhY2staGFybW9ueS1kYW5lLWhpbGxhcmQiXX0sICJ2ZXJzaW9uIjogMX0AA
AYg5Hy4F5xzeUzkpdwef6O92R8LvSQ5m6yIn03esMOastQ
```

For security reasons this token will only appear once. **Copy it now.**

Copy token **Remove token**

Figure 7.14 The one-time page displaying a newly added PyPI API token.

After you add the secret, you should see it listed in the Repository Secrets table (shown in figure 7.15).

Repository secrets

🔒 PYPI_API_TOKEN   Updated now   **Update**   Remove

Figure 7.15 The GitHub Actions secrets interface displaying an added secret

You can reference the PYPI_API_TOKEN secret from the secret context variable in your job. Now you have all the credentials in place to automate your package publishing.

Whereas all the checks, tests, and distribution builds you've added to your workflow so far are triggered directly by pushed commits and tags, the publishing step is one you'll want to restrict from running as regularly. As an example, you probably wouldn't want to publish a new version of the package on each new commit pushed to your repository, especially when the branch is from an untrusted author. Someone with malicious intent could open a pull request with a security flaw and exploit your pipeline to publish that code. A tag representing a milestone in the Git history is a common triggering event for publishing a package version that also enables you to be very deliberate about the exact moment in the code history from which to publish a version. To restrict the publishing job to only tags, you'll make use of an expression to check for the right conditions. If the conditions aren't met, GitHub Actions skips the job.

Your publishing job must do all of the following:

1 Wait for all the other jobs to finish. You don't want to publish something that fails the other checks.
2 Run only if the Git ref for the triggering event is a tag starting with v, using the `if` key and the `startsWith` function to check the `github.event.ref` context variable value. This will allow you to create tags like `v3.4.0` to trigger publishing, but tags unrelated to releases won't trigger publishing.
3 Use the `actions/download-artifact@v3` action to download the wheel and source distribution files you built and uploaded as artifacts in the previous jobs. You can use the `with.path` key to tell the action where to download the artifacts. The dist/ directory is a good choice because the next step will look there by default.
4 Use the `pypa/gh-action-pypi-publish@1.5.0` action from the PyPA to take care of the publishing details. This action uses twine under the hood, but reduces the amount of configuration you need to manage.

The configuration for the publishing job should look something like the following listing when you're done.

Listing 7.5 A job for publishing a Python package and its distributions to PyPI

```
...

publish:
  name: Publish package
  if: startsWith(github.event.ref, 'refs/tags/v')          Runs this job only if triggered by specific tags
  needs:                                                    Waits for all other jobs to finish first
    - format
    - lint
    - typecheck
    - test
    - build_source_dist
    - build_wheels
  runs-on: ubuntu-latest

  steps:
    - uses: actions/download-artifact@v3                    Used to download artifacts from the previous jobs
      with:                                                 Downloads all artifacts into a single directory
        - name: artifact
          path: ./dist/                                     Puts artifacts in a directory the next step will use by default

    - uses: pypa/gh-action-pypi-publish@1.5.0               Uses an API token instead of user/password authentication
      with:                                                 Used to publish package artifacts to PyPI
        user: __token__
        password: ${{ secrets.PYPI_API_TOKEN }}             References the repository secret you added
```

This time, after you commit and push your changes, you should expect the new job to be skipped (see figure 7.16). This is because the commits you push don't match the `if` expression you added.

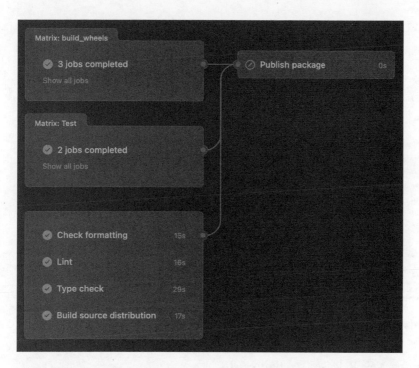

Figure 7.16   You can configure jobs in a workflow to be skipped under conditions you specify.

To trigger the publishing job, you need to create a tag with a matching name; otherwise, the pipeline won't be triggered. You also need to ensure you don't try to publish a version that already exists; otherwise, you'll wait through all the jobs of the pipeline only to receive an error during the publishing job. Your earlier twine upload likely published version `0.0.1` if you've been following this book closely. Update the `version` value in your setup.cfg file to the next highest version, such as `0.0.2`, now. After updating the version, commit and push the change. Then trigger the publishing job using the following steps to create a GitHub *release*. A *release* is a GitHub-specific construct that is associated with a tag and allows you to add relevant notes and attachments.

> **NOTE**   You can achieve the same effect as a GitHub release by manually creating a Git tag and pushing it to GitHub. For public projects, the release workflow is nice because it gives you an opportunity to enter useful release notes from your change log. More on this later in the book.

To create a release, click Releases near the bottom right. This link can be hard to spot; you can always visit https://github.com/<you>/<repo>/releases as well (see figure 7.17).

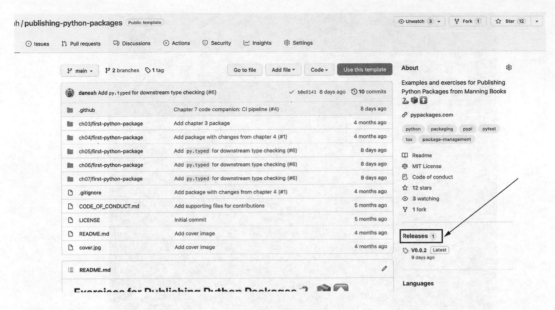

Figure 7.17   Navigating to the releases for a GitHub repository

Click Draft a New Release (see figure 7.18).

Figure 7.18   Starting a new release for a GitHub repository

Click the Choose a Tag dropdown menu, enter a new version such as v0.0.2 into the box, and then click + Create New Tag: v0.0.2 on Publish (see figure 7.19).

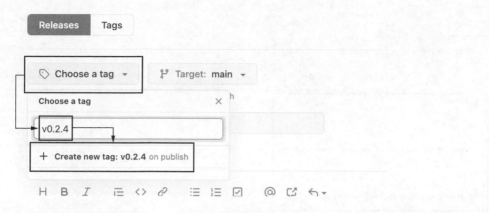

Figure 7.19   Specifying the tag to create for a GitHub release

Click the Target dropdown menu, and choose the Git branch you're using (see figure 7.20).

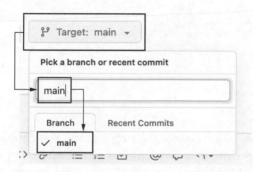

Figure 7.20   Specifying the point in the Git history from which to create a tag

Enter the version in the Release Title box, and optionally add a description for the release describing the changes. Finally, click Publish Release (see figure 7.21).

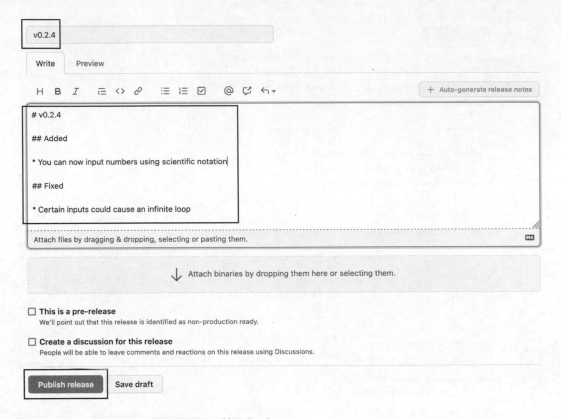

Figure 7.21   Populating and publishing a GitHub release

After you publish the release, visit the Actions tab of your repository. You should see a new workflow run with your new tag name next to it instead of a branch name. This run will meet the condition on the publishing job, and it will not be skipped this time (as shown in figure 7.22).

Congratulations! You just published your first fully automated package version. How does it feel? If you're like me, you're probably tired and a little bit grumpy, but in that way that turns into excitement after a night's sleep. What you've achieved here can't be overstated. Your team is free from the confines of their local development environments, and you're delivering prebuilt distributions for a wider variety of platforms than ever before. Even though the folks at CarCorp use a variety of computer vendors, you can have some confidence that they'll be able to use your work. You've also finally gotten the distributions published to PyPI so that others can even install them in their Python applications using familiar tools like pip. Well done, you.

Now that you're an expert in automation and have a package you want people to use, you need to make sure they know *how* and *why* to use it. Continue to the next chapter to learn about building and maintaining documentation.

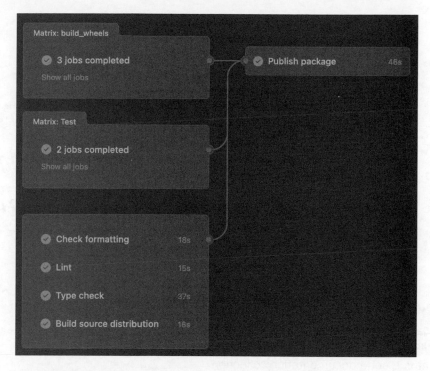

Figure 7.22 A job succeeding after meeting the conditions specified

Summary

- Continuous integration gives you frequent, reliable feedback in a shared environment for high confidence in changes.
- Use a continuous integration solution that works closely with your version control system and deployment infrastructure.
- Check each change you make by configuring your continuous integration solution to run several high-level tasks in parallel, each composed of a few specific commands.
- Be conservative in triggering your publishing process because you want to make sure the code is perfect. Keep a manual trigger in the way of this process until you build very high confidence in the system.

Authoring
and maintaining
documentation

This chapter covers

- Writing prose documentation using reStructuredText
- Automating code documentation collection using sphinx-apidoc and sphinx-autodoc
- Building an HTML documentation site using Sphinx
- Publishing documentation using Read the Docs

At the end of the previous chapter, you achieved the important milestone of publishing your package to the Python Package Index (PyPI) for others to use. The truth is that PyPI already has more than 350,000 packages and will only continue growing. Your work on the functionality, quality, and logistics of packaging has ensured that people *can* use it, but you're going to need to put in some more work if you want to ensure they *will* use it. You already have a captive audience at Car-Corp, but as you try to scale to more clients, they will come to expect more.

Documentation is one of the major hurdles to package adoption. Without ample rationale, people may not understand why they need to use your package. Even with sufficient justification, people may not understand how to use the package, even if they want to. In this chapter, you'll learn what effective package documentation looks like and how to create a setup that will support your project as the code evolves.

> **IMPORTANT**   You can use the code companion (http://mng.bz/69A5) to check your work for the exercises in this chapter.

8.1   *Some quick philosophy on documentation*

Users come seeking documentation with typically one of a few distinct goals in mind:

- They want to learn about the code for the very first time.
- They know the code well but want to achieve a specific task they haven't done before.
- They know the behavior of the code well but still need to reference details like signatures and syntax.
- They want to understand the reasoning that brought the code to the point it's at today.

Although there may be overlap in what kinds of information might benefit a user from one goal to another, the way that information is presented must cater specifically to just one goal at a time to be effective. The Diátaxis framework (https://diataxis.fr/) from Daniele Procida spells out the nuances of each goal and the kind of documentation that helps achieve each goal, as described here:

- Tutorials help a new reader through a worked problem to learn the general ideas and approach of a project.
- How-tos help a reader accomplish a specific task they came into the documentation to find.
- Discussions help a reader understand the history and decisions in a project.
- References help a reader find very specific information, such as syntax or allowed arguments.

The ideas on the Diátaxis site and Procida's corresponding presentation make a compelling argument for separating these concerns, maximizing the efficacy of documentation. The natural result of this approach is that some documentation will be nearly all prose, whereas another will be nearly all code, and others still will be a mix of both. You need a documentation system that can easily combine prose and code documentation while supporting a clear demarcation between the two concepts.

Although the full depth of pedagogy, cognitive science, and didactics are outside the scope of this book (for more of that, check out *The Programmer's Brain* by Felienne Hermans, Manning, 2021, http://mng.bz/lRxd), there are some tools out there that will help your teaching thrive. Sphinx (https://www.sphinx-doc.org) is a documentation framework that builds on the power of reStructuredText (http://mng.bz/BZMw) to create paginated, cross-referenced documentation sites in a variety of output formats.

> **Other great documentation frameworks**
>
> Although Sphinx is one of the most popular frameworks for Python documentation due to its use in Python's documentation and the power of reStructuredText, it isn't the only player in the space.
>
> Python provides a built-in `pydoc` module (https://docs.python.org/3/library/pydoc .html) that can generate documentation files from docstrings found in Python modules. It doesn't have a great way to include prose documentation, but if your project just needs a bare minimum, it might work.
>
> MkDocs (https://www.mkdocs.org/) is another third-party documentation framework that uses Markdown and YAML to create a documentation site, and there's a mkdoc-strings plugin (https://github.com/pawamoy/mkdocstrings) for working with Python docstrings.

Sphinx is incredibly powerful and can be extended through its plugin-based architecture. It's such a valuable choice for Python projects that even the official Python documentation (https://docs.python.org) uses it.

NOTE   The full capabilities and customizations Sphinx provides are outside the scope of this book, but Sphinx has—as you might imagine—excellent documentation. If you enjoy this chapter, you might like to explore more of what Sphinx can do.

Read on to learn how you can use Sphinx to create an HTML documentation website that you can serve on Read the Docs (https://readthedocs.org/), the most popular place to host documentation for Python projects.

8.2 *Starting your documentation with Sphinx*

Start by creating a new tox environment for your documentation. Remember that you can configure tox environments by adding a new section in your setup.cfg file called `[testenv:docs]`, which enables you to run it using `tox -e docs`. Add the `sphinx` package (https://pypi.org/project/Sphinx/) as a dependency for the environment using the `deps` key. Then add the `commands` key with the following command to the environment, which creates a docs/ directory in the root of your project and fills it with the initial documentation configuration and directory structure:

```
[testenv:docs]
...

commands =
    sphinx-quickstart docs
```

One of the files Sphinx's quickstart generates is docs/index.rst. This file is the entry point to your documentation. The quickstart version of the index.rst file creates a table of contents with nested headings and a caption, as shown in the next listing.

Listing 8.1   A basic table-of-contents directive in Sphinx

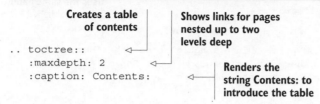

```
.. toctree::
   :maxdepth: 2
   :caption: Contents:
```

The table of contents is an important Sphinx concept, because just like in a book, the reader should be able to find their way to the content they're interested in reading. Each page of documentation you add should be part of the table of contents tree, so Sphinx's quickstart process starts you off following this pattern.

Run your environment using the `tox -e docs` command. Sphinx prompts you for the following basic information about the package:

1 *Directory structure*—You can choose the default that places a _build/ directory in the docs/ directory alongside the raw documentation, or you can choose to have nested source/ and build/ directories to keep the raw and built documentation totally separate. The default works just fine here; the rest of this chapter will assume this structure.

2 *Project name*—This should match the name under which you publish your package so people recognize that they're reading the correct documentation for a package they're considering installing or have installed.

3 *Author name*—This is your name or another identifier such as your company's name.

4 *Project release*—You can leave this empty for now. Later in this chapter, you'll get the package version dynamically in the documentation configuration.

5 *Project language*—This is the two-letter ISO 639-1 code (http://mng.bz/de2g) for the natural language in which you're writing your documentation. Sphinx will adjust some of its output into the selected language as well; English is the default.

The full output of the quickstart process will look something like the following listing.

Listing 8.2   The initial setup for a Sphinx-driven documentation project

```
Welcome to the Sphinx 4.4.0 quickstart utility.

Please enter values for the following settings (just press Enter to
accept a default value, if one is given in brackets).

Selected root path: docs                                         Uses the default
                                                                      structure
You have two options for placing the build directory for Sphinx output.
Either, you use a directory "_build" within the root path, or you separate
"source" and "build" directories within the root path.
> Separate source and build directories (y/n) [n]:        ◁
```

```
The project name will occur in several places in the built documentation.
> Project name: pubpypack-harmony-dane-hillard              ◁─── Uses the same name
> Author name(s): Dane Hillard                                    as the published
> Project release []:                     ◁─── Leave this         package
                                               empty for now.
```

Uses the same name as the published package

Leave this empty for now.

```
If the documents are to be written in a language other than English,
you can select a language here by its language code. Sphinx will then
translate text that it generates into that language.

For a list of supported codes, see
https://www.sphinx-doc.org/en/master/usage/configuration.html#confval-language.
> Project language [en]:                    ◁─── Chooses your
                                                  preferred
                                                  language
```

Chooses your preferred language

```
Creating file /.../first-python-package/docs/conf.py.
Creating file /.../first-python-package/docs/index.rst.
Creating file /.../first-python-package/docs/Makefile.
Creating file /.../first-python-package/docs/make.bat.

Finished: An initial directory structure has been created.

You should now populate your master file
/.../first-python-package/docs/index.rst and create other documentation
source files. Use the Makefile to build the docs, like so:
   make builder
where "builder" is one of the supported builders, e.g., html, latex or linkcheck.
```

Uses your name or another appropriate identifier

You should now see the docs/ directory in the root of your project, and inside it you should see the following files and directories:

- *conf.py*—This file contains the Sphinx configuration for building your documentation.
- *index.rst*—When you build the documentation, this file acts as the main entry point for Sphinx to find all your documentation. Its content will be the home page of your documentation.
- *Makefile*—You can use this to build your documentation manually on Unix systems where GNU Make (https://www.gnu.org/software/make/) is installed. You can remove this file for now; you won't use it in this book.
- *make.bat*—You can use this to build your documentation manually on Windows systems. You can remove this file for now; you won't use it in this book.
- *static/*—You can add CSS or image files to this directory to use within your documentation. You can remove this directory for now; you won't use it in this book.
- *templates/*—You can add to or override Sphinx's default templates to this directory to change how your documentation is presented. You can remove this directory for now; you won't use it in this book.

You won't need to use the sphinx-quickstart command again unless you want to start your documentation over from scratch. The sphinx-quickstart command will produce an error if it finds existing documentation to avoid overwriting what you've already created. Going forward, you want the tox environment to build the documentation instead. You can use the `sphinx-build` command to build the documentation from the docs/ directory as HTML in the docs/_build/ directory. In addition to converting the index.rst file to HTML, Sphinx also builds indices that support searching the documentation as well as letting other Sphinx-based documentation sites cross-reference it—more on this later in this chapter. Remember that you configured pytest and mypy to fail explicitly if you accidentally add nonexistent or unused references. The `sphinx-build` command also has some options to help ensure your documentation doesn't have any broken references. Each of the following options changes the behavior of Sphinx and the output it logs to the console:

- *-n*—Nit-picky mode makes Sphinx output missing references as warnings in the logged output.
- *-W*—This option turns all warnings generated during the build into errors. You might like to enable this to decrease the chances that you introduce issues into your documentation that silently allow the build to succeed.
- *--keep-going*—This option runs the full documentation build, collecting all errors along the way instead of failing after the first one. This is useful so you can see multiple errors to fix at once instead of repeatedly building and getting new errors each time.

Update the `commands` value for your documentation tox environment to run the following command, which builds the documentation from the docs/ directory as HTML in the docs/_build/ directory:

```
sphinx-build -n -W --keep-going -b html docs/ docs/_build/
```

Run the `docs` tox environment again. This time, Sphinx should find the existing configuration in conf.py and the content of the index.rst file and use them to build the documentation, as illustrated in the next listing.

Listing 8.3 Sample output of building HTML documentation using sphinx-build

```
Running Sphinx v4.4.0
making output directory... done          ◄── Creates the _build/
building [mo]: targets for 0 po files that are out of date    directory if not present
building [html]: targets for 1 source files that are out of date   ◄── The index.rst source file
updating environment: [new config] 1 added, 0 changed, 0 removed
reading sources... [100%] index          ◄──
                                              A line for each
looking for now-outdated files... none found   source file is printed.
pickling environment... done
checking consistency... done
preparing documents... done
writing output... [100%] index          ◄── An output file for each
                                              source file is created.
```

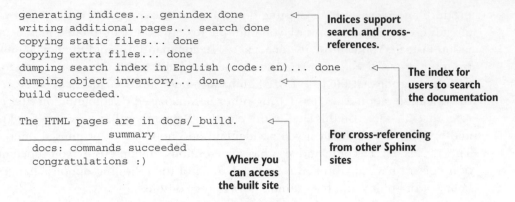

```
generating indices... genindex done
writing additional pages... search done
copying static files... done
copying extra files... done
dumping search index in English (code: en)... done
dumping object inventory... done
build succeeded.

The HTML pages are in docs/_build.
_____ summary _____
  docs: commands succeeded
  congratulations :)
```

Indices support search and cross-references.

The index for users to search the documentation

For cross-referencing from other Sphinx sites

Where you can access the built site

Now that you've built the documentation as HTML, you can view it in your browser. Although you have just one index.rst file right now, in addition to a corresponding index.html file in the docs/_build/ directory, Sphinx built HTML files for the documentation search page and the indices. You can view the index.html file directly in your browser and even run a search, but a better way to view the documentation with all its features is with Python's built-in `http.server` module. This module runs a small HTTP server, simulating how the files would be accessed on a server on the internet. You can run the following command from the root of your project to serve the documentation at http://localhost:9876:

```
$ py -m http.server -d docs/_build/ 9876
```

Visit http://localhost:9876 in your browser now. This shows the documentation home page, which contains some of the information you provided to Sphinx during the quick start process (see figure 8.1).

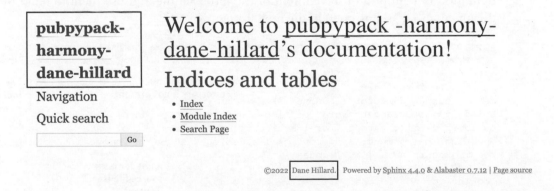

Figure 8.1   The bare-bones HTML site created by Sphinx for a new documentation project. It includes the package name and the author name.

Now that you have Sphinx running successfully, the next step before going further into writing documentation is building automation for a few things to speed up your documentation efforts.

8.2.1   Automating documentation refresh during development

You can leave the Python HTTP server running as you make updates to your documentation throughout this chapter so that you can always access them in your browser, but this can be difficult to remember to do each time you work on the documentation in the future. You can manage this using the `sphinx-autobuild` package (https://pypi.org/project/sphinx-autobuild/) and the `sphinx-autobuild` command it provides instead of `sphinx-build` when you're working on the documentation locally. The `sphinx-autobuild` command starts an HTTP server as well, but it will watch the documentation source files for changes and refresh the documentation in your browser automatically. This is really helpful to save time when you're iterating quickly on the wording or structure of your documentation. Create a new `devdocs` tox environment that has a similar configuration as the `docs` environment with the following changes:

- Add the `sphinx-autobuild` package as a dependency in addition to the `sphinx` package.
- Change the `sphinx-build` command to `sphinx-autobuild`.
- Remove the `--keep-going` option; `sphinx-autobuild` will keep serving the documentation even if an error occurs and prints a warning that the built documentation is out of sync with the source. When you fix the error, the build will catch back up to the latest source.
- Add a `--port` option, if desired, to choose an available port on your machine to serve the documentation. The default is `8000`.

Now you can serve your documentation locally using the `tox -e devdocs` command instead of running the documentation tox environment and Python HTTP server in tandem. You can still run the `docs` tox environment to build the documentation statically, which is used later in this chapter to validate the documentation. For now, keep moving forward on fleshing out the documentation itself.

8.2.2   Automating extraction of code documentation

Low-level documentation of code is most effective when it lives as close to the code as possible. Otherwise, the documentation is sure to become outdated just about the time you finish writing it. Ideally, the code documentation would be interleaved into the code itself, associated directly with the code it documents. Python supports this through some of its language constructs. At the same time, delving into the code isn't always the best option for your users when their goal is only to read the code at a high level. You need a process that allows you to keep code reference documentation close to the relevant code for maintainability, but also enables you to pull it up to a higher level for the reader's usability.

In chapter 6, you configured mypy to validate the type hints in your code. Although type hints are valuable for automated validation, they also help developers reading the code understand what data types they can expect to pass in or receive from a function. You should extract these as part of the code documentation because of their value as reference information. More on this shortly.

Python allows you to add *docstrings,* or free-standing strings meant to document code, to Python modules, classes, methods, and functions. You may have seen or used docstrings before—maybe serving a similar purpose to code comments—but they're quite a bit more powerful. Python parses docstrings as part of the structure of the objects they document. In particular, the __doc__ attribute of any module, class, method, or function contains the value of its docstring if present. An example Python module called shapes.py is shown with docstrings at each level in the following listing.

Listing 8.4   Docstrings for modules, classes, methods, and standalone functions

```python
"""                    ◁——⌐  A module
shapes.py                 |  docstring

This module contains utilities for dealing with shapes.
"""

from math import pi


class Circle:               ⌐  A class
    """              ◁——┘      docstring
    A class for calculating
    the circumference and area of a circle.
    """

    def __init__(self, radius: int = 1):
        self.radius = radius
                            ⌐  A method
    def area(self):         |  docstring
        """          ◁——┘
        Return the area of this circle.
        """

        return pi * self.radius**2

    def circumference(self):
        """
        Return the length of the perimeter of this circle.
        """

        return 2 * pi * self.radius
```

You can observe the behavior of the docstrings by inspecting the __doc__ attribute of the objects in the shapes.py module, including the module itself (see the next listing). Note that because the docstrings are multiline Python strings, they're faithfully reproduced in the __doc__ attribute with the same newlines and indentation as the original string.

> **Listing 8.5 Introspecting docstrings using the __doc__ attribute**

The docstring starts and ends with a newline

The docstring at the start of the module file

```
>>> import shapes
>>> shapes.__doc__
'\nshapes.py\n\nThis module contains utilities for dealing with
 shapes.\n'
>>> shapes.Circle.__doc__
'\n    A class for calculating
 \n    the circumference and area of a circle.\n    '
```

The docstring just inside the Circle class

The docstring contains more indentation because it is inside a class.

This association makes docstrings useful in automated systems because they can extract the name, signature, and docstring of a function for documentation purposes, putting the focus on the API and the prose documentation you add in your docstrings instead of forcing users to sift through the implementation details of the source code. Sphinx provides tools for this kind of extraction, which would otherwise be an insurmountable task in a project with more than a handful of objects to document.

To get Sphinx to extract your code's documentation, you must add an additional command to your documenation tox environments. Sphinx provides a sphinx-apidoc command (http://mng.bz/rnJx) that discovers all the modules, classes, methods, and functions in your project and extracts any documentation they have. The command provides a large number of options affecting how the final documentation renders, but these often come down to a matter of personal taste. I recommend the following options for their effects:

- *--force*—This will cause sphinx-apidoc to overwrite any existing extracted documentation. Because you're generating these files directly from the code continuously rather than building them just once in a while, you want to make sure the generated documentation is in sync with the source code it comes from. Without this option, sphinx-apidoc will conservatively avoid writing to files that exist already.

- *--implicit-namespaces*—When searching for modules, you want Sphinx to find any modules that are in an implicit namespace, as defined in PEP 420 (https://www.python.org/dev/peps/pep-0420/). This supports a wider variety of package configurations so that it won't break on you later if you add implicit namespaces to your project.

- *--module-first*—Usually people learn best by reading about high-level concepts before low-level concepts. By default, Sphinx outputs documentation with the lowest-level code documented first; this option puts the highest-level documentation first instead.
- *--separate*—Some readers can become overwhelmed if too much content is presented on one page. By default, Sphinx groups documentation together; this option splits the documentation for each module onto its own page instead.

The next few options are necessary to tell the sphinx-apidoc command where to discover and output the documentation:

- The -o option indicates the output directory for the documentation. A directory with a name like docs/reference/ is a decent choice for the output directory, but you can name it something else if you like. This name will appear in the URL for the extracted documentation, and you should add the directory to your .gitignore file to avoid checking in the generated documentation files.
- The positional arguments are the directory in which to start discovering code, followed by zero or more patterns of files to ignore during the search. You want Sphinx to look in your src/imppkg/ directory where your package's source code is located, and you want it to ignore all src/imppkg/*.c and src/imppkg/*.so files because those are non-Python files generated by Cython.

The final incantation for the sphinx-apidoc command may be a bit intimidating, but you understand the moving parts of it now. It should look like the listing shown here.

Listing 8.6   Automatically extracting code documentation using sphinx-apidoc

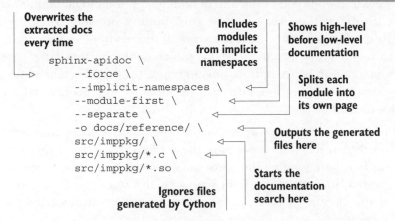

Add this new sphinx-apidoc command as the first command in each of the docs and devdocs tox environments so that they extract the code documentation into the docs/reference/ directory before building and watching the full documentation. You're almost ready to extract some code documentation, but before you do, you need to configure two more things.

WARNING The sphinx-autobuild command you set up in the devdocs environment can detect changes only to existing documentation files. If you add a new Python module while the devdocs environment is running, any code documentation in the new module won't get automatically extracted by Sphinx. When this happens, you can stop and rerun the tox -e devdocs command.

The sphinx-apidoc command generates several files in the docs/references/ directory that use directives from Sphinx's autodoc extension (http://mng.bz/VyMN), and that extension isn't enabled by default. In the docs/conf.py module, look for the empty extensions list and add the extensions shown in the next listing to interpret the extracted docstrings and type hints from the source code.

Listing 8.7   Extracting documentation from source code using Sphinx

```
extensions = [
    "sphinx.ext.autodoc",          ◁── The files output by sphinx-apidoc use this extension.
    "sphinx.ext.autodoc.typehints",  ◁── This extension will render type hints in the documentation.
]
```

One of the files the sphinx-apidoc command generates is called docs/reference/modules.rst. Just as index.rst acts as the main entry point to all your documentation, the modules.rst file acts as an entry point to the code documentation generated by the sphinx-apidoc command. You need to link the index.rst file to the modules.rst file so that your documentation home page will link to the code documentation.

Version control for generated documentation

In my experience, the automated documentation Sphinx extracts from your code should be ignored from version control systems, because the documentation regenerates any time the code changes and will mostly add noise to code review. That being said, you could put them in version control if you work on a project whose documentation needs careful attention to validate its contents. You need to decide on the trade-off between completeness and overhead that this choice has for your projects.

When you first rendered the documentation and viewed it in your browser, there was no content; you hadn't added any documentation yet. Because you're about to build code documentation in the docs/reference/ directory, where the modules.rst file will be an entry point to all documentation in that directory, you can add it to the table of contents directive in index.rst. In reStructuredText, you can use relative links to files and omit the extension for other files if they're also reStructuredText. That is, if you want to reference docs/reference/modules.rst from docs/index.rst, the relative path is reference/modules.rst, and you can use the shorter reference/modules because it's a reStructuredText file. Add this value to the `toctree` directive now, separating it with a blank line from the `:maxdepth:` and `:caption:` properties, as shown in the next listing.

Listing 8.8   Linking other documentation in a table of contents

```
.. toctree::
   :maxdepth: 2
   :caption: Contents:        ┐ Links documentation
                              │ found in this file in the
   reference/modules    ◁─┘   table of contents
```

In addition to one .rst file for each Python module, Sphinx generates an .rst file for each import package. The import package's file links to the .rst file for each module in that package. In turn, the top-level module.rst file links to the .rst file for each import package. This creates a graph of links, and when Sphinx builds them into an HTML site, they create a browsable page structure, as shown in figure 8.2.

> **WARNING** Sphinx uses the terms *module* and *submodule* interchangeably with *import packages* and *modules*, respectively. If you've named things clearly and know the structure of your project well, this doesn't prove to be too big an issue, but it's good to keep an eye out for this.

Now that your tox environments are configured to run the `sphinx-apidoc` command, and Sphinx is configured to interpret the output of that step using the `sphinx.ext.autodoc` extension during the HTML build, run the `devdocs` tox environment again. This time you should see additional output from the `sphinx-apidoc` command indicating the creation of new documentation files (see the following listing).

Listing 8.9   Output from automated generation of documentation using sphinx-apidoc

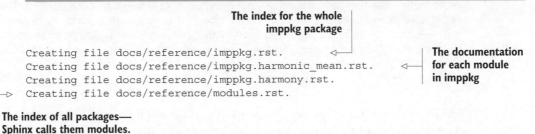

```
                        The index for the whole
                        imppkg package
                                                          The documentation
Creating file docs/reference/imppkg.rst.          ◁─┐    for each module
Creating file docs/reference/imppkg.harmonic_mean.rst.  ◁─┤ in imppkg
Creating file docs/reference/imppkg.harmony.rst.
Creating file docs/reference/modules.rst.
  ▷
The index of all packages—
Sphinx calls them modules.
```

View the documentation again in your browser. You should now see the `imppkg` package linked on the home page (see figure 8.3).

1. Prose documentation lives in the docs/ directory and can be cross-referenced using links and table of content directives in reStructuredText.

2. Documentation can link to code references, but they exist only after Sphinx builds them using sphinx-apidoc.

3. The documentation is a graph; every page should be reachable from some other page, starting at the main index.

5. For simplicity, this diagram depicts the documentation strictly as a tree with leaf nodes; any document may reference any other document.

4. Sphinx generates a page for each Python module and package, as well as a top-level entry point file for all the code documentation.

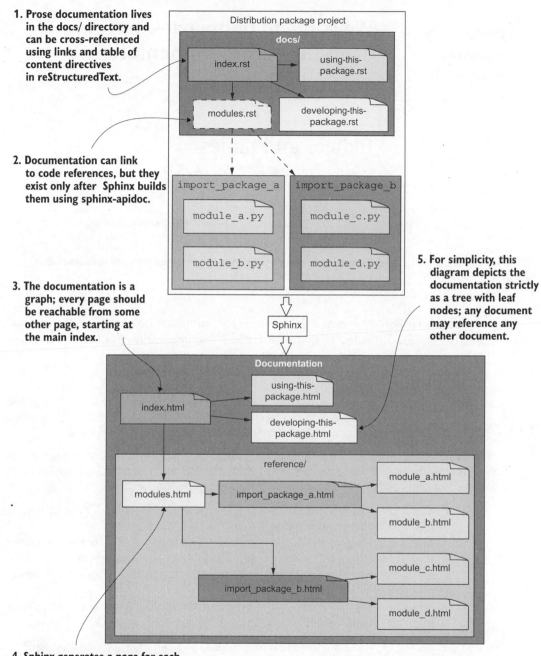

Figure 8.2   Sphinx processes interlinked prose documentation and code documentation into a browsable graph of HTML pages.

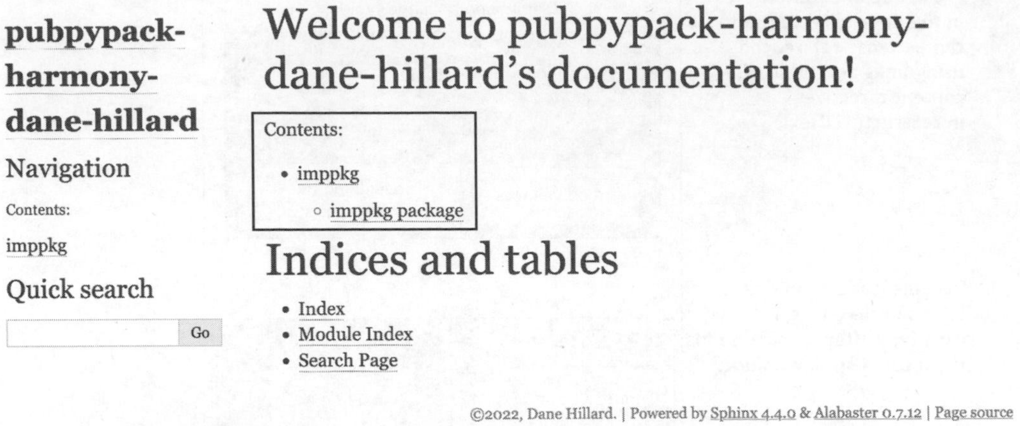

pubpypack-harmony-dane-hillard

Welcome to pubpypack-harmony-dane-hillard's documentation!

Navigation

Contents:

* imppkg
    * imppkg package

imppkg

Quick search

[   ] Go

Indices and tables

* Index
* Module Index
* Search Page

©2022, Dane Hillard. | Powered by Sphinx 4.4.0 & Alabaster 0.7.12 | Page source

Figure 8.3   A Sphinx table of contents built using the automated sphinx-apidoc code documentation extraction approach

You can also follow these new links to view the documentation specific to the `harmonic_mean` or `harmony` modules. Remember that the documentation is a browsable graph.

Exercise 8.1

Although it doesn't look like much yet, your documentation setup is already equipped to build fairly rich documentation. You need to do the hard work by adding more prose documentation in the docs/ directory and docstrings to your Python code.

Take a moment to practice adding docstrings to your code, and see how Sphinx reflects these in the documentation as a result. Add the following documentation to your project, and observe how the built HTML documentation changes:

* Add a module-level docstring to the `harmony.py` module explaining how to use it as a command-line tool.
* Add a docstring to the `harmonic_mean` function in the harmonic_mean.pyx Cython file linking to a resource about the use of harmonic means.
* Add an introduction about the harmony package to the index.rst file before the table of contents.
* Add a new .rst file explaining the project's structure to a developer who wants to add or change features, and link it in the table of contents.

In addition to using reStructuredText in .rst files, you can also use reStructuredText in your docstrings. If you want to see how to achieve something specific in reStructuredText, check out Sphinx's reStructuredText primer (http://mng.bz/xMn7). You will need to rerun the `devdocs` or `docs` environment when adding or changing docstrings in the source code.

Finally, you should configure the package version so Sphinx and Read the Docs can associate a particular build with its corresponding package version. You can use the `importlib` module (https://docs.python.org/3/library/importlib.html) to retrieve the version of your installed package. `importlib.metadata.version` accepts the installation name of a distribution package and returns the installed version as a string. Add the code shown in the next listing to the `docs/conf.py` module, entering the name you chose for publishing your package.

> **Listing 8.10   Configuring Sphinx to understand the version of your installed package**

```
from importlib import metadata

PACKAGE_VERSION = metadata.version('pubpypack-harmony-
➥ <firstname>-<lastname>')
version = release = PACKAGE_VERSION
```

Note that the default theme for Sphinx doesn't display the package version in the documentation. Some of the other built-in themes do, and you can customize the theme to show the version if you prefer; more on themes and customization later. When you're feeling satisfied with the quick first pass of your documentation, you can commit those changes to your project and push them to GitHub. The next step is getting your documentation published on Read the Docs.

8.3   Publishing documentation to Read the Docs

> **TIP** Before proceeding in this section, you must create an account on Read the Docs (https://readthedocs.org/accounts/signup/). You can use either your email or your GitHub account; I connect with GitHub because it makes importing an existing GitHub project that much easier.

You have a great start on your documentation, but if it only lives in your repository in plain text files, it still isn't reaching its full potential to help your users. You don't want to force the people trying to use your code to build the documentation themselves, distracting them from their true goals. Read the Docs is a great hosting platform that publishes your Sphinx-built HTML documentation online. It supports Sphinx directly, along with a few other documentation systems, and as of this writing, it's always free for open source projects.

> **Publishing documentation for private projects**
>
> Do you have a private package for use within your organization? Read the Docs has a paid business-class solution (https://readthedocs.com), which is a great way for your organization to give back to them. If your organization is more likely to pay for your time and some private infrastructure, you can also build the Sphinx documentation in a Docker container and serve it yourself using nginx (https://nginx.org) or the Apache HTTP Server (https://httpd.apache.org/). This works because the Sphinx build ultimately converts all your documentation to static HTML.

After you log in on Read the Docs, you arrive on the dashboard page. If you've never used Read the Docs before, there won't be much there. The important part is the Import a Project button (see figure 8.4). Click there to begin importing your project.

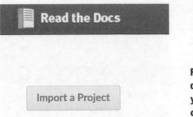

Figure 8.4   The Read the Docs dashboard shows you any projects you've already imported, with a callout to import new projects.

On the first import page, Read the Docs prompts you to select a repository to import. You can select any public repository owned by you or one of your organizations (see figure 8.5). Choose your package's repository from the list by clicking Add (+). If you don't see your repository, click refresh or double-check that your repository is public on GitHub.

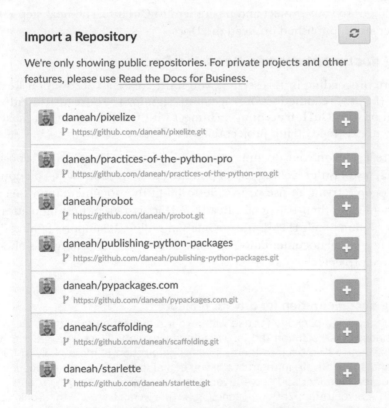

Figure 8.5   Read the Docs can import any public repositories from your account or any organizations you're in.

When you add your repository, Read the Docs prompts you for some project information. This page is already populated with default values, but you should change the following:

1 Change the Name field to match the name you used to publish your package on the Python Package Index. This should be something like `pubpypack-harmony-<firstname>-<lastname>`.

2 Ensure the Default Branch field is set to your repository's default branch, which is typically `main` for new GitHub repositories. If you are still working on your documentation on a branch other than the default branch, set this field to your documentation branch for now so Read the Docs can find your documentation code. You can switch this setting back to `main` when you're ready to merge the documentation branch.

3 Select the Edit Advanced Project Options: option.

Your settings should look something like figure 8.6 before proceeding. When you're ready, click Next.

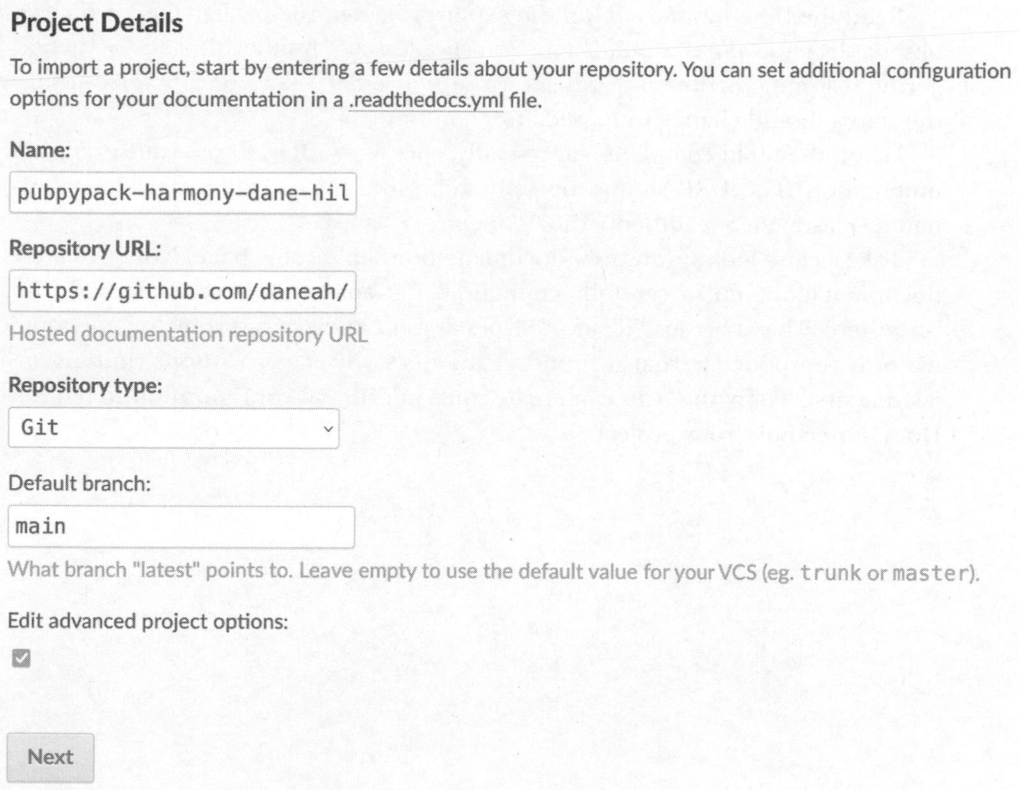

Project Details

To import a project, start by entering a few details about your repository. You can set additional configuration options for your documentation in a .readthedocs.yml file.

Name:

```
pubpypack–harmony–dane–hil
```

Repository URL:

```
https://github.com/daneah/
```

Hosted documentation repository URL

Repository type:

```
Git                              ⌄
```

Default branch:

```
main
```

What branch "latest" points to. Leave empty to use the default value for your VCS (eg. `trunk` or `master`).

Edit advanced project options:

☑

Next

Figure 8.6 The main Read the Docs settings when importing a project

The next page prompts you for advanced settings about the project, which is also populated with some default values. Change the following:

1 Update the description to match the description from your project's README file, if you choose. This is shown only on the Read the Docs site.
2 Ensure the Documentation Type field is set to Sphinx HTML.
3 Ensure the Language field is set to the language in which you wrote your documentation.
4 Ensure the Programming Language field is set to Python.
5 Add some tags of your choosing. These tags help others discover your project. Add a pubpypack tag so all the readers of this book can find each other's projects.

Your settings should look something like figure 8.7 before proceeding. When you're ready, click Finish.

When you finish the import process for the project, Read the Docs brings you to the project's page. There isn't a lot of information yet; it mostly reflects the settings you just entered. Importantly, you can see that the Last Built field says "No builds yet" and the status badge shows an Unknown status (see figure 8.8).

Read the Docs has started building your project in the background, which you can observe by choosing the Builds tab. You should see a build with a status such as Triggering, Cloning, or Building (as shown in figure 8.9). Periodically refresh this page; the status should change to Passed after a minute or so.

When the build completes successfully, click View Docs to see your published documentation. The URL should be something like https://pubpypack-harmony-<first-name>-<lastname>.readthedocs.io/<language>/latest/.

Take a close look at your new documentation site's home page. Notice that the code documentation you so carefully configured the `sphinx-apidoc` command to extract isn't there. This is because Read the Docs doesn't know about your tox environment—it's only reproducing what it found in the docs/ directory without running `sphinx-apidoc` first. To fix this, you can create some additional configuration to tell Read the Docs more about your project.

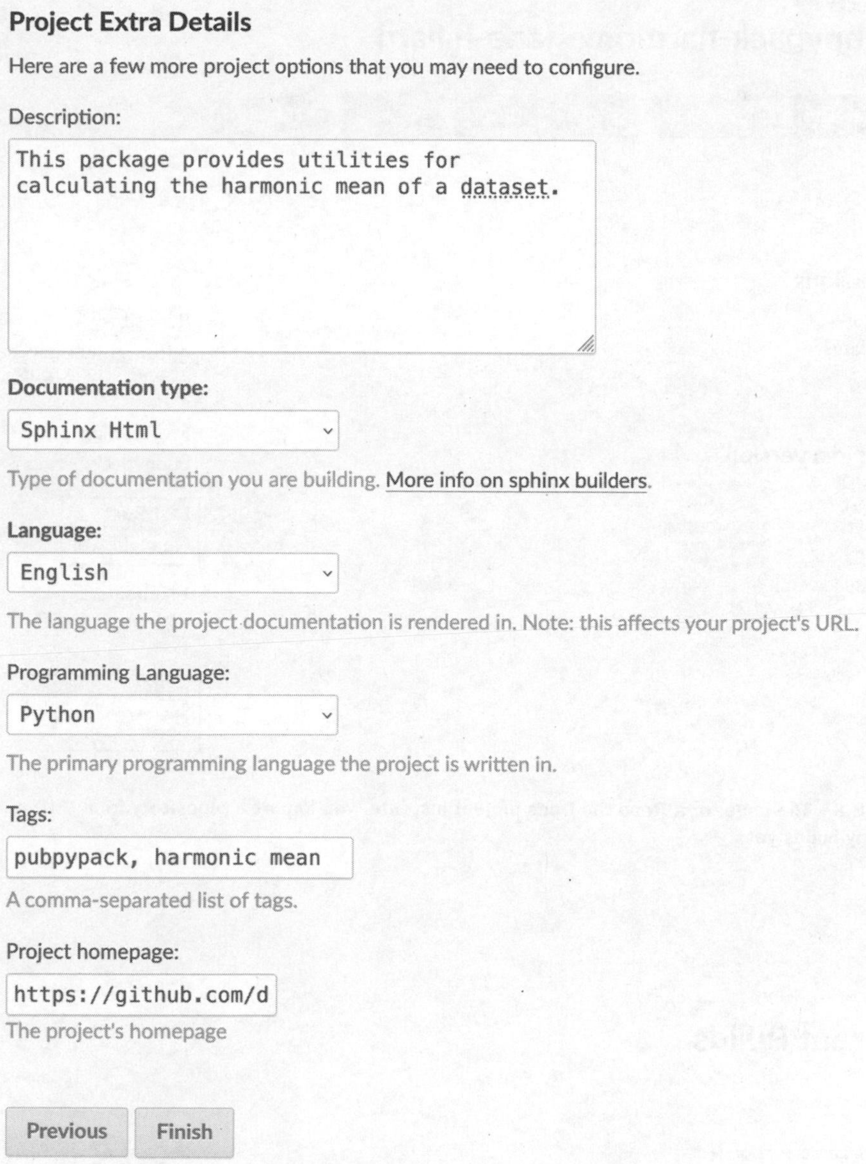

Project Extra Details

Here are a few more project options that you may need to configure.

Description:

```
This package provides utilities for
calculating the harmonic mean of a dataset.
```

Documentation type:

```
Sphinx Html                    ⌄
```

Type of documentation you are building. **More info on sphinx builders**.

Language:

```
English                        ⌄
```

The language the project documentation is rendered in. Note: this affects your project's URL.

Programming Language:

```
Python                         ⌄
```

The primary programming language the project is written in.

Tags:

```
pubpypack, harmonic mean
```

A comma-separated list of tags.

Project homepage:

```
https://github.com/d
```

The project's homepage

[Previous] [Finish]

Figure 8.7   The advanced Read the Docs settings when importing a project

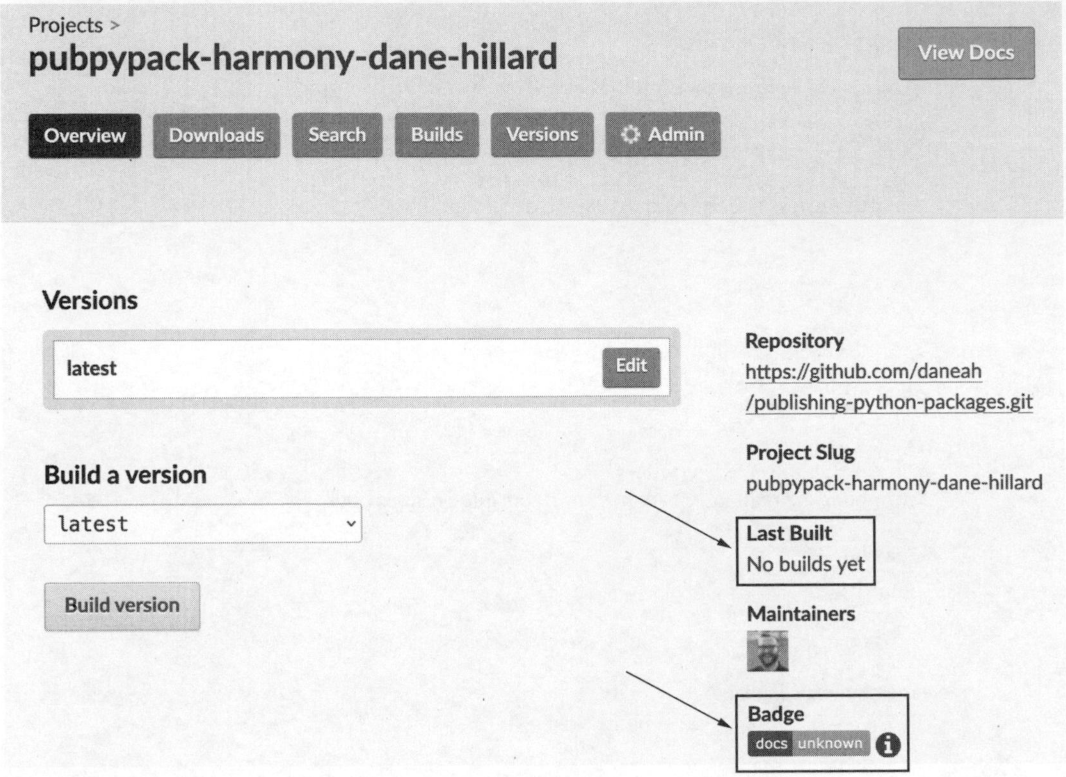

Projects >
pubpypack-harmony-dane-hillard

View Docs

Overview   Downloads   Search   Builds   Versions   ⚙ Admin

Versions

latest   Edit

Repository
https://github.com/daneah
/publishing-python-packages.git

Build a version

latest ⌄

Project Slug
pubpypack-harmony-dane-hillard

Build version

Last Built
No builds yet

Maintainers

Badge
docs unknown ⓘ

Figure 8.8   The page for a Read the Docs project just after you import a repository from GitHub. It may not have any builds yet.

Recent Builds

Build Version: latest ⌄

Triggered version latest (html)   0 minutes ago

Figure 8.9   The Builds page shows the status of past and current builds.

8.3.1 Configuring Read the Docs

Your current configuration has the following two drawbacks:

1 Read the Docs won't run your tox environment or a `sphinx-apidoc` command before building your documentation, causing the missing code documentation you observed earlier (http://mng.bz/AVye).
2 Sphinx doesn't install your package into the Python environment like your tox environment does. If your package has any third-party dependencies, those also won't be installed, and Sphinx may fail during the build of the documentation when it runs into unknown package imports.

You must handle both of these cases to ensure smooth operation moving forward.

Read the Docs will read configuration from a YAML file called .readthedocs.yaml (http://mng.bz/ZpAN) in the root directory of your project. The Read the Docs build uses operating system images, much like the GitHub Actions you set up earlier. The YAML configuration file can change the operating system, the versions of tools used during the build, and so on. Read the Docs also found your Sphinx documentation files automatically, but you can explicitly configure where those files are located so Read the Docs doesn't get confused later on.

Create an empty .readthedocs.yaml now. For your project, you need to add the following:

- *version*—The version of the Read the Docs configuration schema you're using. The latest version is 2 at the time of this writing and is a required field.
- *sphinx.configuration*—The relative path from the project root directory to the Sphinx conf.py file.
- *formats*—A list of the output types to build. Sphinx supports EPUB and PDF output in addition to HTML. If you want to build just the HTML, specify `htmlzip`.
- *build.os*—The operating system to build on. Use the latest Ubuntu LTS release, which at the time of this writing is `ubuntu-20.04`.
- *build.tools.python*—The Python version to build on. At the time of this writing, the default is Python 3.7. You should use one of the Python versions your package supports. Specify something like `"3.10"`, including the quotes; YAML interprets `3.10` without quotes as a decimal number, resulting in `3.1`.
- *python.install[0].method*—How to install dependencies for the documentation build. Read the Docs supports using pip or Setuptools to install packages; you should use pip because the Setuptools approach is a legacy one, and you properly configured your package to be installable using the latest build system approach for Python. Specify `pip`.
- *python.install[0].path*—The relative path to the directory of the package project. Your package project is the same as the root directory, so specify the current directory using a dot character (`.`).

Your Read the Docs YAML configuration file should look like the following listing when you finish.

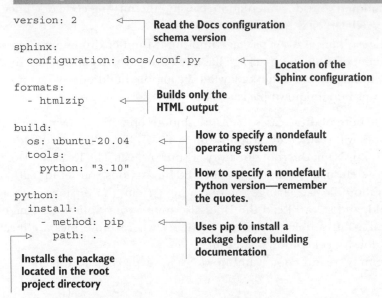

Listing 8.11   A Read the Docs configuration file

```
version: 2              ◁──  Read the Docs configuration
                             schema version
sphinx:
  configuration: docs/conf.py   ◁──  Location of the
                                     Sphinx configuration
formats:
  - htmlzip            ◁──  Builds only the
                            HTML output
build:
  os: ubuntu-20.04     ◁──  How to specify a nondefault
  tools:                    operating system
    python: "3.10"     ◁──  How to specify a nondefault
                            Python version—remember
                            the quotes.
python:
  install:
    - method: pip      ◁──  Uses pip to install a
  ▷   path: .               package before building
                            documentation
Installs the package
located in the root
project directory
```

With this configuration in place, you can add dependencies to your project later and be confident that Sphinx won't fail because of unknown imports. Next, you need to get Read the Docs to run the `sphinx-apidoc` command.

RUNNING SPHINX-APIDOC ON READ THE DOCS

In your tox environment, you added the `sphinx-apidoc` command before the `sphinx-build` and `sphinx-autobuild` commands, respectively, so that the code documentation is extracted before the full build. When your project gets built on Read the Docs, Read the Docs is running its own separate set of commands that aren't related to or aware of your tox environment. You can't tell Read the Docs to change its process directly, but you can tell Sphinx to do something before every build.

As part of its plugin-based architecture, Sphinx exposes a series of "events" (http://mng.bz/Rv4R) with which extensions can interface. One such event is called `builder-inited` (http://mng.bz/2rro), which is triggered just before the build occurs. Sphinx will call a `setup` function defined in your configuration during the build, where you can connect with any events you need to listen for. You can leverage this architecture along with the programmatic API for sphinx-apidoc to achieve the same behavior as calling the `sphinx-apidoc` command in your tox environment.

> **NOTE**   What follows may feel redundant given what you already added in your setup.cfg file, but I recommend keeping both configurations. The duration of the sphinx-apidoc step grows linearly with the number of Python modules

your project contains, so it only grows slower and slower over time. Running it before each and every build locally can be tiresome, especially when you're making changes to only your prose documentation.

Your programmatic configuration of sphinx-apidoc should happen only when the build is executing in the Read the Docs environment. You can determine this by inspecting the value of the READTHEDOCS environment variable, which has a value of "True" in the Read the Docs build environment. When you detect that the build is happening on Read the Docs, you can then define your setup function to hook into sphinx-apidoc. sphinx-apidoc's programmatic API accepts the same arguments as the command-line interface because it exposes a main function as a console script—similar to the one you created for your harmony command. The only difference when using it in the docs/conf.py module is that the paths to the source code, output directory, and ignored files need to be relative to the module rather than to the root directory of the project. You can use Python's os.path module (https://docs.python.org/3/library/os.path.html) or the newer pathlib module (https://docs.python.org/3/library/pathlib.html) to achieve this.

Add the code in the next listing to the bottom of the docs/conf.py module.

Listing 8.12 **Making sphinx-apidoc run as part of the Read the Docs build process**

```
if os.environ.get("READTHEDOCS") == "True":          ◁──  Only run this in the Read
    from pathlib import Path                                the Docs environment.

    PROJECT_ROOT = Path(__file__).parent.parent       ◁──  Calculates the
    PACKAGE_ROOT = PROJECT_ROOT / "src" / "imppkg"          needed project
                                                            paths
    def run_apidoc(_):                                ◁──  A function to run
        from sphinx.ext import apidoc                      sphinx-apidoc
        apidoc.main([                                 ◁──
            "--force",
            "--implicit-namespaces",                  Calls sphinx-apidoc with
            "--module-first",                         the same arguments as
            "--separate",                             elsewhere
            "-o",
            str(PROJECT_ROOT / "docs" / "reference"), ◁──  Paths must be
            str(PACKAGE_ROOT),                              properly relative
            str(PACKAGE_ROOT / "*.c"),                      and must be strings.
            str(PACKAGE_ROOT / "*.so"),
        ])
                                                      Calls run_apidoc
    def setup(app):                                   just before the
        app.connect('builder-inited', run_apidoc)     main build  ◁──
```

Imports sphinx-apidoc → *(points to `from sphinx.ext import apidoc`)*

Called by Sphinx during the build → *(points to `def setup(app):`)*

When you finish adding the changes to the docs/conf.py module, you're ready to commit your changes and push them to GitHub. When those changes arrive on the branch you specified on Read the Docs, it triggers a new build. When this build completes, you should see your documentation in full fidelity.

NOTE   Read the Docs has an effective caching policy in place for documentation sites. You typically need to perform a hard refresh in your browser to see fresh content after a build.

Before moving on, Read the Docs offers one other convenience you should take advantage of.

AUTOMATING READ THE DOCS BUILDS FOR GITHUB PULL REQUESTS

Read the Docs can build your documentation for every pull request you open, much like the GitHub Actions workflow you already have in place. To add this, take the following steps:

1   Visit your project's page in Read the Docs.
2   Click Admin.
3   Click Advanced Settings.
4   Select the Build Pull Requests for This Project option at the bottom of the Global Settings section.
5   Click Save at the bottom of the page.

The next time you push a change, Read the Docs will add a status to your pull request indicating whether the documentation built successfully (see figure 8.10).

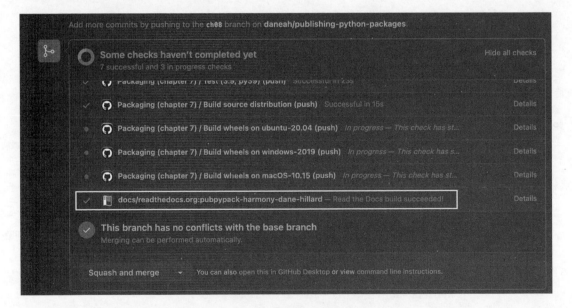

Figure 8.10   Read the Docs build status on a GitHub pull request

You can click the Details link on the Read the Docs pull request status to see an ephemeral version of the documentation. Read the Docs adds a warning to the HTML to indicate the documentation is not the live version (as shown in figure 8.11).

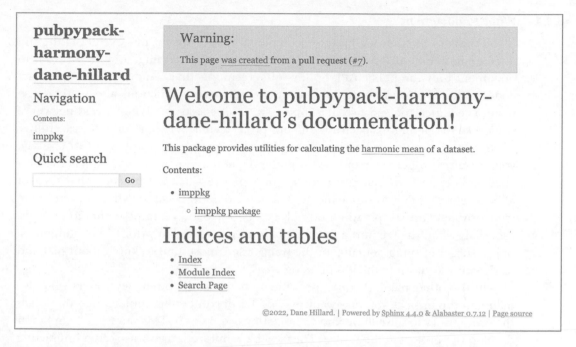

Figure 8.11   Read the Docs builds an ephemeral version of the documentation for pull requests.

You now have a documentation system that covers the following:

- Prose documentation with rich interlinking and stylization powered by reStructuredText and Sphinx
- Code documentation complete with type hints, which also supports reStructuredText syntax
- Automated builds and publishing via Read the Docs

This is valuable for you and your users at CarCorp and beyond, but the value moving forward will be in your commitment to keeping the documentation thorough and updated. Any time you make changes to your code—in particular, to the public API—consider what impact the change has on the documentation and act accordingly. The last sections of this chapter cover best practices and a few additional tips. If you're feeling energized about documentation, have a look now; otherwise, you can move to the next chapter and revisit them when you're ready for more.

8.4   Documentation best practices

At the beginning of this chapter, you learned about the Diátaxis framework, which aims to stratify documentation into distinct goals for the user. Some practices transcend this model and are applicable in almost any situation to ensure stellar documentation.

8.4.1   *What to document*

If you think of the thoroughness of documentation as a spectrum—excluding the "no documentation at all" case—one end is to document everything, and the other is to document only the public API. Sphinx offers features that can automatically extract code documentation even for undocumented or private functions and methods, so from a technical perspective, it supports the full spectrum. When deciding where you'd like to fall on this spectrum for your project, consider your audience carefully.

If you expect the audience to be *end users*, or people who only want to leverage your features to get their own work done, documenting the public API is the best choice. This has two benefits: people won't be overwhelmed by code that doesn't affect them, and they won't be inclined to depend on it. Because Python doesn't have truly private code, people will inevitably come to depend on implementation details, especially when they're in the documentation. If you need to prioritize documenting only a subset of things, document the things users most want to know about first and work your way down to the less pressing areas.

On the other hand, if you expect the audience to be other developers who also maintain the project, you may want to consider documenting implementation details that were tricky to solve, have known limitations, and so on. This can help them better develop the project in the future. They will have different priorities, often interacting with the code from an architectural perspective to determine good paths forward for the project. Because good documentation helps people understand beyond the "what" into the "why" of the code, you have an emphasized duty to ensure project maintainers understand the design and history of the project.

8.4.2   *Prefer linking over repetition*

Aside from choosing which areas of your own project code to avoid documenting, it's important to avoid documenting other projects' code in too much depth as well. Keeping code up to date in your own project is already fairly challenging, but documenting other projects adds a new layer of complexity on top. Projects outside your control may change at any time, so behavior you document on Monday might change on Thursday, and you might not realize it for days or weeks or months. Instead, consider alluding to a major feature of a project and link to that project's page for the feature. This has the additional benefit that people can understand the high-level flow in your documentation, and then they can jump over to the detailed documentation to learn more if and when needed.

By default, Sphinx enables you to link to specific classes, functions, and so on using roles like `:class:` and `:ref:` (http://mng.bz/199Q), but these references will only work within your own project. Fortunately, Sphinx provides an extension called inter-sphinx (http://mng.bz/Poo8) that enables references to work across other Sphinx-powered documentation sites. The only requirement for intersphinx is for any documentation sites you connect to be accessible over the network when building your project documentation.

You can see intersphinx at work in a number of different Python projects. As an example, pytest-django (https://pytest-django.readthedocs.io) cross-references both the pytest documentation (https://docs.pytest.org) and the Django documentation (https://docs.djangoproject.com). Those projects in turn link to Python's documentation (https://docs.python.org). The interlinked sets of documentation ensure that users can always get the latest information available, directly from the official source. With well-structured documentation, this can create an almost Wikipedia-like experience where users can browse in and out of different topics.

8.4.3   Use consistent, empathetic language

Documentation benefits from many of the same practices as writing an essay, book, or other work. Tenses should be consistent. Grammar should be correct. References to things should be spelled and capitalized correctly. Any typos or confusing passages put cognitive load on a user who is already potentially facing a challenge by learning the material.

Further, certain language can create frustration for users. Imagine someone is having a tough time understanding a concept and can't get their code to work. When they visit the project's documentation, it mentions that it should work in "just a few easy steps" or that it "obviously doesn't work for this use case." Things aren't easy or obvious for this user, and seeing that phrasing might cause them to flip their desk over. Always make an effort to stick to the facts and remove weasel words, ambiguous phrasing, gendered language, and so on.

Check your documentation for some of the following words and see whether they're adding value:

- Basic
- Easy/easily
- Simple/simply
- Obvious
- Just
- Automatic/automated
- Magic
- Fast/slow

The following example shows how a passage might look before and after applying this practice:

```
We created this easy API as a way to make international taxes simple.
We created an international taxes API that solves some problems other APIs
weren't handling.

The developer can use his code to calculate how much manpower is needed.
The developer can use the code to calculate how large a workforce is needed.

This package magically tells you which stock to buy.
This package uses the Bloomberg API and machine learning to recommend a stock
with strong odds of increasing in value.
```

8.4.4   *Avoid assumptions and create context*

Users often land on documentation after performing a search on Google or another search engine. They may crash-land on any page of your documentation without context, and they may not even know what they're looking for. When you can, avoid relying on context from other sections or pages. If you do need to assume prior knowledge from another location, mention it explicitly, and link to it if possible. This will help users more quickly locate the information they need and do further reading if necessary to gain a solid understanding of the material.

The following example shows how a passage might look before and after applying this practice:

```
Make sure to use BCNF when modeling your database.
```

```
Using `BCNF <https://en.wikipedia.org/wiki/Boyce%E2%80%93Codd_normal_form>`_
will help ensure that your data model addresses some specific concerns,
listed below.
```

8.4.5   *Create visual interest and coherent structure*

Massive walls of text are hard to absorb. If you get lost or need to pause in the middle of a 20-line paragraph, you will also have difficulty finding your place when you pick back up. Breaking up the information with new paragraphs, figures, and so on helps people find and maintain their bearings, reducing cognitive load so they can stay engaged.

Some passages are difficult to break up—I apologize for any in this book—but as a general rule, try to limit passages to one focused topic per paragraph, and use lists for things that are naturally amenable to listing. Use parallel structure (http://mng.bz/wyyB) so people can logically group phrases and concepts.

8.4.6   *Powering up your documentation*

Because authoring documentation can be a high-friction activity, some of the best tools for creating great documentation improve the authoring process specifically. They may make the syntax for writing stylized text less tedious, help check whether your documentation is outdated, or help you cross-reference things more effectively. The following quick tips are some avenues to explore further:

- If you see some Sphinx-powered documentation you like because of its stylization or features, you can almost always take a look at the source code that produced it. Many Sphinx-powered sites link directly to the relevant file in GitHub. You can also look at that project's Sphinx configuration to see if it uses any interesting extensions or techniques that you can adopt in your own project. Django's configuration (http://mng.bz/qooN) is a lot to take in, but it has a lot of valuable things you can explore.
- If you prefer Markdown over reStructuredText, or your project just needs both, check out the MyST project (http://mng.bz/N59n).

- Python's `doctest` module (https://docs.python.org/3/library/doctest.html) can test code examples in your code's docstrings to ensure they still function. This can be a nice way to ensure your documentation stays up to date.
- Read and observe the structure of documentation for big projects, even if they aren't a Python project. The documentation for the Vue JavaScript framework (https://v3.vuejs.org/guide/introduction.html) is a good one to check out.
- The napoleon extension (http://mng.bz/m22y) enables you to use some alternate formats for docstrings that will still be parsed correctly into structured documentation.
- If you don't like the default Alabaster theme, Sphinx has other available built-in themes (http://mng.bz/5mmZ), and there's an entire community of Sphinx documentation themers out there (https://sphinx-themes.org/). You can also customize Sphinx from the ground up or alter an existing theme to fit your project's needs.

Summary

- Documentation is necessary for the successful adoption of a project.
- Different users may have different goals, and documentation should be focused on catering to one goal at a time.
- Use a technology that supports linking and cross-references to support readers browsing the documentation.
- Keeping documentation updated is challenging, so find ways to automate what you can. Keep code reference documentation close to the code, and extract it automatically for higher-level use.
- Sphinx is an extensible framework for building documentation out of prose and code documentation.
- Read the Docs is a popular public documentation platform that supports Sphinx.
- Keep the reader in mind as you write; what's the clearest, most honest way to say what needs to be said?

Making
a package evergreen

In previous chapters, you successfully built a package locally and then published it so developers at all your client companies could benefit from all your hard work. You might imagine at this point that you've done most of the work, but releasing a project is often just the beginning for many developers. After people start using your package, new and broken use cases start to surface. A popular open source project might turn into a years-long endeavor.

Even when the dust settles and a project reaches a stable level of maturity, the occasional update or bug fix comes along. If none of the maintainers have cracked the project open in a while, these moments can prove costly. If the ecosystem of dependencies and tools around the project has evolved significantly since the last update, what might have been a simple one-line change can balloon into a days-long excursion to update dependencies to compatible versions and get the project sputtering along again. In the worst cases, this happens in the face of a security vulnerability; the high stress and high stakes won't do you any favors in making careful updates.

This picture I'm painting is not meant to scare you; rather, I hope it will imprint upon you the continued importance of upkeep and automation. If you want to remain productive, stave off software rot, and sustain your projects a long time into the future, you need to keep a well-stocked toolbox of practices. This chapter covers a selection of tools and philosophy but should not be taken as comprehensive; the point is to practice continuous learning as your project evolves, so it will stay *evergreen*—the way conifers stay evergreen throughout the winter.

> **IMPORTANT**   You can use the code companion (http://mng.bz/69A5) to check your work for the exercises in this chapter.

9.1 Choosing a package-versioning strategy

You first created your package and its distribution metadata, including the *version*, in chapter 3. The version of a distribution package release helps distinguish it from other releases. You started by giving your package a version of `0.0.1`, and in chapter 7, you published a release to the Python Package Index with this version. In the first stages of a project, versions are often a detail of logistics, acting simply as a unique identifier so each release is distinguishable. But over time, people who use your project expect it to convey information about what's contained in the release. You need to define a strategy for versioning your releases. Before diving directly into those details, you first need to understand the interplay between dependencies and release versions in the Python ecosystem.

9.1.1 Direct and indirect dependencies

Not all dependencies are equal. When you think about your package and its dependencies, you likely think about those you specified in the `install_requires` metadata list or those you specified in the `deps` list for your tox environments. These are dependencies you import directly in your code, or that you use directly during the development of your project. As an example, your package depends on the `termcolor` package to provide stylized output, and you depend on packages like `mypy` and `black` when you develop your package. These are *direct dependencies*, because you reference them explicitly by name.

Your project's direct dependencies may themselves depend directly on yet other packages, which may depend on yet other packages, and so on. Those dependencies a layer or more down from your project's direct dependencies are *indirect dependencies*.

> **NOTE**   You may encounter sources that use different terminology around dependencies. Some sources may use "concrete/abstract" or "dependency/subdependency" to refer to direct and indirect dependencies, respectively.

Because Python only allows one version of a package to be installed in a particular environment, these words are mostly interchangeable.

A dependency can be both direct and indirect at the same time; your project may depend directly on package A and package B, and package B may depend directly on package A. In this way, a project's dependencies produce a graph (as shown in figure 9.1).

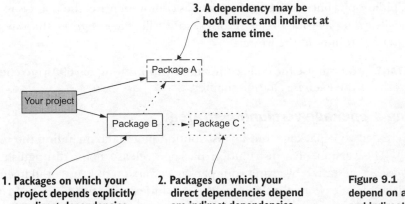

3. A dependency may be both direct and indirect at the same time.

1. Packages on which your project depends explicitly are direct dependencies.

2. Packages on which your direct dependencies depend are indirect dependencies.

Figure 9.1   Python projects depend on a graph of direct and indirect dependencies.

Keep this graph model in the back of your mind whenever you start using new dependencies in your projects. It isn't a concept most tools will point out to you directly, so you need to commit it to your own understanding. The graph model comes in handy when resolving certain dependency issues, as discussed in the following section.

DIRECT AND INDIRECT DEPENDENCIES IN PRACTICE

The asymmetry of direct and indirect dependencies shows up occasionally in Python tooling. When you use the `python -m pip install` command to install a package, you specify the direct dependency only. When you use the `python -m pip list` command to list packages, it lists all installed packages, whether direct or indirect. This can lead to mistakes. Imagine you added `package-a` as a direct dependency some time ago. You haven't worked on your project in a while, and when you come back to it later, you want to see what's installed. When you list the installed packages, you see that `package-a` and `package-b` are installed. `package-b` is installed only because `package-a` depends on it; unless you double-check your direct dependencies, you might mistakenly believe you can use `package-b` safely in your project. This mistake could break your project later on if a new version of `package-a` stops depending on `package-b`, causing Python to produce an `ImportError` when the application runs.

Differentiating direct and indirect dependencies

Although direct and indirect dependencies get flattened into one list by pip at the time of this writing, other tools do track the distinction between the two types of dependencies. As an example, poetry (https://python-poetry.org) provides a `poetry show --tree` command that lists the installed dependencies; it uses a tree instead of a graph for the sake of listing the packages linearly.

There are also other approaches to dependency installation, such as the pip-tools flow (http://mng.bz/xMdX). This can be valuable because you still have to manage your direct dependencies explicitly, but you also get a more repeatable build because pip-tools generates a static list of direct and indirect dependencies instead of resolving them again each time you install your dependencies. Though powerful, I recommend getting used to the core behavior of dependency management before adding this complexity to a project.

Think of dependencies as an API for a moment. The direct dependencies are part of the public API, and the indirect dependencies are part of the private API. You should depend only on the public API, because the private API is subject to change without notice (see figure 9.2).

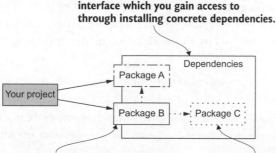

1. Think of package dependencies as an interface which you gain access to through installing concrete dependencies.

2. Concrete dependencies are exposed as a public part of the interface, and you can access them directly in your application and development tooling.

3. Abstract dependencies should be treated as a private part of the interface. They are inaccessible to your application and development tooling.

Figure 9.2   Thinking about dependencies as an interface between public and private behavior

Always ensure that any package you import into your runtime application is specified in the `install_requires` metadata, and ensure that any package you use to develop your project is specified in the `deps` list for the appropriate tox environment. This practice will ensure your project never breaks because of a shift in indirect dependencies. If you do run into such an issue down the road, your understanding of the graph model of dependencies will lead you to check that all imported packages are direct dependencies.

Distribution package release versions come into play with the dependency graph when tools like pip need to determine which set of dependency versions to install.

> **Dependency resolution is nontrivial**
>
> It can be difficult to satisfy all the constraints in a project's dependencies. There's more to consider than you might think. Although dependency resolution algorithms are outside the scope of this book, the story of pip's dependency resolution algorithm update is an interesting one (check out Podcast.__init__, episode 264, http://mng .bz/woKQ).

9.1.2 *Python dependency specifiers and dependency hell*

In chapter 4, you added the `termcolor` package as a dependency. Recall that you specified allowing any version greater than 1.1.0 and less than 2.0.0, as shown in the following snippet:

```
install_requires =
    termcolor>=1.1.0,<2
```

PEP 440 (https://www.python.org/dev/peps/pep-0440/) covers the variety of ways you can version a package and, in turn, how you can specify dependency versions. In the most common cases, projects specify dependencies in the following ways, from most restrictive to least restrictive:

1 An exact match version, often called *pinning*. `termcolor==1.1.3` is an example of an exact match for version 1.1.3.
2 A lower and upper bound, which may be exact matches or prefix matches. `termcolor>=1.1.0,<2` or `termcolor~=1.1` allows for any version greater than or equal to 1.1.0 but less than 2.
3 A lower bound only. `termcolor>=1.1.0` allows for any version greater than or equal to 1.1.0.
4 No version. `termcolor` without any additional specification allows for any version of `termcolor` to be installed.

Think about the set of all available release versions of the `termcolor` package. They may range from version 0.0.1, like your own package, all the way to version 5.6.2, or 10.8.19, or 1000.5.2. By specifying the range of versions you allow to be installed, you restrict the installer to a smaller set of versions to resolve. In addition to the constraints you place on your project's direct dependencies, the packages your project depends on may also constrain the set of allowed versions further. As shown in figure 9.3, these constraints may not always play well together.

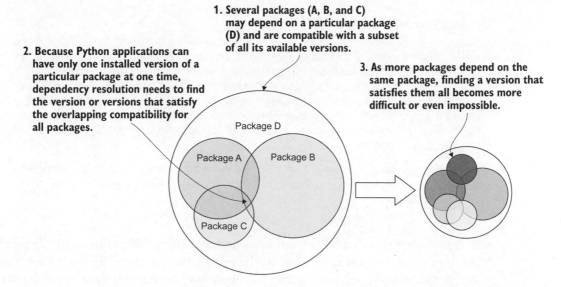

1. Several packages (A, B, and C) may depend on a particular package (D) and are compatible with a subset of all its available versions.

2. Because Python applications can have only one installed version of a particular package at one time, dependency resolution needs to find the version or versions that satisfy the overlapping compatibility for all packages.

3. As more packages depend on the same package, finding a version that satisfies them all becomes more difficult or even impossible.

Figure 9.3   Dependency version specifiers act as constraints on the set of all available release versions for a given package.

When resolution becomes impossible because of dependency version constraints, the course of action is often to investigate a potentially cascading set of tests to check if upgrading one of your direct dependencies fixes the issue. Because the graph of this situation sometimes looks like a diamond, this situation is sometimes referred to as a *diamond dependency conflict* (figure 9.4).

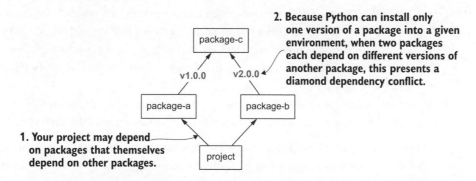

2. Because Python can install only one version of a package into a given environment, when two packages each depend on different versions of another package, this presents a diamond dependency conflict.

1. Your project may depend on packages that themselves depend on other packages.

Figure 9.4   Dependency resolution is sometimes impossible due to conflicts, and a diamond dependency conflict is one of the most common types.

Because this is rarely fun to fix and almost always frustrating, it's also sometimes referred to as *dependency hell*.

> **Managing dependency hell**
>
> Dependency hell is, frankly, part of the reality of software development. But it's often exacerbated by packages that unnecessarily constrain their dependencies to a narrow range. If you use features introduced in a specific version of a dependency, it makes sense to specify that version as the lower bound of allowable versions. Upper bounds make less sense; they should generally be used only when your library has a known incompatibility with a newer version (see Henry Schreiner, *Should You Use Upper Bound Version Constraints?*, http://mng.bz/099v for a profound exploration of the danger of upper bounds).
>
> By leaving the range of allowed versions as wide as possible in your direct dependencies, you maximize the options for those using your package alongside other dependencies.

Now that you've got a solid foundation of understanding about direct and indirect dependencies, the dependency graph, version specifiers, and the tensions these can produce, you're equipped to start thinking about the strategy you want to use for versioning your own package.

9.1.3   *Semantic versioning and calendar versioning*

By far the two most prominent approaches to package versioning in the Python ecosystem are *semantic versioning* (https://semver.org/) and *calendar versioning* (https://calver.org/). Both of these approaches are compatible with the PEP 440 specification, but they each emphasize different information about a distribution package release.

Semantic versioning aims to communicate the degree to which the API of the behavior changed in the release. It focuses on the following:

- If installed, will this release version break any existing behavior? If so, it's a *major* change. The most significant version identifier number should increase by 1.
- If existing behavior is maintained, does this release version add new behavior? If so, it's a *minor* change. The next most significant version identifier number should increase by 1.
- If no new behavior is added, the change must fix broken behavior, so it's a *patch* change. The least significant version identifier number should increase by 1.

This scheme helps you discern that version 2.0.1 fixes something that was broken in version 2.0.0, or that you might need to update your usage when upgrading from version 2.7.3 to version 3.0.0. This can be a very helpful scheme when navigating a wide variety of packages.

> **Exercise 9.1**
> Write down the resulting semantic version for a major, minor, and patch release that comes after each of the following:
>
> - 17.8.3
> - 0.4.6
> - 1.0.19

An issue with semantic versioning is that a particular version may overpromise what users can expect, whether due to human error from the maintainers or too much user confidence in the versioning scheme. If you fix a bug, but fixing the bug also breaks existing behavior, should it be a patch or a major version release? Strictly speaking, you should issue a major version release. But even the semver specification says to "use your best judgment." If you choose to issue a patch release and users believe that you would never break functionality without a major release, there is a communication breakdown and, therefore, the potential for frustration.

Another less impactful issue with semantic versioning is that it doesn't give you a sense of when a particular version was released. You can typically look this up in the package repository where it's published, but that may be tedious when you're interested in looking at multiple packages or versions. Semantic versioning might even cause users to believe a particular version was released before another because of the version numbers, which isn't guaranteed; you could release version 4.0.0 one day and release a fix for version 2.1.0 as version 2.1.1 the next day. The fact that the timeline isn't guaranteed and that even the semantics of semantic versioning aren't guaranteed is partly what gave rise to calendar versioning.

Calendar versioning is a less precise specification, but in general, projects using calendar versioning schemes start each version with the current year or month, followed by a more specific version number. Often, projects that use calendar versioning also release new versions on a set schedule, fitting in as many updates and fixes as they can until the next release. This gives predictability to the timeline but doesn't necessarily promise anything about changes to the API.

> **Single-sourcing the package version**
> You might discover some articles online discussing the value of single-sourcing the package version. This is a valuable thing to do, because if you keep the version stored in multiple places, you'll inevitably update one and forget the other at some point. Historically, this discussion arose because project authors had a practice of providing the version of the package as a `__version__` attribute in the package's root `__init__.py` module. Because the version also needs to be specified in a file such as setup.cfg or setup.py in order for the package build tooling to recognize it, approaches for specifying the version once and using it in both places were necessary (see the *Python Packaging User Guide*, "Single-sourcing the package version," http://mng.bz/qYp2).

(continued)

The `__version__` attribute is only a common practice and is not standardized—its only mention is in the rejected PEP 396 (https://www.python.org/dev/peps/pep -0396/). A best practice going forward is to use the `importlib.metadata.version` function, as you did in your Sphinx documentation configuration in chapter 8. Using this approach, you need only specify the version in your package's static metadata for it to be readable elsewhere in your code or your users' code.

Of the two approaches, semantic versioning is still overwhelmingly the most common. It does make sense to use a sequential version scheme, so you need to decide which is intuitive to you and your users. The most important thing in the end is communication, and communication often requires a little bit more elbow grease. One of the best ways to communicate about releases is through a consistent and thorough change log, which you'll read more about in chapter 11.

The next section covers some of the features GitHub provides for managing dependency versions.

9.2 *Getting the most out of GitHub*

As a popular collaboration platform for software project changes, GitHub is positioned as a useful place to do software project maintenance as well. Over the last few years, they've developed or acquired several useful tools for managing software dependencies: security scans, automated vulnerability fixes and dependency updates, and a dependency graph. Learn more about each of these features in the following sections.

> **NOTE** The availability of features similar to those covered in the following sections differs from platform to platform. If you want to use another platform for your software collaboration, you'll need to read their documentation to see what they offer.

9.2.1 *The GitHub dependency graph*

GitHub inspects the files in your repository and extracts structured knowledge about dependencies from it. This works across several languages, and even works for some workflow- and framework-level things like GitHub Actions. Across all repositories, GitHub then uses this structured data to produce a graph of dependencies and dependents. The dependency graph is enabled for all public repositories, and you can enable it for private repositories as well in the repository settings. Because your repository is public, the dependency graph is already enabled.

Visit the GitHub page for your repository now. Click the Insights tab; then, in the left-hand navigation, click Dependency Graph. GitHub shows you, on a per-file basis, the dependencies it was able to identify. For each dependency, it links to that project's repository and shows the version your project depends on. Figure 9.5 shows that GitHub found a dependency on version 2 of the `setup-python` action in the GitHub Actions YAML file in a project and provides a link to the repository for that action.

Figure 9.5   The dependencies in GitHub's dependency graph from a project using GitHub Actions

NOTE   GitHub doesn't support dependencies defined in `install_requires` in the setup.cfg file at the time of this writing (http://mng.bz/7yAy). Please help projects get better support in the GitHub dependency graph by upvoting and joining my feature request discussion on the topic (http://mng.bz/K00O).

You can also click the Dependents tab to see any projects that depend on yours. You likely don't have any users of the package you've created for this book, but you can see examples of this in action on other popular projects like the requests package (http://mng.bz/9VVr). As of this writing in March 2022, over one million projects depend on requests (figure 9.6)!

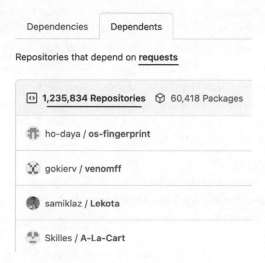

Figure 9.6   The dependents in GitHub's dependency graph from a popular project

In addition to displaying the dependencies of your project, GitHub can check them for security vulnerabilities.

9.2.2   *Mitigating security vulnerabilities with Dependabot*

Navigate to the settings page of your project's GitHub repository. In the left-hand navigation, click Code Security and Analysis. On this page you can find the variety of features GitHub offers for dependency security in addition to the dependency graph, as described here:

- *Dependabot alerts*—GitHub can create automated notifications of vulnerable packages you depend on, with suggestions for mitigation. This is on by default.
- *Dependabot security updates*—When Dependabot finds a vulnerable dependency, enabling this option will open a pull request automatically to update to a non-vulnerable version, if available. This is off by default.
- *Code scanning*—GitHub can scan your project code for vulnerabilities as well. This is off by default.
- *Secret scanning*—GitHub scans your code for potentially leaked passwords, API keys, and so on to protect you from attackers who scrape and use the information. This is always on.

> **NOTE**   Dependabot security alerts aren't easy to generate for the sake of example, and any existing vulnerabilities are sensitive private information to project maintainers. Refer to GitHub's own documentation to see examples and read about interacting with the alerts themselves (http://mng.bz/mOM2).

This may seem like a lot to take in, but these features are all automated and provide actionable alerts or pull requests that you can respond to as necessary. Security is best performed as a many-layered process, because each layer has its own focus and shortcomings (James T. Reason, "The Contribution of Latent Human Failures to the Breakdown of Complex Systems," *Philosophical Transactions of the Royal Society*, http://mng.bz/jAAe). The more variety you can introduce to your security strategy, the better.

ENABLING DEPENDABOT SECURITY UPDATES

Click Enable next to Dependabot Security Updates. Dependabot will open a pull request to update vulnerable dependencies when it can. Dependabot opens pull requests from the @dependabot user, and the pull request includes the following useful pieces of information in addition to the code change:

- Which dependency is being updated
- Where the dependency was found in the project
- The version of the dependency before and after the change
- Release notes, change log, and commits that happened between the old and new version
- How likely it is that the new version introduces breaking changes, if known

You can also interact with the pull request through comments to have Dependabot take additional actions. Importantly, Dependabot does not indicate in the pull request that the change addresses a vulnerability, because this would alert malicious actors to try exploiting the vulnerability. An example pull request description from the `black` package's repository is shown in figure 9.7.

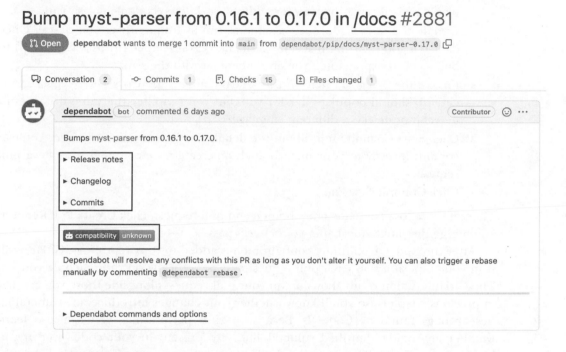

Figure 9.7   Dependabot opens pull requests to update vulnerable dependencies and provides information to assess the compatibility of the new version.

After Dependabot opens a pull request, you can assess the compatibility of the change by observing the status of your tests and code quality checks. You can also check out the code locally to do any manual verification. If the change appears to be compatible, you can merge the pull request. Dependabot detects the updated dependency and removes any associated vulnerability alerts. Next, you'll configure GitHub's code scanning to scan your own code for security issues and bugs.

ENABLING GITHUB CODE SCANNING

GitHub uses a system called CodeQL, short for "code query language," that enables developers to query their code base for particular code constructs (https://codeql .github.com/). CodeQL works similarly to tools like mypy, black, and flake8 that use Python's abstract syntax tree to find issues. As an example, you could use CodeQL to find areas in a Django project that are vulnerable to SQL injection because the code passes unvalidated user input directly into a database query. People can submit CodeQL queries to the community identifying common security issues and bugs. You can enable CodeQL scanning in your repository in a few steps, as shown here:

1 Navigate to the Code Security and Analysis settings for your repository.
2 Click Set Up next to Code Scanning.
3 Click Set Up This Workflow in CodeQL Analysis. GitHub takes you to a prepopulated new file creation view for .github/workflows/codeql-analysis.yml.
4 Update the `on.schedule.cron` value to run as frequently as you desire. Once daily is a good starting place; use a site like Cron Helper (https://cron.help) to build a cron expression if you aren't familiar with the syntax.
5 Ensure the `language` field in the YAML configuration is set to [`'python'`]. GitHub should populate this for you, but you can alter the value if it doesn't detect it or detects a different language.
6 Click Start Commit, and fill out the details for the commit as desired. You can commit directly to your main branch or create a new branch to open a pull request.
7 Click Commit New File.

Then, if you chose to create a new branch and pull request, click Create Pull Request, and merge the pull request after your checks pass.

After the CodeQL scanning configuration is added to your repository, GitHub will scan your repository on each pull request and periodically on the schedule you set. The GitHub Action result shows up on your pull request alongside those you created in previous chapters, so you'll know whether your changes introduce any vulnerabilities or bugs found by CodeQL. Because it runs periodically, you can also learn whether any newly identified vulnerabilities are present in your code, even if you haven't opened a pull request recently. This proactive scanning is particularly helpful for mature projects that aren't being updated every day.

With Dependabot alerts, automated updates, and code scanning in place, you can feel confident that your dependencies and your code changes won't impact your project with security vulnerabilities in the future. There's still one threat model to your project, though: *the threat model of decay.*

UPDATING DEPENDENCIES AUTOMATICALLY WITH DEPENDABOT

The threat model of decay (the first known usage of this phrase was by YCombinator user javajosh, https://news.ycombinator.com/item?id=29474932) states that one of your biggest threats will be not from an outside malicious actor but from your own software and ecosystem crumbling around you due to lack of maintenance. In addition to your project's dependencies having vulnerabilities, you should keep them updated so you don't run into dependency hell or "big bang" updates that leave you pulling your hair out. Dependabot was originally created for precisely this use case.

You can configure Dependabot to automatically bump dependency versions for you, even when the existing versions aren't vulnerable (http://mng.bz/WMMW). To do so, you can configure aspects such as the software ecosystem, project location, strategy, and frequency of the updates in a .github/dependabot.yml file. Note that many of these settings are rather subjective; you will need to adjust them for the pacing that works for you and your team to avoid frustration.

A good minimum viable place to start with Dependabot updates for your package is to check for updates for your GitHub Actions and your Python dependencies once per day. You will need to use the following fields:

- *version*—The current Dependabot configuration version. At the time of this writing, the version is 2.
- *updates*—The list of configurations to check for available updates.
- *package-ecosystem*—The ecosystem for a given configuration. You will have one for github-actions and one for pip.
- *directory*—The directory in which to check for the current dependency versions. You can use "/" for both your configurations.
- *schedule.interval*, *schedule.day*, *schedule.time*, *schedule.timezone*—The frequency at which to check for updates. A check every Monday morning may be a good starting place.

TIP For a comprehensive list of all available configurations, refer to the GitHub documentation (http://mng.bz/5QV1).

Create the dependabot.yml file in the .github/ directory of your project now. Note that it should not live in the .github/workflows/ directory next to your GitHub Actions, because it isn't a GitHub Action. When you're done, your configuration should look something like the following listing.

Listing 9.1 An example configuration that updates on a weekly basis

```
version: 2

updates:
  - package-ecosystem: "github-actions"
    directory: "/"
    schedule:
      interval: "weekly"
      day: "monday"
      time: "09:00"
  - package-ecosystem: "pip"
    directory: "/"
    schedule:
      interval: "weekly"
      day: "monday"
      time: "09:00"
```

The Dependabot configuration version

The list of configurations for update checks

An update configuration for GitHub Actions dependencies

Checks for dependencies starting at the root of the project

Checks dependencies on Mondays

Checks dependencies at 09:00

Checks for dependency updates weekly

An update configuration for Python dependencies

Commit and push this new file to your repository. After the file is added, Dependabot will check for opportunities to update your dependencies on the schedule you specified. If Dependabot finds any updates that meet your parameters, it opens a pull request that looks exactly like those it opens for security vulnerability updates.

Now that you've covered a variety of practices around your dependencies, read on to take a look at other aspects that affect your project's evergreen status.

9.3   *Thresholding test coverage*

In chapter 5, you added unit testing and test coverage measurement to your package using pytest and pytest-cov. This configuration helps you understand how much of your code is untested and which files have the least coverage. Although this is useful information, it lacks any enforcement.

It's natural for many projects to outpace their test coverage. Not all contributors will include tests, and repeatedly telling people to write tests can cast you in a bad light, even though you're just trying to protect the project. As you can probably guess, having an automated process tell people this instead helps a lot. They'll be informed, and you won't need to intervene in the majority of cases. If your project has already fallen way behind on coverage, it may seem insurmountable to start enforcing test coverage, but it turns out the opposite is true. Your goal should be to first stop the bleeding, so the coverage can't get any worse, and then add enforcement that ensures the coverage only gets better.

Recall that 100% coverage is not necessarily the end goal; it can be difficult to achieve and has diminishing returns. By instead focusing on *monotonically increasing* coverage, you don't need to think so anxiously about the gap between where you are now and the end state you want. Instead, you can ensure the coverage is, at worst, staying the same, and incrementally improve it over time. This system is like a ratchet that tightens in only one direction. Any time new tests are added that increase the coverage, you need a way to say that the coverage will never drop back below that new value again (see figure 9.8).

You can build in a test coverage thresholding mechanism for your project with a single line of code. Open your setup.cfg file and locate the `[coverage:report]` section. Recall that you used this section in chapter 5 to control how the coverage is reported when you run the tox environment for tests. You can add a `fail_under` key to this section with a float value between 0.0 and 100.0. If the test coverage percentage is below the value you specify, the step that reports coverage after your tests run will fail with a message similar to the following snippet:

```
FAIL Required test coverage of 78.9% not reached. Total coverage: 33.33%
```

Exercise 9.2
Run your tests now. They should still be at 100% coverage from your work in earlier chapters. Set the `fail_under` value to 100.0, and run the tests again. Do they pass? Try deleting a test or two temporarily. Do they pass now?

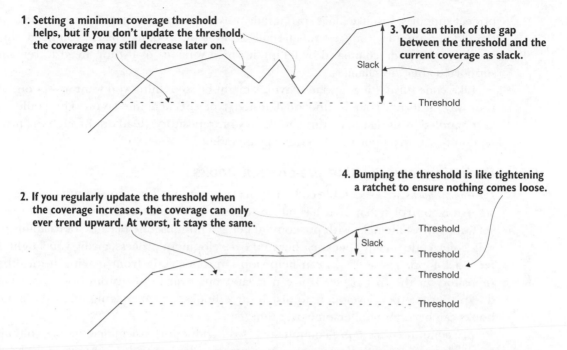

1. Setting a minimum coverage threshold helps, but if you don't update the threshold, the coverage may still decrease later on.

3. You can think of the gap between the threshold and the current coverage as slack.

Slack

Threshold

2. If you regularly update the threshold when the coverage increases, the coverage can only ever trend upward. At worst, it stays the same.

4. Bumping the threshold is like tightening a ratchet to ensure nothing comes loose.

Threshold

Slack

Threshold

Threshold

Threshold

Figure 9.8   Prioritize monotonically increasing coverage for sustained, incremental improvement over time.

Any time your coverage improves, you should update your `fail_under` value to the new threshold. When others contribute new code without new tests, the GitHub Action for tests will fail due to decreased coverage, letting them know they need to test their work.

> **TIP**   Make sure to observe the coverage percentage for all combinations of the testing matrix. Different dependencies may cause the coverage percentage to be slightly different, and you'll need to set `fail_under` to the lowest value among them so they don't fail to meet the threshold.

With security and test coverage under your belt, turn next to an aspect less often thought about: the Python syntax you use.

9.4   *Updating Python syntax using pyupgrade*

Part of what makes a language evolve is not only the features it provides but the syntax you use to write programs. Syntax sugar is added over time to make certain constructs easier, and sometimes using the built-in syntax of a new language version is faster or more correct than an older, manual way of doing the same thing. In some cases, new syntax even makes things possible that simply weren't before.

pyupgrade (https://github.com/asottile/pyupgrade) updates the syntax of your Python code to take advantage of newer syntax available in the Python versions your project supports. Just like black, pyupgrade uses the abstract syntax tree to ensure that the old and the new code are functionally equivalent. Also, like black, you need only run the pyupgrade command by telling it which versions of Python need to remain supported after any changes.

Like code formatting, updating syntax might be something you want to stay out of your way until your code is functional, tested, type checked, and so on. This could be best handled by using pre-commit hooks in your repository. Read on through the next section to set up a hook that leverages pyupgrade.

9.5   *Reducing rework using pre-commit hooks*

Pre-commit hooks are executable code that runs when you attempt to commit changes to a version-control system. Git has native support for hooks into various parts of the version-control lifecycle, with pre-commit being a popular one because of its ability to shift some code quality checks earlier in the development process, giving you a tighter feedback loop. These hooks can help stop improper code from making it into the repository in the first place. You can create your own fully custom hooks, but Git doesn't force other developers to install these hooks, and managing many disparate hooks can become cumbersome over time.

pre-commit (https://pre-commit.com/) is a framework for managing pre-commit hooks. It provides several nice improvements over dealing with Git hooks natively, as described here:

- Hooks can be installed from repositories on the internet, creating a plugin-based architecture.
- Most hooks run in an isolated container, decreasing the likelihood that they act on anything but the repository in which they're installed.
- Most hooks run only on changed files, which is useful for expensive checks. You can still run them across all files when desired.

IMPORTANT   Before reading on, visit appendix B to install the tools you'll need for this chapter.

To get started configuring pre-commit, create a new .pre-commit-config.yaml file. In this YAML file, you need to use the following keys:

- `repos`—The list of repositories from which to fetch pre-commit hooks.
- `repo`—The repository for a specific hook, such as a URL.
- `rev`—The revision of the hook to use. This revision is typically one of the Git tags in the specified repository.
- `hooks`—The list of hooks to use from the specified repository.
- `id`—The unique identifier of a hook supplied by the specified repository.
- `args`—Additional arguments to pass to the hook when it runs.

TIP   For a comprehensive list of all available configurations, refer to the pre-commit documentation (http://mng.bz/822D).

Create your first hook configuration for pyupgrade. Fill in the .pre-commit-config.yaml file with the following information:

- The repository for pyupgrade is https://github.com/asottile/pyupgrade.
- The latest revision available as of this writing is `v2.31.0`.
- The identifier for the hook is `pyupgrade`.
- The arguments to pyupgrade indicate the Python versions you want to support. As an example, `--py37-plus` supports Python 3.7 and up. `--py3-plus` supports all versions of Python 3. The versions you specify here should agree with the versions you specified for black in pyproject.toml as well as the versions you specified in your tox `envlist`.

After you finish your pyupgrade configuration, it should look similar to the following listing.

Listing 9.2 An example pre-commit configuration that uses pyupgrade

```
                    The list of all
                    hooks repos                                          The pyupgrade
repos:                                                                   repository
  - repo: https://github.com/asottile/pyupgrade
    rev: v2.31.0
  hooks:                          The version of the
                                  pyupgrade hooks
    - id: pyupgrade
      args: ['--py39-plus']
                                     Arguments to pass to
                                     the hook's command
```

The list of hooks to use

pyupgrade's main hook

After you create a configuration for your repository, install pre-commit into your repository so it can manage pre-commit hooks by running the `pre-commit install` command in the root directory of your project. After you install pre-commit hooks, any new commits you make will trigger the hooks to run against the changed files. To run pre-commit hooks against all files in your project, you can run the `pre-commit run --all-files` command. Run it now, and observe whether pyupgrade makes any syntax changes.

Exercise 9.3

A growing number of tools provides pre-commit hooks. flake8 (https://github.com/pycqa/flake8) and black (https://github.com/psf/black) both provide pre-commit hooks. The configuration of these hooks is nearly identical, with any specifics for `args` or other keys being tool-specific. Add a hook for flake8 and black to your pre-commit configuration now. black and flake8 configurations are included in the code companion. You should read the documentation for your favorite tools to see whether and how to use them as pre-commit hooks.

Although pre-commit hooks might feel like they're a big productivity boost, it's important to recognize that if they become too expensive and slow to run, they can have a nasty backfire effect. Even though your intent is to provide a tighter feedback loop on small, independent commits, slow commit hooks can encourage people to avoid committing until they've done all their work. Find a balance between how valuable each of the checks you install are and how long they take to execute.

You now have security scanning for your code and its dependencies, monotonically increasing test coverage, the latest and greatest Python syntax, and a way to prevent some common mistakes from even being committed to the repository in the first place. This will reduce a fair amount of noise in your project over its lifetime and help you proactively evolve over time to avoid the threat model of decay. In the next chapter, you'll revisit some of what you've learned and extract a template so you can create this same experience across any new project you create.

Answers to exercises

9.1

- 18.0.0, 17.9.0, 17.8.4
- 1.0.0, 0.5.0, 0.4.7
- 2.0.0, 1.1.0, 1.0.20

Summary

- Software dependencies form a graph, and project authors should take care to constrain their dependencies as little as possible for maximum interoperability with other packages.
- Dependencies impact your project through security vulnerabilities and staleness. Update them regularly to avoid headaches down the road.
- Don't try to achieve 100% test coverage, especially on existing projects. Instead, use coverage thresholds for incremental and monotonically increasing coverage over time.
- Pre-commit hooks help you prevent improper code from being committed in the first place, but you should use them judiciously to encourage frequent, small commits.

Part 4

The long haul

By this point in the book, you're operating at least one well-oiled Python package project. Whether you plan to apply what you've learned to another existing project or to new projects you create in the future, there's a lot of information to remember and a lot of configuration, syntax, and directory structure to get right. If you come back a few months from now, you could find yourself having to relearn the material from scratch. If you're trying to grow your group of maintainers and your user base at the same time, it can all become a bit much.

This part helps you create a repeatable process for new projects so you can get up and running quickly and focus on the software unique to each project. You'll also learn some of the aspects of a successful user community that maximize the likelihood of others contributing to and maintaining your project.

10
Scaling and solidifying your practices

This chapter covers

- Extracting a project template to create future packages using cookiecutter
- Publishing and installing packages with a private package repository server
- Using namespace packages to split large projects across several packages

You've spent the majority of this book working up to the act of publishing a package. Throughout this book, I've emphasized the value of a repeatable process and automation, but so far what you've focused on is for only a single package. Now that you have a solid process in place for your package, what about the next package you want to create? Whether you're interested in maintaining open source projects or becoming the subject matter expert on Python packaging in your organization, you'll inevitably create and publish more packages. Although you might want to reinforce some of what you've learned by building another package from scratch, the process will start to feel pretty monotonous after the fourth or fifth one.

In this chapter, you'll learn how to extract the common elements from your existing package and some techniques for working with private and large distributed package projects at scale.

IMPORTANT   Before reading on, visit appendix B to install the tools you'll need for this chapter.

You can use the code companion (http://mng.bz/69A5) to check your work for the exercises in this chapter.

10.1   *Creating a project template for future packages*

As a general rule, each project you create should have one clear responsibility. This helps you have tough conversations with people asking for new features, because you can more easily determine what does and doesn't belong in the project. It also allows your users to compose several small packages to achieve their specific goals, rather than installing a huge package and using only a small subset of its available behavior.

Although your projects may each have unique responsibilities supported by different code, many parts will look the same from package to package. These common pieces of code and configuration, called *boilerplate*, are necessary for a project to work but seldom need special attention other than to fill in some values.

Imagine you need to create five new packages for CarCorp from scratch by following the process you've learned so far in this book. Think about all the different configuration files and the directory structure that you have to create. Where would you slip up? How would you verify that you did everything correctly? How long do you think it would take? You likely thought of a few things off the top of your head, and in practice, you often run into a few more issues that you didn't anticipate. With so much room for human error, the lack of repeatability of package creation could hinder the pace at which you develop new value.

Instead of creating packages from scratch each time, you can use a templating system that contains all the boilerplate a project needs and helps you fill in the project-specific information where needed. You can even put your project template in version control and make improvements to it over time, imparting your latest standards on each new package you create. You can make a template specific to CarCorp and each of your other clients if you notice that they differ enough to codify those differences. In the following sections, you'll use cookiecutter (https://cookiecutter.readthedocs.io), a Python-based project for creating language-agnostic project templates.

10.1.1   *Creating a cookiecutter configuration*

Like a real cookie cutter, the cookiecutter project is so named because you use it to create a template and then use that template to stamp out several similarly shaped things. Although the core shape of the projects you create will be similar, you can also signify certain parts as dynamic and fill the values in when creating new projects (see figure 10.1). This is a bit like decorating cookies with different icing and sprinkle combinations.

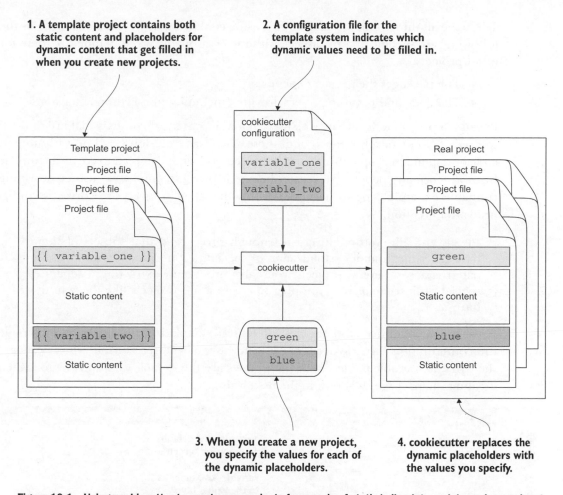

1. A template project contains both static content and placeholders for dynamic content that get filled in when you create new projects.

2. A configuration file for the template system indicates which dynamic values need to be filled in.

3. When you create a new project, you specify the values for each of the dynamic placeholders.

4. cookiecutter replaces the dynamic placeholders with the values you specify.

Figure 10.1   Using cookiecutter to create new projects from a mix of static boilerplate and dynamic user input

Throughout the following sections, you'll make changes to this new directory to turn it into a cookiecutter template project.

The first step toward making this project work with cookiecutter is configuring the dynamic values that must be filled in. To understand which values those are, think about the things that are currently specific to your project but would need to be changed to other values in any new project, such as the following:

- The project name, `first-python-package`
- The import package name, `imppkg`
- The description of the project's purpose
- The project author's name and email
- The license under which you provide the project

These are all things that you can address using cookiecutter. Other things, such as the following, are specific to your project, without a reasonable way to templatize them for other projects:

- The packages the project depends on
- The code and tests the project provides, including non-Python extensions

Because a project template may be used in a wide variety of contexts that are difficult to predict, you typically want to omit these. That way, you don't end up with unused code or dependencies polluting a newly created project. If you plan to create a template from which many people will create their own projects, you can consider providing runnable example code to help users verify that their projects are correctly configured after creation.

> **TIP** Eventually, you might create enough projects so that subsets of them have the same kind of customization or specialization. After you notice these patterns across several projects, you can think about extracting a separate, special project template if you plan to create more projects like those in the future.

Once you've identified all the values you want to templatize, the next step is to create the configuration file. cookiecutter looks for a cookiecutter.json file whose keys are the dynamic variable names and whose values are the default values presented when creating the package, as shown in the next listing.

Listing 10.1   A small cookiecutter JSON configuration with two variables

```
{
    "variable_one": "green",        ◁——  variable_one defaults
    "variable_two": "blue"          ◁——  to the value "green".
}
                                          variable_two defaults
                                          to the value "blue".
```

You can reference the `variable_one` and `variable_two` variables throughout your project template, and cookiecutter will replace them with the default or user-specified values when creating a project.

PROMPTING A USER FOR INPUT

You can create a project from a project template by running the `cookiecutter` command and passing it the path to your project template directory. When you run the command, cookiecutter will prompt you to accept the default value or enter a custom value for keys in the cookiecutter.json file, as shown in the next listing.

Listing 10.2   Example output from running cookiecutter with two variables

```
$ cookiecutter python-project-template       Variable name and default
variable_one [green]: red            ◁——    value, with alternative supplied
variable_two [blue]:
                                  ◁——  You can press Enter to
                                       accept the default value.
```

For variables with a string as the default option, you can input any arbitrary alternative input to use something other than the default value. In addition to a string, cookiecutter enables you to configure a list of values for a given variable. Unlike a string variable, a list variable will display all the available values when you run the cookiecutter command and default to the first one; you must choose one of those options and can't enter an arbitrary value. This is useful when your project template needs to restrict the possible options or you want to make it convenient to select from a few options.

Following from the earlier example, the following listing shows how to add a list of options for a variable.

> **Listing 10.3 Specifying a list of possible options for a cookiecutter variable**

```
{
    "variable_one": "green",              ⊲── Uses a string to provide
    "variable_two": "blue",                   a default value
    "variable_three": ["foo", "bar", "baz"]   ⊲── Uses a list to provide
}                                                  an enumeration of
                                                   allowed options
```

Running the `cookiecutter` command with this configuration results in the same output for the first two variables as before and additionally displays all the options for the third variable (shown in the next listing).

> **Listing 10.4 Example output from running cookiecutter with a mix of variable types**

```
$ cookiecutter python-project-template
variable_one [green]:
variable_two [blue]:
Select variable_three:       ⊲── Indicates you must
1 - foo         ⊲──              make a selection
2 - bar             Displays all
3 - baz             available options
Choose from 1, 2, 3 [1]:   ⊲── Enter the index of the option,
                               or default to the first one.
```

The string and list variable options give you enough power to make a template of the dynamic parts of your package, but there's one more convenient feature of cookiecutter you can make use of.

BUILDING ON PREVIOUS VALUES

Quite often, a value in your project configuration will be similar, but not identical, to another value. One prominent example is that the distribution package name is often similar to the import package name, but the distribution name is hyphenated, whereas the import name has the hyphens removed or replaced with underscores. As an example, a package with a distribution package name like `flask-tools` might have an import name like `flasktools` or `flask_tools`.

When you need to create a template for two similar values like package names, ask yourself the following questions:

- Is one of the two values more "canonical" than the other? That is, does one feel like a derivation of the other?
- If so, can the canonical value be readily transformed programmatically into the other?

If the answer is yes to both these questions, you can consider prompting only for the canonical value and generating the other automatically. The cookiecutter template system uses Jinja2 (https://palletsprojects.com/p/jinja/) to inject dynamic content, and Jinja2 enables you to use Python expressions when generating that content; more on this shortly. You can use a Python expression in the value of one variable to calculate a value based on an earlier variable.

> **WARNING** Note that because cookiecutter prompts for the variables in the order they appear in the cookiecutter.json file, any variables that depend on another variable must come after the variables they depend on.

As an example, you can prompt the user for a distribution package name and then use the provided value to generate valid import package name options. The following listing shows how you can use Python's `str.replace` function to replace each hyphen in a user-supplied distribution package name with either the empty string or an underscore character and offer them as options for the import package name.

Listing 10.5   Generating a cookiecutter variable value from another variable value

```
{
    "distribution_package_name": "my-python-package",        ◁   A Python distribution
    "import_package_name": [                                       package name often
        "{{ cookiecutter.distribution_package_name                 contains hyphens.
  ➥ .lower().replace("-", "") }}",                          ◁
        "{{ cookiecutter.distribution_package_name                 Removes hyphens
  ➥ .lower().replace("-", "_") }}"          ◁                      for a valid import
    ]                                                              package name
}          Replaces hyphens with underscores
           for a valid import package name
```

Running the `cookiecutter` command using this configuration results in the output shown here.

Listing 10.6   Output from a cookiecutter configuration with dependent variables

```
$ cookiecutter python-project-template              The value chosen here
distribution_package_name [my-python-package]:  ◁   is used to generate
Select import_package_name:       ◁                 later values.
1 - mypythonpackage
2 - my_python_package        These values are
Choose from 1, 2 [1]:        generated from
                             the first variable.
```

You now have all the configuration tools you need to turn the copy of your package into a Python package project template. The next step is to create the cookiecutter configuration and update the package contents to reference the configured variables, but before diving into creating templates, you need to understand the flow of the variables and Jinja2's syntax more deeply.

10.1.2   *Extracting a cookiecutter template from an existing project*

Jinja2 works under a *rendering context*, or a set of available variables containing values it can inject into the content. The cookiecutter tooling adds a `cookiecutter` variable to the context, which in turn has attributes corresponding to the variables configured in the cookiecutter.json file. Jinja2 *renders* output by parsing input as a string and then identifying and operating on the following two special expression types:

- *Placeholder expressions* are enclosed in double curly braces ({{ ... }}) and contain references to context variables. A placeholder expression may further manipulate a context variable value using Python string operations; you saw an example of this earlier when offering transformed options for an import package name based on a distribution package name.
- *Block expressions* are enclosed in a curly brace and percent sign ({% ... %}). Block expressions can conditionally render content or render a piece of content repeatedly with different values from the rendering context.

As an example, you could render one of two different pieces of content based on a context variable value using the syntax in the next listing.

Listing 10.7   A Jinja2 control flow using conditional block expressions

```
{% if variable_one == "green" %}
It's green!
{% else %}
It isn't green.
{% endif %}
```

This is useful if your project template should render different content in a file depending on one of the options you configure.

After Jinja2 parses expressions and renders the content, cookiecutter creates an output project containing the rendered content. Figure 10.2 depicts the flow you saw earlier with more specifics about cookiecutter and Jinja2.

Another powerful aspect of the cookiecutter templating setup is that it also works in the names of files and directories. Because your package directory names are also dynamic and important to the proper functioning of the package, you need to be able to templatize these as well.

Importantly, cookiecutter expects the root directory of your project template to be a wrapper around the template for the output project. Put another way, your template project must contain a directory that will become the root directory of the output project. Like your `first-python-package` project, that output directory typically has

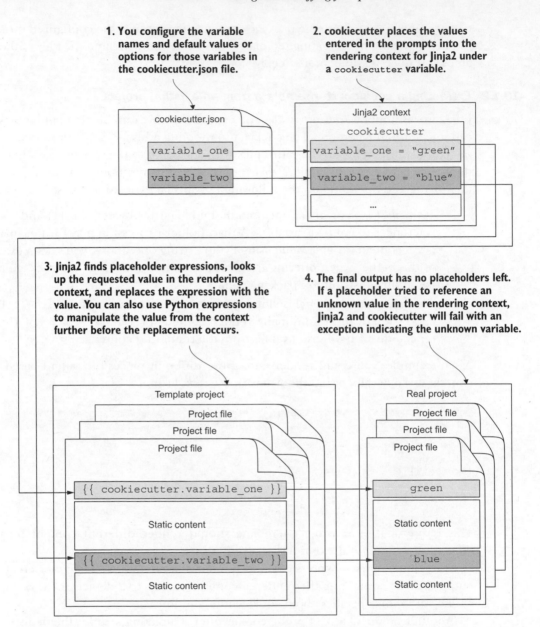

1. You configure the variable names and default values or options for those variables in the cookiecutter.json file.

2. cookiecutter places the values entered in the prompts into the rendering context for Jinja2 under a `cookiecutter` variable.

3. Jinja2 finds placeholder expressions, looks up the requested value in the rendering context, and replaces the expression with the value. You can also use Python expressions to manipulate the value from the context further before the replacement occurs.

4. The final output has no placeholders left. If a placeholder tried to reference an unknown value in the rendering context, Jinja2 and cookiecutter will fail with an exception indicating the unknown variable.

Figure 10.2   Jinja2 renders values from a dynamic context into placeholder expressions within static content.

the same name as the distribution package. You can achieve this using the following steps:

1   Create a new directory for your template project called python-project-template/ alongside your original package project.

2 Add an empty cookiecutter.json file to the python-project-template/ directory, which you'll configure shortly.

3 Copy the first-python-package/ directory into the python-project-template/ directory.

4 Rename the first-python-package/ directory to {{cookiecutter.package_distribution_name}}/ using Jinja2 placeholder syntax to refer to the package's distribution name.

The next listing shows what the directory structure should be for your project template.

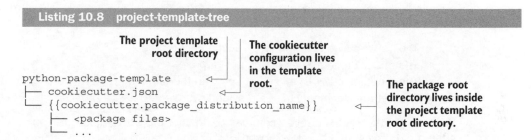

Listing 10.8   project-template-tree

```
                         The project template          The cookiecutter
                          root directory               configuration lives
                                                        in the template
                                                        root.
python-package-template  ◄──┘                                              The package root
├── cookiecutter.json    ◄────────────────────                            directory lives inside
└── {{cookiecutter.package_distribution_name}}          ◄──               the project template
    ├── <package files>                                                    root directory.
    └── ...
```

You're now equipped with the knowledge you need to complete the conversion of your package into a project template.

Exercise 10.1

Make a template from the rest of your project. You'll need to configure the cookiecutter.json file to prompt for the following:

1 `package_distribution_name`.

2 `package_import_name`; generate an option with and without underscores from the value of `package_distribution_name`.

3 `package_description`; use the value of `package_distribution_name` in the description.

4 `package_license`; suggest a subset of open source licenses, using names from the list of OSI approved classifiers (https://pypi.org/classifiers/).

5 `package_author_name`.

6 `package_author_email`.

After configuring cookiecutter to prompt for those values, you need to replace all of the following hard-coded references in your project with the placeholders so they'll be rendered dynamically:

- The import package directory inside the src/ directory needs to be determined dynamically from the cookiecutter variables. Rename it to depend on a `package_import_name` variable.

(continued)

- Replace references in the following files with their placeholder variable counterparts:
  - setup.cfg
  - README.md
  - docs/index.rst
  - docs/conf.py

Then, use conditional block expressions to change the content of the LICENSE file to provide the proper license content for the chosen `package_license`. Finally, remove the following pieces that you might not want in your project template:

- The `[options.entry_points]` section in setup.cfg
- The `install_requires` option in setup.cfg
- The modules other than `__init.py__` in the src/ and test/ directories
- The Cython machinery in setup.py and pyproject.toml

You can run the `cookiecutter` command with your project template periodically to generate a project and check your work.

After cookiecutter generates a project from your template that's to your liking, you can commit the template to version control and continue to use it to create new projects in the future.

10.2 *Using namespace packages*

The package you've built in this book is a small, isolated piece of functionality. Sometimes, a project grows large enough that it no longer makes sense to keep it in a single package, even if all the behavior is still related in a broad way. As an example, think about a large plugin-based framework like Django (https://www.djangoproject.com/) or Flask (https://flask.palletsprojects.com/en/2.0.x/). These projects have a core responsibility to provide tools for creating web server applications but can also do a lot more.

Other times, you may be working on packaging within your organization and want to clearly delineate all your organization's packages from third-party packages. It can be nice to maintain separate, small packages that share a common top-level import name so the team is certain they're using organizational code. This pattern is extremely common in Java applications (see "Naming a Package," The Java Tutorials, http://mng.bz/N5md), but less so in Python until an organization has wide adoption of Python and packaging.

Recall that packages should generally have one clear responsibility. Following this rule rigidly has consequences; you can imagine needing to install hundreds or even thousands of packages, all with their own distribution and import package names, just to accomplish a simple task. The NPM ecosystem (https://www.npmjs.com/) for JavaScript follows this philosophy. You don't want to shove all behavior into one large package that no longer has a clear purpose, but you also might not want to break that behavior up so much that people can't remember where to get what they need.

PEP 420 (https://www.python.org/dev/peps/pep-0420/) defines the specification for *implicit namespace packages*, which make it possible to provide granular behavior without sacrificing the ergonomics of importing behavior from a common namespace. Namespace packages enable you to break up a distribution package into multiple distribution packages while keeping them under a single namespace (see figure 10.3).

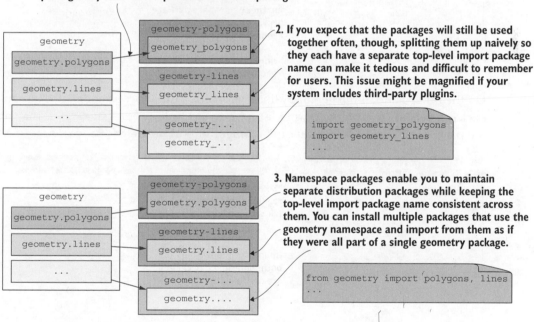

Figure 10.3 Namespace packages break up an existing distribution package into multiple distribution packages while maintaining a single, top-level namespace.

Namespace packages differ from regular packages in one key way: they provide a directory containing one or more regular packages, but that is not itself a package. That is, a directory is a namespace package if it contains Python packages but doesn't contain its own __init__.py module. Through this mechanism, multiple directories in different locations may share a common name but contain different packages. The name those directories share acts as the namespace, and the packages those directories contain are all importable under that namespace.

Namespace packages may also be nested, but the structure of namespace and regular packages needs to match across different directories to be compatible. If a directory is a namespace package in one directory but is a regular package in another directory, Python will favor the regular package and the namespace package won't work. As an example, the directory structure shown in the following listing results in being able to import `geometry.lines` as well as `geometry.polygons`.

Listing 10.9   A directory structure with a single namespace package

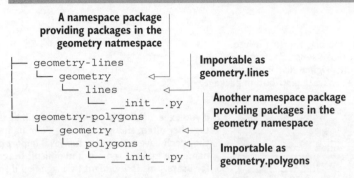

On the other hand, if the geometry-lines/geometry/ directory is made to be a regular package, as shown in the following listing, you can still import `geometry.lines` and the packages it contains, but you can no longer import `geometry.polygons`.

Listing 10.10   A regular package taking precedence over a namespace package

```
├── geometry-lines
│   └── geometry
│       ├── __init__.py       ◁──  Makes geometry a
│       └── lines                  regular package and
│           └── __init__.py        takes precedence
└── geometry-polygons
    └── geometry
        └── polygons          ◁──  No longer importable if
            └── __init__.py         both namespace packages
                                    are on the path
```

When you attempt to import a package, Python works to resolve the requested import by checking the paths it knows about for matches. Python's resolution algorithm will prefer regular packages, because looking for namespace packages takes more effort due to the additional nesting that may be involved for a namespace package. When one package on the system path is a regular package, Python will make it available over anything else, even when there are matching namespace packages on the system path as well.

Now that you understand the mechanics of namespace packages, you need to get some practice with them.

10.2.1 Converting an existing package to a namespace package

To convert an existing distribution package that provides a regular package into one that provides a namespace package, you need to take the following two actions:

- Update the directory structure for the namespace:
  - If the regular package is currently named the same as the namespace, remove the __init__.py module from the src/<package>/ directory to make it a namespace package.
  - If the regular package is a package that should live inside the namespace, create an empty src/<namespace>/ directory, and move the src/<package>/ directory inside it.
- Update the [options] section in the setup.cfg file:
  - Change the packages key from find: to find_namespace:.
  - Add a namespace_packages key with a value equal to the new namespace's name.

With these two changes, you turn a package from one that "consumes" its original namespace into one that can interoperate with other distribution packages that provide packages within the same namespace.

> **TIP** Using the setup you've learned in this book, you can generally use find_namespace: in place of find: without affecting anything. You can use this as the default in your project template, even if your distribution package doesn't provide any namespace packages.

> **Exercise 10.2**
> Using the project template you created earlier in this chapter, create two new packages. After you're done creating them, convert them both to provide packages within the same namespace. Install them both into a virtual environment, and check that you can import the code from both of them using a single namespace.

Now that you have a way to create many packages that follow your standards, as well as a way to create many packages that work well together using a single namespace, you might also be curious about how you can publish all these new packages in a private setting so that your team can install them within your organization.

10.3 Scaling packaging in your organization

There's no one right way to share code, and organizations will solve the problem of code reuse across projects in whatever way necessity dictates in the moment. Some organizations, like Google, end up putting all their code in a single repository with a complex build system. Others keep each project modular in its own repository with its own build process. If you suspect that decoupled delivery of behavior that people can opt into is going to be a priority for you, you should consider creating a private packaging ecosystem that mirrors how the Python Package Index and others work using the tools people are already familiar with.

10.3.1 *Private package repository servers*

Recall that PyPI is a package repository whose main job is to store and serve distribution packages. People can publish packages to it and install packages from it. This functionality seems basic, but as you learned in chapter 1, it's the core of the opt-in update model for installed dependencies that makes packaging so valuable. Even when you can't use PyPI because you're working on proprietary software or because your organization has restrictions about external access, you can consider running a private package repository within the walls of your organization.

PyPI works with pip because they each adhere to a particular contract about the paths the packages are served at in the index. Any private package repository you choose should adhere to this same contract to ensure that it is compatible with pip as well. The pypiserver package (https://github.com/pypiserver/pypiserver) provides a plug-and-play, open source solution for running a PyPI-compatible package index server. If you foresee needing other kinds of package repositories for JavaScript, Docker, Ruby, and so on, you might want to consider running a multilanguage package index using a solution like Artifactory (https://jfrog.com/artifactory/).

> **TIP** You can also look specifically for solutions that will automatically pull packages that have never been requested before from PyPI automatically and then cache them thereafter. This can speed up downloads for future installations and also gives you some resilience if PyPI servers are unavailable. pypiserver and Artifactory both support this.

Setting up and operating a private package repository server are outside the scope of this book, but the solutions mentioned and linked in this section have documentation about configuration and hosting that will help you do so. Assuming you have such a server, you need to know how to get your packaging tools to speak to it.

CONFIGURING TWINE AND PIP TO USE A PRIVATE REPOSITORY

Recall that you first used twine (https://twine.readthedocs.io) to publish your package before using GitHub Actions. GitHub Actions can't publish packages to a private package repository unless you specifically allow it to access the server through your network. If this is a limitation for you, you can use twine to publish your package instead. By default, twine and pip will communicate with PyPI when you ask it to install a package. Both tools accept configuration that will make them communicate with a server of your choosing. You can read about the variety of possible ways to configure twine (http://mng.bz/DDZV) and pip (http://mng.bz/lRJo), but the following is my personal recommendation for being explicit in your projects to make clear whether the project publishes or installs packages from a private server.

To publish packages to an alternate repository server using twine, you can create a new `publish` tox environment in your setup.cfg file that does the following:

1 Installs the `build` package to build the package
2 Installs the `twine` package to upload the built package to the repository server
3 Allows the external `rm` command so you can clean up the dist/ directory before building and uploading packages
4 Runs commands to clean, build, and publish the package

You can pass the `twine upload` command a `--repository` flag with the URL to your repository server's Python package repository upload endpoint, along with a `--username` flag and `--password` flag if your server requires authentication. The following listing shows an example of this setup using Artifactory.

Listing 10.11 Adding an alternate package repository URL via twine

```
[testenv:publish]
skip_install = True
deps =
    build                       Installs twine for
    twine                       publishing the
                                package
whitelist_externals =
    rm                          Allows the external
commands =                      rm command to be
    rm -rf dist/                used
    pyproject-build .
    twine upload \              Cleans up any existing
        --username="" \         built packages before
        --password="" \         proceeding
        --repository-url=
    https://artifactory.mycompany.org/artifactory/
    api/pypi/pypi \             Uploads the package to an
        dist/*                  alternate repository server
```

Builds the package

With the `publish` tox environment in place, you can publish the package manually from your machine or create a continuous integration workflow on a self-hosted solution like Jenkins (https://www.jenkins.io/) or GitLab CI/CD (https://docs.gitlab.com/ee/ci/) that runs the environment when you create a tag on the code repository.

After you publish a package to your alternate repository server, you then need to tell pip how to retrieve packages from that same server. If you're installing packages in a Python runtime application that uses a requirements.txt file, you can add an `--index-url` flag with the repository server's Python package repository download endpoint to either the `pip install` command or into the requirements.txt file itself. Imagine you publish a private package called my-private-package to your private package repository, and you need to install it as well as Django in a project you're working on. Listing 10.12 shows an example requirements.txt file that instructs pip to look at the private package repository, where it will be able to find my-private-package. The repository server may have a copy of Django available, or it may need to fetch it from

PyPI first; this is an implementation and configuration detail of your private repository solution of choice.

Listing 10.12   Adding an alternate package repository URL via pip

```
# requirements.txt

--index-url https://artifactory.mycompany.org/artifactory/api/pypi/pypi/simple   ◁

my-private-package==2.5.1    ◁
Django==3.2.12   ◁
```

pip looks here for packages, alternative to PyPI

Resolves because you published it to the private server

Either resolved on the private server or fetched from PyPI

By putting these URLs explicitly into the project source code, you ensure that developers who check out and work from the code repository will publish and fetch packages from the expected package repository servers. If you use configuration methods that live outside the project, you must trust developers to properly configure tools like twine and pip to use the proper package repository servers.

You've now learned how you can proliferate the use of packages, even within an organization that might have limitations on using the broader open source packaging ecosystem. You can create new packages using your cookiecutter project template and create a set of namespace packages so people can install smaller pieces of software using a consistent prefix for the imports, and you can do this all on a self-hosted server internal to your organization. You're almost ready to go forth and prosper! But don't miss out on the last chapter, which will help you put some final important polish on things if you're heading in the direction of open source projects.

Summary

- Don't just focus on automating a single project; when it comes to modular software ecosystems, consider automating the creation of the projects themselves using a project template.
- Using a project template helps others adopt the system, and you can keep it up to date to ensure the latest standards make it into each new project.
- Some things in a specific project won't map to all projects you create, so you need to refine your project template over time for maximum productivity.
- Packages can get too big, but too many namespaces can also be confusing. Consider using namespace packages to find a happy medium for your users.
- Each public solution you've used in this book has a private or self-hosted corrolary, and you can use these to build out a proprietary packaging ecosystem in your organization.

Building a community

This chapter covers

- Creating a user-to-maintainer funnel
- Adding a code of conduct to your project
- Communicating the status of your project to users
- Using templates and labels to streamline GitHub issue management

Imagine you've just created another valuable software package and can't wait to share it with the world. You make the repository publicly available on GitHub, and you send out a blast of tweets and emails to everyone who might be interested. You sit back and wait for the hype to build, but it never comes. Although you've reached a milestone by completing the implementation of your project, it turns out this is rarely the final milestone. If you want people to use your work, and especially if you want them to contribute new features, bug fixes, or documentation, you need to provide guidance and vision for the project so everyone can head in the same direction together. This is a lot like building a product.

I've released a few different projects as open source over the years, and I can tell you now that the most successful among them have a few things in common.

Occasionally, some work might become popular purely out of interest or accident, but there are some measures you can take to give a project its best chance at success. Whether you're keen on providing your work to others so they can benefit, building a portfolio to gain notoriety, or both, building a community is important. If you expect your project to grow outside the captive audience of your coworkers or clients, and if you want your projects to live a long time without constantly doing the work yourself or holding people's hands, this chapter is for you.

11.1   *Your README needs to make a value proposition*

The README is often the landing page for your project. Whether a user finds your project on the Python Package Index, GitHub, or a Google search, the README will be one of the first things they see. Many projects don't leverage this to its full potential, stopping short of the opportunity to draw people in to give the project a try.

In the midst of the absolute sea of projects online today, it's no longer enough to merely state *what* your project accomplishes. Think instead about *why* someone should choose to use your project, especially compared to the competition. If your project is entirely novel, say so. As in most other arenas of life, each project is vying for user attention, and you only have a precious few moments to give your "elevator pitch" before someone moves on to the next project. Many successful teams treat projects as products and build a brand that may encompass multiple projects. Developing a brand is a careful craft and involves studying the emotional connection to users over time (see Kevin L. Keller, "Brand Synthesis: The Multidimensionality of Brand Knowledge," *Journal of Consumer Research*, https://www.jstor.org/stable/10.1086/346254). Think about incorporating a bit of yourself and the team into the README and include the motivation behind the project so people feel like they can engage with you instead of simply consuming software.

Visual aids can be a big help in catching the eye—pictures are worth a thousand words, after all—so think about what you can show instead of tell. The rich package (https://github.com/Textualize/rich) does a great job of showing up front what it's capable of, enticing people to read on about how they can build beautiful command-line interfaces using it. The rich README then covers several of the use cases it supports, so potential users can get a high-level sense of what it would be like to work with. Note that this is not intended as, or in place of, proper documentation; its express purpose is to get people to try rich, and the full documentation is elsewhere. Finally, the README ends with some social proof to show that others are already happy users of the project (for more on social proof, see Robert B. Cialdini, *Influence: Science and Practice* [Allyn and Beacon, 2000]).

Many of the most valuable contributions to a project come from its most engaged users, and the more contributions someone makes, the more likely they are to make another contribution in the future. To maximize the funnel of people coming back to contribute to a project, you then need to maximize the number of people who use it regularly. You can expect each level of the funnel to drop off by an order of magnitude.

Making your README as captivating as possible ensures that the loss of potential users who don't become actual users is as small as possible (see figure 11.1).

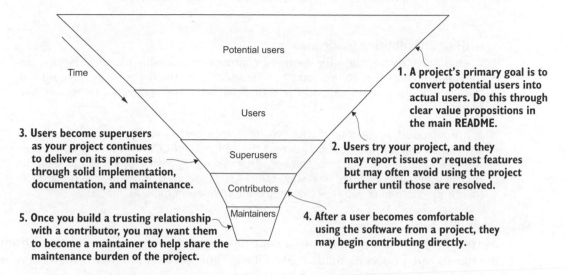

Figure 11.1 A project's community goes through a funnel over time. Each level of the funnel is much smaller than the last, often by an order of magnitude.

This mental model can be important as you share your latest endeavors, because it will help you identify who might be the most interested and who might be able to help evangelize using your solution to address real problems they have. As an example, the folks at CarCorp might want to use one of your newest packages in general, but they may not be interested in telling others about how useful it is in the air travel industry. By identifying the types of users coming your way, you can better stratify their motivations and desired outcomes and optimize for those that make sense for the project. Each level of the user funnel has different needs when it comes to your project, and they'll need documentation to support those needs.

11.2 Provide supporting documentation for different user types

You learned in chapter 8 that documentation supports several modes of activity:

- Learn how to use the project
- Achieve a specific task
- Find syntax details and other reference material
- Understand the history and direction of the project

Early users of the project are best supported by the first three types of documentation. Because such a significant band of your user funnel needs these types of documentation, don't skimp on them. Be sure to create how-tos, tutorials, and automated code reference documentation to cover as many bases as possible. Especially in the early life of a project, focusing most of your effort here will have the most impact.

GitHub contribution guidelines

GitHub provides a feature for surfacing contribution guidelines to new users when they open issues and so on. You can leverage this feature by putting your contribution guidelines in a file called CONTRIBUTING.md in the .github/ directory in your project.

If you provide the majority of your project's documentation the way you learned in chapter 8, you may be best off keeping the contents of CONTRIBUTING.md concise with a link to your main documentation. This way users will be prompted to read the documentation when opening issues but will be directed through to your main documentation instead of you maintaining the information in multiple places.

As your project matures, superusers, contributors, and maintainers will benefit from the fourth type of documentation. They'll want guidance on whether certain features should even be considered for addition to the project and what kind of experience users will want. They'll also need an increasing understanding about the decisions leading up to the current state of the project so they can support and evolve the system's design in an aligned way.

Imagine someone loves your project and wants to contribute after they find a bug. They head over to your project's repository and see all the great documentation about how to *use* the software, but after half an hour looking for documentation about *developing* the software and an hour struggling to get things set up on their own, they give up. Unfortunately, they may be too frustrated to give you feedback about this, and you won't know it needs to be improved. You've also lost a valuable contribution.

If you don't provide this level of guidance, your project is also likely to grow in ways you didn't expect. When a contributor makes a change that doesn't agree with your vision, but the vision isn't documented, you end up having a tough and potentially frustrating conversation to make the change conform. You can reduce the time and effort you spend on these conversations by providing the vision up front where possible.

The vision and status of a project are another facet where treating it like a product can help the community of users. What's next for this project? What's the ultimate goal for the project? Is that goal accomplished, close to being accomplished, or somewhere on the horizon? Answering these questions in your documentation will help the right users take the right actions at the right time and minimize frustration as much as possible.

> **Documenting architectural decisions**
>
> For the broadest decisions you make in a project about architecture and system design, it can be valuable to record the decision along with the context under which the decision was made so that when the context inevitably changes in the future, new decisions can be made without reconstructing the entire context from scratch. Architectural decision records (ADRs) are a popular framework for capturing this information (see Michael Nygard, "Documenting Architecture Decisions," http://mng.bz/BZl2).
>
> I've been using ADRs on a few projects lately, and our team has come to like them quite a bit. In the same way that a linter separates the feedback about code quality from the human aspect, ADRs can serve as reminders to put in the extra effort for specific reasons without too much rehashing of reasoning.
>
> Some tools, like adr-tools (https://github.com/npryce/adr-tools), help automate the process of creating, linking, and evolving your architecture decisions over time.

Despite mitigating as much as you can up front, inevitably someone will get unreasonably upset about the state of things. They may even do or say something inappropriate that can damage the community if left unaddressed. You should prepare for this inevitability with a code of conduct that includes a clear plan of enforcement.

11.3   Establish, provide, and enforce a code of conduct

The Zen of Python (https://peps.python.org/pep-0020/) states that "explicit is better than implicit." A plethora of projects out there don't provide any particular code of conduct, and because the platforms where those projects are developed have very generous terms of service, users get away with a lot of behavior that ultimately undermines project communities.

Imagine a newer user opens a request for a new feature in good faith, not realizing that the feature has been requested and rejected more than once in the past. You're about to respond with a friendly welcome and the context about the past rejection, when another member of the community jumps in and very rudely tells the new user off. This user may never come back to the project again. In the best case, they'll be nervous about requesting features going forward. You give some private feedback to the member who responded rudely, but you've seen them do this a few times and are worried it will continue to happen.

These situations are always uncomfortable, but they don't need to be unstructured. A code of conduct helps clearly define the expected and unacceptable behaviors of members of the community and what repercussions can come when a member acts outside those bounds. These users may face temporary or permanent bans that disallow them from engaging further in a project. Having these rules clearly spelled out and available to the community ensures that the project maintainers are both empowered and accountable to enforce them.

A great starting place for a code of conduct is the Contributor Covenant (https://www.contributor-covenant.org/), which has been adopted by some of the largest technology companies for their open source projects. The Contributor Covenant provides a template code of conduct that you can adapt and adopt for use in your project and outlines the escalation policy of enforcement against inappropriate behavior. Projects as large as Vue (https://github.com/vuejs/vue) are using the Contributor Covenant as their code of conduct.

Although discussions can still get heated and sometimes even negative, a code of conduct protects both the maintainers and the community from the kinds of behavior that can have a lasting negative impact on a project's community. Adding the text of your code of conduct to a file called CODE_OF_CONDUCT.md in the root of your project repository will display a link to it in some parts of the GitHub interface, such as when a new user is about to open an issue (see figure 11.2).

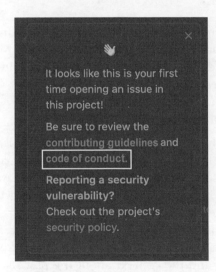

Figure 11.2   GitHub will display a link to your code of conduct to new users when they open issues.

Take a look at the codes of conduct for some large projects like Django (https://www.djangoproject.com/conduct/) or Python (https://www.python.org/psf/conduct/) for inspiration. Although their enforcement process may be more involved than something you can handle, they likely cover cases they've seen in real life that you can anticipate instead of experiencing as surprises later on. Stick to the codes of conduct for free and open source software, ideally from nonprofit organizations, because they're more likely to have robust codes than for-profit projects.

Now that you have a few pieces of homework for creating a welcoming space and supporting your users' needs through documentation, you can take a few additional actions to promote effective contributions.

11.4 Conveying the project's road map, status, and changes

You've already covered the project vision in your documentation, but this should be as evergreen as possible to support ongoing design and decision-making. When it comes to how the project is tracking against the vision at any point in time, it helps to have a road map and a way to track the status of activities on that road map.

11.4.1 Using GitHub projects for kanban management

If you haven't worked in an agile software development environment before, you may not have heard of kanban. Kanban is a lean approach to work tracking originally developed for inventory management in Toyota's manufacturing process (see Taiichi Ohno, *Toyota Production System: Beyond Large-Scale Production* (Productivity Press, 1988)). Kanban was adapted to software to track the queue of work within a team. Today's kanban products offer visibility into the following attributes:

- The status of a given task (often "to do," "in progress," and "done" for simple projects)
- The category of the work to be done (sometimes called *swimlanes*)
- Who's working on which tasks

As a project progresses, the visibility into these attributes can then provide the following signals:

- A lack of focus (too much work in progress at one time)
- Misalignment (low-priority work done before high-priority work)
- Challenges (task in progress for a long time)
- Common bottlenecks and blockers

These signals become increasingly important as you work through new releases users are anticipating. GitHub offers a projects feature on top of GitHub issues (https://github.com/features/issues) that provides a kanban-style workflow for issue management. You can combine user story card descriptions, issues, pull requests, and some light automation into a rich tracking and reporting system for your project (see figure 11.3).

11.4.2 Use GitHub labels to track status for individual tasks

Whereas the kanban board features in GitHub issues are useful for the high-level progress of an entire project, each individual task in the project goes through a life cycle as well. Because maintainers and contributors alike often look at these tasks through the lens of the associated pull request, GitHub labels can be a useful, visible way to indicate the status of the pull request. GitHub comes with a default set of labels, but you can create your own labels on the labels page of your repository (https://github.com/<owner>/<repo>/labels). You can even change or add default labels to a

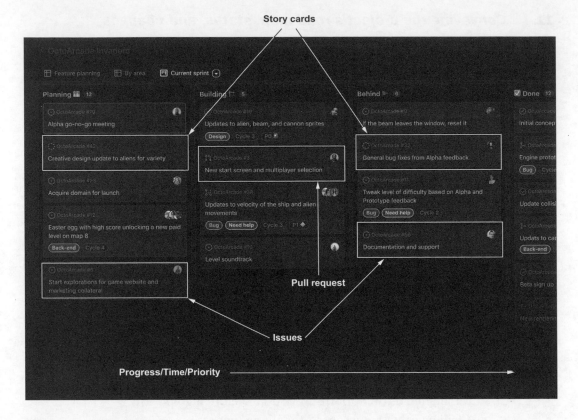

Figure 11.3   GitHub issues

GitHub organization so that new repositories you create conform to your organization's needs. Replace <organization> with the name of your organization: https://github .com/organizations/<organization>/settings/repository-defaults.

You might think of a pull request as being in one of three states: open, merged, or closed. For changes to critical areas of code or larger changes that require more careful review and a few iterations of development, the "open" state might actually be several distinct states, as shown here:

1 *In progress*—The code is about there but is still being worked on. Reviewers might look at it, but the code is subject to change.
2 *In review*—The code should be reviewed with all the usual scrutiny the project requires. Any specific reviewers who need to look at the area of code being changed should do so.
3 *Reviewed*—The code change is deemed fit for release but may not be ready for the actual act of releasing yet.
4 *Ready to be released*—The code should be included in the next appropriate release.

5   *On hold*—Whatever state the code is in, it's not ready for other activity. The maintainers may need time to think about it, or the contributor has been inactive, or something else.

These are just some possible states; pull requests in your projects may go through more or different states, and they may flow back and forth between some states as the maintainers and contributors collaborate on the change (see figure 11.4).

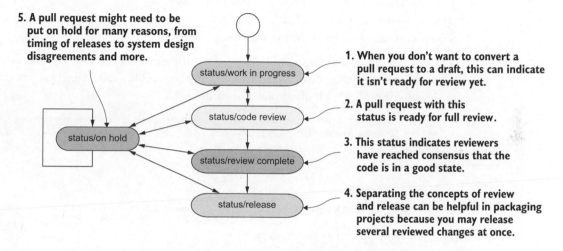

5. A pull request might need to be put on hold for many reasons, from timing of releases to system design disagreements and more.

1. When you don't want to convert a pull request to a draft, this can indicate it isn't ready for review yet.

2. A pull request with this status is ready for full review.

3. This status indicates reviewers have reached consensus that the code is in a good state.

4. Separating the concepts of review and release can be helpful in packaging projects because you may release several reviewed changes at once.

Figure 11.4   Pull requests in a project may transition through many different states and can be thought of as a state machine.

A clearly defined status-labeling system can help everyone, new and experienced with the project, understand where in its life cycle a pull request is at a quick glance. It can also help a pull request move through these states more efficiently because people can tell more easily whether a pull request might benefit from their attention.

Another area where people can benefit from a quick glance is seeing what changed in the past. For that, look to the humble changelog.

11.4.3 *Track high-level changes in a log*

For projects with a regular cadence of releases, especially for packaging projects with versioned releases, the biggest thing people will want to know about any release is what changed. For major version releases, this becomes critical because consumers may need to react to those changes as they upgrade to keep their own projects working.

Keeping track of what changed in which release becomes increasingly difficult as more and more releases go out, to the point that going back and making release notes retrospectively gives diminishing returns. If you can develop a process early on that enables you to keep track of changes as they happen, you'll avoid late nights doing archaeology on your own project.

One helpful system is the creatively named Keep a Changelog (https:// keepachangelog.com). In the Keep a Changelog system, you create a file in the root of your repository, typically called CHANGELOG.md, that keeps high-level notes about your releases in a strict conventional format. This format provides the following:

- The version of the release
- The exact date of the release in YYYY-MM-DD format
- One or more sections of changes, which may be additions, changes, deprecations, removals, bug fixes, or security fixes

Keep a Changelog also encourages you to keep a running tally of the as-yet unreleased changes you've merged into your project so that they're readily available when you do make a release. An example changelog is shown next.

> Listing 11.1 The Keep a Changelog format with several historical entries

A running list of features in the next release

```
# Changelog

All notable changes to this project will be documented in this file.

The format is based on [Keep a Changelog](
➥ https://keepachangelog.com/en/1.0.0/),
and this project adheres to [Semantic Versioning](
➥ https://semver.org/spec/v2.0.0.html).

## [Unreleased]          List of new
### Added          ←     features added
- Half-Life 3
                               Specific release with
                               an exact release date
## [2.7.1] - 2022-04-05   ←
### Fixed
- Stop mining Bitcoin in the emergency phone call feature

## [2.7.0] - 1914-08-15
### Added
- New colors for the Model T including Dark Black and Midnight Black
```
List of fixes made

If you're used to writing READMEs and other Markdown files, the Keep a Changelog syntax and format should feel comfortably familiar.

My personal changelog approach
For personal projects, I quite like Keep a Changelog. I tend to slowly build up my changelog as I merge features, and when it comes time to make a release, I'll manually copy the contents of the latest changelog into the body of the GitHub release.

If I've sufficiently sold you on the value of automation, you might like to explore automated solutions for this problem. I've used Atlassian's changesets project (https://github.com/changesets/changesets) happily for an organizational project, but note that it's geared toward the JavaScript ecosystem. In the Python ecosystem, I've heard good things about towncrier (https://github.com/twisted/towncrier). These both produce changelogs in similar formats, with slight differences in their power and presentation. The main thing is to choose a tool you'll actually use; an imperfect changelog is often better than no changelog.

Although Keep a Changelog isn't an automated system, it's a nice plaintext approach that renders readable notes in Markdown and provides just enough of a reminder that people can remember to do it. You can add an item to your pull request checklist to remind folks to fill out the changelog.

One of the more difficult challenges with changelogs is knowing how much detail to record in them. Repeating the detail from the individual changes that went in might be too much for users to sift through, but saying that "something changed" isn't going to cut it either. You should adjust your level of detail according to the changes in question. As an example, a breaking change should include explanation of the steps to migrate to the new way of doing things. It can also be a fruitful but tedious practice to include a link to the pull request(s) that achieved a change so users can look deeper if they want to.

So far you've been given a lot of homework that will benefit the community, but the last section will benefit you significantly as well.

11.5 Gather consistent information with issue templates

Some people have a knack for reporting bugs. Without prompting, they'll provide all the details of their operating system, software versions, what they had for lunch leading up to experiencing the bug, and more. Others will provide an error message without much additional context to go off of, and other still may just report a bug that says, "It's broken when I use it."

You can take measures to make sure your project community is comfortable reporting issues and contributing pull requests, but left to their own devices, they'll provide a wide variance in type and amount of contextual information. This ends up being frustrating for you as you engage in a back-and-forth conversation to gather more detail. You can increase your chances of success by creating issue templates in GitHub.

GitHub supports templates for pull requests, which populate the description field when a contributor starts the pull request creation workflow. You can use this to ensure that contributors are prompted with things like

- The problem statement pertaining to the change
- The details of how the change addresses the problem
- Any additional context that's useful for reviewers

An example of a pull request template and how it appears in GitHub is shown in figure 11.5.

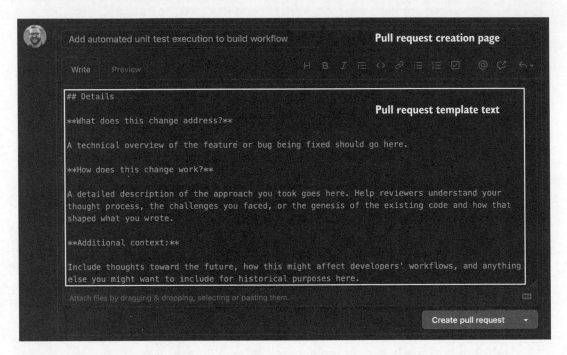

Figure 11.5 Pull request templates help extract useful information from contributors to promote more effective collaboration.

To create a pull request template, create a file named PULL_REQUEST_TEMPLATE .md in the .github/ directory of your repository. Add the content you want to appear in the pull request description by default as the contents of the file, and commit it. New pull requests will use the PULL_REQUEST_TEMPLATE.md file contents as the pull request description.

TIP Indicate with uncommon characters like <<>> specific values or sections people should fill in, and keep it short so people fill it all out instead of filling it partially out or replacing the entire contents with something of their choosing.

The listing that follows shows a pull request template I usually favor as a starting place for new projects. It's short enough that people are inclined to fill it out fully, but thorough enough to understand the change better than with no prompting.

Listing 11.2 A good pull request description including context

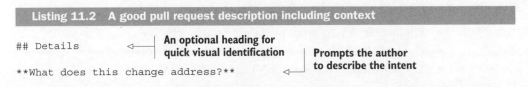

```
A technical overview of the feature or bug being fixed should go here.

**How does this change work?**        ◄──┤  Prompts the author to
                                          explain the approach

A detailed description of the approach you took goes here.
Help reviewers understand your thought process, the challenges you faced,
or the genesis of the existing code and how that shaped what you wrote.

**Additional context:**              ◄──┤  Prompts the author for lateral
                                          and long-term thoughts

Include thoughts toward the future, how this might affect developers'
workflows, and anything else you might want to include for historical
purposes here.
```

GitHub also provides issue templates for reporting bugs, requesting features, and so on. With issues, you can even create forms that restrict and structure the information users provide. The unique nature of your project's needs and depth of possibility in this area put issue template coverage outside the scope of this book, but in the end, it's a matter of adding and configuring a file for each issue type you want users to file. See the official GitHub documentation on issue templates (http://mng.bz/deJw) for a detailed walkthrough and examples. I encourage you, as with documentation, to consider your users' goals when filing issues and to create an issue type for each of those distinct goals. This will guide users to the right experience, which helps immensely when they're feeling frustrated or confused or both.

For a deep dive into all the community features GitHub offers, many of which you learned about in this chapter and earlier in this book, check out the official documentation (https://docs.github.com/en/communities).

11.6 Go forth

If you're reading this, you've made it successfully through a gauntlet of trials and tribulations on the way to developing a successful Python package project and community. That, or you skipped a bunch and you need to go back and revisit the previous chapters.

I've poured as much of my experience onto these pages for you as I can think of, but that doesn't mean that's all there is to learn. The Python packaging ecosystem continues to evolve in amazing ways, and I'd love to keep in touch with you about it. Tag me (@daneah) in a GitHub issue or discussion if something isn't working, you need advice, or you just want to show off what you've made. I'll be there to set you on the right path or cheer you on, as the case may be. Until then, happy coding!

Summary

- Your community has a funnel, and as you build the community, you want to keep the mouth of the funnel as wide as possible. Provide support through documentation and issue management to the distinct users in each level of the funnel.

- Communities benefit from systems and structure so members know what to expect. So do you.
- Above all, your community needs communication to function. Communicate the project vision, status, and needs. Communicate architectural decisions. Communicate progress. Communicate change.
- You've been a wonderful audience, and you deserve to go out and do something nice for yourself.

appendix A
Installing asdf
and python-launcher

In this book, you'll need to manage the installation of multiple Python versions and virtual environments and the switching between them. This appendix covers the installation of tools to ease this burden, which you'll learn more about in the chapters.

> **Important**
>
> The tools covered in this appendix are recommendations I give for convenience to people looking for an easier way to manage environments on macOS, and they're the ones I use myself. If you're already deeply familiar with installing base Python versions and managing virtual environments, you don't need to use them. If you're on Windows or Linux, you may need to install additional dependencies for these tools to work, and you may want or need to consider some of the alternatives that follow. For brevity and consistency in the book, examples will leverage them, so be sure to at least read through this appendix to best understand the examples in the chapters. In the end, if you want to work through this book agnostic of any other tools or ecosystem, you can install Python versions manually, create virtual environments manually, and activate them manually.
>
> Alternatives to asdf that I would recommend for base Python version management follow in order of preference based on my experience with them:
>
> 1 pyenv (https://github.com/pyenv/pyenv) or pyenv-win (https://pyenv-win .github.io/pyenv-win) for Windows users
> 2 Direct installation from source or a prebuilt binary for your platform (https:// www.python.org/downloads/)
> 3 Homebrew (https://brew.sh/) or your platform's official system package manager

(continued)

Alternatives to python-launcher and venv that I would recommend for virtual environment management follow in order of preference based on my experience with them:

1 pyenv-virtualenv (https://github.com/pyenv/pyenv-virtualenv)
2 poetry (https://python-poetry.org/)
3 virtualenv (https://virtualenv.pypa.io/en/latest/) and virtualenvwrapper (http://mng.bz/rndy) for added management convenience
4 pipenv (https://github.com/pypa/pipenv)

Anywhere the `py` command appears in this book, unless stated otherwise, you should treat it as meaning you need to have your project's virtual environment active or otherwise ensure you're using the `python` command associated with your project.

A.1 *Installing asdf*

asdf (https://github.com/asdf-vm/asdf) is a tool for installing multiple versions of languages, frameworks, and tools and switching between them. Although you can install base versions of Python from the source code or a prebuilt binary for your operating system, asdf manages installed versions and per-directory configuration nicely. In addition to Python, it also does this across other languages and frameworks like NodeJS, Ruby, and more.

You'll use asdf to install multiple base versions of Python, from which you'll create isolated environments for your projects. You can use asdf on macOS, Linux, or the Windows subsystem for Linux.

> **NOTE** The following instructions are provided as a convenience so you can stay here in the context of the book. You may also want to check asdf's official documentation for getting started (https://asdf-vm.com/guide/getting-started .html) to see if anything has changed.

To install asdf, first determine the most recent tagged version (https://github.com/ asdf-vm/asdf/tags). Then, clone the branch corresponding to that version into the $HOME/.asdf/ directory. As an example, if the latest release is `v1.2.3`, you would run the following command:

```
$ git clone \                                        The asdf repository
    https://github.com/asdf-vm/asdf.git \            on GitHub
    $HOME/.asdf \            The destination for
    --branch v1.2.3          the cloned code
        The version of the
        code to use
```

After cloning the code, you need to source it during your shell's startup. For macOS, where the default shell is zsh, add the following lines to `$HOME/.zshrc`. For bash, add them to `$HOME/.bash_profile`:

```
if [ -f $HOME/.asdf/asdf.sh ]; then
    source $HOME/.asdf/asdf.sh
fi
```

After saving your startup file, open a fresh shell session. Verify that asdf was installed properly using the following command:

```
$ asdf --version
```

You should see a version that matches the branch you checked out when you cloned the repository. Now that you have asdf installed, install the Python plugin using the following command:

```
$ asdf plugin add python
```

This will make the plugin available immediately. Verify the plugin is working, and see which versions of Python are available using the following command:

```
$ asdf list all python
```

You should see several hundred versions listed, including PyPy, Anaconda, and others. Scroll up to the versions that are only numbered without any name—these are the standard CPython implementation versions.

You'll test your project on the three most recent minor versions of Python, so install these next. As an example, if the most recent version of Python is 3.11.X, you should install the most recent versions that match the following:

- 3.11.X
- 3.10.Y
- 3.9.Z

You can install these with asdf using the following commands, replacing the versions with those you'd like to install:

```
$ asdf install python 3.11.X
$ asdf install python 3.10.Y
$ asdf install python 3.9.Z
```

WARNING
macOS Big Sur and later may cause issues installing older versions of Python. If you see compilation errors when trying to install a Python version, you can patch Python with the following approach:

```
ASDF_PYTHON_PATCH_URL=\                  ◁── Instructs asdf to apply a patch to
                                             the Python code before compiling
"https://github.com/python/cpython/commit/
➥ 8ea6353.patch?full_index=1" \         ◁── This specific patch fixes a common
asdf install python 3.11.X                   compilation issue on macOS Big Sur.
```

After you've installed your desired versions of Python, you can list them all using the following command:

```
$ asdf list python
```

You should see output similar to the following, with slightly different versions based on what you installed:

```
3.11.X
3.10.Y
3.9.Z
```

Finally, make all the Python versions you've installed available on your `$PATH` using the following command, replacing the versions as appropriate:

```
$ asdf global python 3.11.X 3.10.Y 3.9.Z
```

This will create a $HOME/.tool-versions file with content similar to the following:

```
python 3.11.X 3.10.X 3.9.X
```

Specifying multiple versions makes them available by default anywhere on your system, which will be useful after you install python-launcher in the following section. You can also pare down the versions available in a given project using `asdf local python` in a project's root directory to create a .tool-versions file specific to that project.

To verify your configuration, start a fresh shell session and invoke the `python` command. This should start an interpreter of the first version of Python you passed to `asdf global python`, because that version has the highest precedence. You should also be able to start an interpreter from any of the installed versions. As an example, if you have Python 3.9 installed, you should be able to invoke the `python3.9` command to get a Python 3.9 interpreter.

A.2 *Installing python-launcher*

It's not too hard to use different versions of Python with asdf alone, but it will become more difficult as you create environments for different projects. python-launcher (https://github.com/brettcannon/python-launcher) is a convenience tool for launching the right Python at the right time. With python-launcher, you can use a single command, py, to invoke the installation of Python you intend based on your current working directory or the presence of a virtual environment directory. This can save you a lot of time because you don't need to constantly activate and deactivate the virtual environment. The examples in this book will use python-launcher for most actions.

> **Warning**
>
> If you're a Windows user, you don't need to install python-launcher yourself. It already comes with Python on Windows (http://mng.bz/VypG) and has since 2012. The python-launcher for Unix-based systems may eventually be brought into the Python core, but no specific plans have been announced as of this writing. The consistency across platforms would be beneficial to those who use Windows and Unix platforms.

To install python-launcher, you can likely use your platform's system package manager (https://github.com/brettcannon/python-launcher#installation).

> **Installing python-launcher manually**
>
> If a python-launcher package isn't available for your platform, or you want finer control, you can install it manually using Rust (https://www.rust-lang.org). As of this writing, the recommended way to install Rust is with the following command (for the latest installation instructions, see "Install Rust," https://www.rust-lang.org/tools/install):
>
> ```
> $ curl --proto '=https' --tlsv1.2 -sSf https://sh.rustup.rs | sh
> ```
>
> After Rust is installed, use Rust's cargo tool to install python-launcher with the following command:
>
> ```
> $ cargo install python-launcher
> ```

You should now be able to verify your installation by starting a fresh shell session and using the following command to list all of the versions of Python that python-launcher knows about:

```
$ py --list
```

You should see output similar to the following, with slightly different versions based on your operating system and what you installed:

```
3.10 | /Users/<you>/.asdf/shims/python3.10
3.9  | /Users/<you>/.asdf/shims/python3.9
3.8  | /Users/<you>/.asdf/shims/python3.8
3.7  | /Users/<you>/.asdf/shims/python3.7
2.7  | /usr/bin/python2.7
```

Note that most of these versions mention asdf, which you made available through the asdf global python command. But the last version points somewhere else—that's the system Python. asdf interacts with your shell's $PATH variable, which is how it can switch where the python command resolves.

python-launcher will, by default, use the highest available version of Python it can find. As an example, if you installed Python 3.10, 3.9, and 3.8, python-launcher would prefer to use Python 3.10 by default. You can also control which base Python version you get using python-launcher's version flag. As an example, if you have Python 3.9 installed, you should be able to invoke the py command with the -3.9 flag to get a Python 3.9 interpreter.

Exercise A.1

If you used asdf to install Python 3.10, 3.9, and 3.8, and ran `asdf global python 3.9 3.8`, which version would the following command return?

```
$ py -V
```

Answer to exercise A.1

A.1—3.9. 3.10 is not on the $PATH unless configured with asdf, so python-launcher won't know about it and finds 3.9 to be the highest version.

appendix B
Installing pipx,
build, tox, pre-commit,
and cookiecutter

In this book, you'll use a few tools frequently, and you'll eventually need them across several projects. This appendix covers the installation of these tools, which you'll learn more about in the chapters. You can run the installation commands from almost anywhere on your system.

B.1 Installing pipx

Several tools are available as Python packages, but you don't want to have to install them in each project where you use them if they're general purpose in nature. You should still install the tools in isolation, though, so that they don't mix with other installed software unnecessarily. pipx (https://github.com/pypa/pipx/) is a management tool for running other Python tools in isolated environments inspired by the JavaScript world's npx (https://docs.npmjs.com/cli/v8/commands/npx). You'll use pipx to install a few general-purpose tools, and you can use it to install other "system-wide" tools you'll want in the future.

Install pipx using the following command, optionally supplying the desired base Python version in which to install it:

```
$ py -3.10 -m pip install pipx
```

Start a fresh shell session after the installation completes to ensure the pipx command provided by the package is available on your $PATH.

> **Installing pipx so that pipx can manage pipx itself**
>
> pipx is all about isolating tools but isn't isolated itself. You can install pipx using the pipx-in-pipx project (https://github.com/mattsb42-meta/pipx-in-pipx) so that even pipx itself is isolated. pipx will also be able to manage itself for version upgrades and so on. To do so, install `pipx-in-pipx` instead of `pipx`. The documentation mentions some sharp edges; I haven't experienced any issues of substance myself.

B.2 *Installing build*

build (https://github.com/pypa/build) is a tool provided by the Python Packaging Authority (PyPA) for building Python packages. Because you might eventually want to use it to build several different packages, installing it with pipx will make it available wherever you might need it. You'll use `build` to build the Python package you develop throughout the course of the book. Install build using the following command:

```
$ pipx install build
```

You should see output similar to the following indicating the `pyproject-build` application was installed:

```
installed package build 0.4.0, Python 3.10.0
  These apps are now globally available
    - pyproject-build
done! ✨ 🌟 ✨
```

To verify your configuration, run the following command:

```
$ pyproject-build --version
```

The version should match the version in the output of the `pipx install` command.

B.3 *Installing tox*

tox (https://tox.wiki/en/latest/) is a testing and task management tool for Python projects. Install tox using the following command:

```
$ pipx install tox
```

You should see output similar to the following:

```
installed package tox 3.23.1, Python 3.10.0
  These apps are now globally available
    - tox
    - tox-quickstart
done! ✨ 🌟 ✨
```

To verify your configuration, run the following command:

```
$ tox --version
```

The version should match the version in the output of the pipx install command.

B.4 *Installing pre-commit*

pre-commit (https://pre-commit.com) is a tool for managing and executing pre-commit hooks for Git repositories. Install pre-commit using the following command:

```
$ pipx install pre-commit
```

You should see output similar to the following:

```
installed package pre-commit 2.17.0, Python 3.10.0
  These apps are now globally available
    - pre-commit
    - pre-commit-validate-config
    - pre-commit-validate-manifest
done! ✨ 🌟 ✨
```

To verify your configuration, run the following command:

```
$ pre-commit --version
```

The version should match the version in the output of the pipx install command.

B.5 *Installing cookiecutter*

cookiecutter (https://cookiecutter.readthedocs.io) is a tool for creating projects from project templates. Install cookiecutter using the following command:

```
installed package cookiecutter 1.7.3, Python 3.10.0
  These apps are now globally available
    - cookiecutter
done! ✨ 🌟 ✨
```

To verify your configuration, run the following command:

```
$ cookiecutter --version
```

The version should match the version in the output of the pipx install command.

index